Shakespeare in the Theatre: Trevor Nunn

SHAKESPEARE IN THE THEATRE

Series Editors

Bridget Escolme, Peter Holland and Farah Karim-Cooper

Published titles

Patrice Chéreau, Dominique Goy-Blanquet
The American Shakespeare Center, Paul Menzer
Mark Rylance at the Globe, Stephen Purcell
The National Theatre, 1963–1975: Olivier and Hall,
Robert Shaughnessy
Nicholas Hytner, Abigail Rokison-Woodall
Peter Sellars, Ayanna Thompson

Forthcoming titles

Cheek by Jowl, Peter Kirwan
The King's Men, Lucy Munro
Peter Hall, Stuart Hampton-Reeves
The Other Place: The RSC and Studio Theatre,
Abigail Rokison-Woodall and Lisa Hammond-Marty
Shakespeare in Berlin, 1918–2018, Holger Schott Syme

Shakespeare in the Theatre: Trevor Nunn

Russell Jackson

THE ARDEN SHAKESPEARE
LONDON • NEW YORK • OXFORD • NEW DELHI • SYDNEY

THE ARDEN SHAKESPEARE
Bloomsbury Publishing Plc
50 Bedford Square, London, WC1B 3DP, UK
1385 Broadway, New York, NY 10018, USA

BLOOMSBURY, THE ARDEN SHAKESPEARE and the Arden Shakespeare logo
are trademarks of Bloomsbury Publishing Plc

First published in Great Britain 2019
Paperback edition first published 2020

Copyright © Russell Jackson, 2019

Russell Jackson has asserted his right under the Copyright, Designs
and Patents Act, 1988, to be identified as the author of this work.

For legal purposes the Acknowledgements on p. ix constitute
an extension of this copyright page.

Cover design: Irene Martinez Costa
Cover image: 1976 production of Macbeth by Joe Cocks Studio Collection
© Shakespeare Birthplace Trust

All rights reserved. No part of this publication may be reproduced or
transmitted in any form or by any means, electronic or mechanical,
including photocopying, recording, or any information storage or retrieval
system, without prior permission in writing from the publishers.

Bloomsbury Publishing Plc does not have any control over, or responsibility for,
any third-party websites referred to or in this book. All internet addresses given
in this book were correct at the time of going to press. The author and
publisher regret any inconvenience caused if addresses have changed or sites
have ceased to exist, but can accept no responsibility for any such changes.

A catalogue record for this book is available from the British Library.

A catalog record for this book is available from the Library of Congress.

ISBN: HB: 978-1-4742-8958-0
PB: 978-1-3501-6457-4
ePDF: 978-1-4742-8960-3
eBook: 978-1-4742-8959-7

Series: Shakespeare in the Theatre

Typeset by Integra Software Services Pvt. Ltd.

To find out more about our authors and books visit
www.bloomsbury.com and sign up for our newsletters.

*To Professor Sir Stanley Wells,
with gratitude and affection*

CONTENTS

List of figures viii
Acknowledgements ix
A note on the text x
Series preface xi
Author's preface xii

    Introduction: 'Controlled flamboyance' and Leavisite analysis 1

1 The Main Stage at Stratford, 1968–72 33

2 The Main Stage at Stratford: After the Romans 87

3 'Chamber' Shakespeare at The Other Place 127

4 1997–2007: The National Theatre, and beyond 171

    Conclusion 197

Appendix: Shakespeare productions directed or co-directed by Trevor Nunn 200
Notes 204
Bibliography 230
Index 239

LIST OF FIGURES

1 In the rehearsal room: Trevor Nunn directing Susan Fleetwood (Regan) (left) and Sheila Allen (Goneril) in *King Lear* (Royal Shakespeare Theatre, 1968). Photo by Reg Wilson © RSC 20

2 *The Winter's Tale* (Royal Shakespeare Theatre, 1969), Act 1, Scene 1: Hermione (Judi Dench), Mamillius (Jeremy Richardson) Leontes (Barrie Ingham) and Polixenes (Richard Pasco) in the nursery. Photo by Reg Wilson © RSC 47

3 *Antony and Cleopatra* (Royal Shakespeare Theatre, 1972): Cleopatra (Janet Suzman) tended by her entourage. Photo by Reg Wilson © RSC 69

4 *Romeo and Juliet* (Royal Shakespeare Theatre, 1976): Romeo (Ian McKellen) embraces Juliet (Francesca Annis) on the edge of the grave (Joe Cocks Studio Collection © Shakespeare Birthplace Trust) 100

5 *All's Well That Ends Well* (Royal Shakespeare Theatre, 1981), 2.3: the King of France (John Franklin-Robbins) gives Helena (Harriet Walter) to Bertram (Mike Gwilym). Photo by Reg Wilson © RSC 119

6 *Othello* (The Other Place, 1989), 3.3: Othello (Willard White) and Iago (Ian McKellen) (Joe Cocks Studio Collection © Shakespeare Birthplace Trust) 152

7 *King Lear* (Courtyard Theatre, 2007), 1.1: Cordelia (Romola Garai) speaks her mind. Photo by Manuel Harlan © RSC 192

ACKNOWLEDGEMENTS

I am grateful to the staffs of the libraries of the University of Birmingham's Shakespeare Institute and the Shakespeare Birthplace Trust. Michelle Morton at the Royal Shakespeare Company and Julia Nottingham at the Shakespeare Birthplace Trust have been helpful in identifying and providing illustrations. The series editors Peter Holland, Farah Karim-Cooper and Bridget Escolme, and Margaret Bartley, Mark Dudgeon and Lara Bateman at Bloomsbury have given me diligent and sympathetic support. My wife Patricia Lennox, whose critical and scholarly gifts include a keen eye for an inappropriately placed preposition, knows what I am indebted to her for.

A NOTE ON THE TEXT

Shakespeare's plays are cited by act, scene and line references corresponding to those in *The Arden Shakespeare: Complete Works*, Revised Edition, eds Ann Thompson, David Scott Kastan and Richard Proudfoot (London: Arden Shakespeare, 2011). Where other editions have been used in a production, the text quoted may differ from that of this edition. The attribution of particular plays to Shakespeare as sole author is that adopted by the productions, rather than adjusted in the light of subsequent scholarship.

Press reviews have been consulted in the cuttings collections of the Shakespeare Institute and the Royal Shakespeare Company's archive at the Shakespeare Centre Library, both in Stratford-upon-Avon. For productions since 1991 I have also drawn on reviews reprinted in *The (London) Theatre Record*: in this source headlines are not included, and consequently some references in the endnotes give only author, publication and date.

SERIES PREFACE

Each volume in the *Shakespeare in the Theatre* series focuses on a director or theatre company who has made a significant contribution to Shakespeare production, identifying the artistic and political/social contexts of their work. The series introduces readers to the work of significant theatre directors and companies whose Shakespeare productions have been transformative in our understanding of his plays in performance. Each volume examines a single figure or company, considering their key productions, rehearsal approaches and their work with other artists (actors, designers, composers). A particular feature of each book is its exploration of the contexts within which these theatre artists have made their Shakespeare productions work. Thus, the series considers not only the ways in which directors and companies produce Shakespeare, but also reflects upon their other theatre activity and the broader artistic, cultural and socio-political milieu within which their Shakespeare performances and productions have been created. The key to the series' originality then, is its consideration of Shakespeare production in a range of artistic and broader contexts; in this sense, it de-centres Shakespeare from within Shakespeare studies, pointing to the range of people, artistic practices and cultural phenomena that combine to make meaning in the theatre.

Series editors:
Bridget Escolme, Peter Holland,
Farah Karim-Cooper

AUTHOR'S PREFACE

Although Sir Trevor Nunn – he was knighted in 2002 – is not a theatrical radical or activist in the usual sense of the words, he has long been committed to the idea that theatre speaks not merely to its audiences, but with and for them. Since the mid-1960s he has been one of Britain's most influential directors of Shakespeare, and during his eighteen years as artistic director of the Royal Shakespeare Company his productions were influential far beyond the company's bases in Stratford-upon-Avon and London. His work represents an approach to Shakespeare's texts that has informed the work of actors and expectations of audiences. It has also been responsive to shifts in the more general cultural and social climate.

This book focuses on the Shakespeare productions he has directed during his years at the Royal Shakespeare Company and the National Theatre, as representing the periods of his greatest influence and exemplifying the various aspects of his approach to the plays. It consequently reflects the ways in which critical opinion has responded to the institutions as well as to his productions and the issues raised by them. Beginning with *The Revenger's Tragedy* in 1966, I saw all but two of his productions at the Royal Shakespeare Theatre, and this informs my account of them: hence the first-person interventions in some chapters.

After the Introduction the organization of chapters is chronological, with the exception of Chapter 3, which deals as a separate group with Nunn's 'chamber' productions directed at The Other Place, the RSC's studio theatre in Stratford: *Macbeth*, *Othello* and (in the 'new' Other Place) *Measure for Measure*. The final chapter discusses his three Shakespeare productions at the National Theatre and three of the several Shakespearean productions he has directed since standing down as its Director, *Hamlet* and *Richard II* at the Old Vic and *King Lear* for the RSC.

Introduction: 'Controlled flamboyance' and Leavisite analysis

Trevor Nunn was born into a working-class family in Ipswich in 1940. Like many thousands of working-class children of the postwar generations he benefitted from the Education Act of 1944, which abolished fees for secondary education. From the city's Northgate Grammar School he went to Cambridge on a scholarship to read English at Downing College in 1959, where he came under the influence of the charismatic lecturer and critic F. R. Leavis. By the time he graduated in 1962 he had directed thirty-four plays, including several by Shakespeare. In 2011 he told a *Guardian* interviewer that during his final term he directed both the Marlowe Society's Shakespeare production and the Footlights revue: 'so you can tell where my concentration went'. He regarded his 2.2 degree as 'a happy trade-off' for his immersion in the university's theatrical life.[1]

In 1965 Peter Hall 'discovered' him at the Belgrade Theatre, Coventry, where he was winning golden opinions as an associate director. A correspondent in *The Stage* reported that his production of *The Caucasian Chalk Circle* – his second as a professional director – was 'a triumph' with a play that 'with 82 characters [was] a challenge to any company'. The play 'moved at great speed' on Christopher Morley's set of 'a circular-raked rostrum with various lowering pillars and simple backings'.[2] Hall appointed him in 1965 as an associate director at the Royal Shakespeare Company. (Before long Morley would be joining his colleague in Stratford.)

Nunn had a disappointing first year, but his directorial debut on the main stage of the Royal Shakespeare Theatre, in October 1966, was another triumph. Produced on a shoe-string at the end of an unspectacular season, *The Revenger's Tragedy*, then still attributed to Cyril Tourneur, set down a marker for what would become recognized as one characteristic of much of the director's subsequent work: his enthusiasm for exciting theatricality in the service of a strong and thoroughly worked-out interpretative approach. In a 1977 *Observer* 'Profile', Robert Cushman recalled that Nunn 'had more or less invented a style', which his productions of *The Relapse* and *The Taming of the Shrew* in the following year had confirmed: 'a controlled flamboyance rare in a generation of young scholastics'.[3]

The opening moments had a thrilling, sinister glamour. The set was that of Peter Hall's 1965 *Hamlet*, revived earlier in the season, with marble-like side walls that could swing back to reveal the full depth of the stage. In flickering torchlight, accompanied by Guy Woolfenden's strident, brassy score, figures clad in silver-encrusted costumes danced towards the front of the stage, parting mid-way to show a dream-like enactment of an assault and rape. When the group formed up in a line facing the audience, Vindice (Ian Richardson) strode down to the centre of the forestage to identify them: 'Duke, royal lecher, go, grey-haired adultery, / And thou his son, as impious steeped as he.'[4] As he spoke each masked figure lowered his or her mask as if in acknowledgement of their character. Left alone on stage, Vindice produced a skull from beneath his cloak: 'Thou sallow picture of my poisoned love, / My study's ornament, thou shell of death, / Once the bright face of my betrothèd lady.'[5] Richardson's voice, clear, trenchant, nuanced and alarmingly detached, established Vindice's bleak-eyed command over the spectacle. Woolfenden, in notes for an

LP of his music from a number of RSC productions, described the effect sought after:

> We were exploring a decadence at once Jacobean and modern. We wanted the music to speak of a world of brittle, glittering sophistication that was also a world of painted vulgarity; to be at times sensual and provocative, at times brassy and megalomaniac.[6]

In a 1978 interview, Nunn reflected that the production 'deplored the vogue while celebrating it', and that in the mid-1960s 'contemporary society was lacerated, but in a self-congratulatory way'.[7]

This production of a play hardly ever seen on stage suited the *Zeitgeist* of the late 1960s. It was especially exciting for those of us in our teens and twenties who had taken David Warner's gangling, aggressively dismissive prince in Hall's *Hamlet* as an endorsement of our own disaffection with the Establishment. Here was a decadent regime more pervasively tainted by vice than that of Elsinore, with a revenger whose assured demeanour and subtle eloquence were those of an experienced insider now in revolt. In *The Stage* 'S.B.' hailed it as 'a savagely satirical picture of a corrupt society so far disintegrated that justice is a meaningless concept and private revenge has become the means of redress'.[8] Reviewing the London revival of the production at the Aldwych in 1969, Ronald Bryden hailed Nunn's achievement as 'the reclamation of a whole lost kingdom of theatrical response, the country where tragic poetry and the popular zest of melodrama once co-existed'.[9]

In its theatricality and energy, the production exemplified what came to be a distinctive development in the RSC's style: unafraid of grand theatrical gestures, but with its acting rooted in naturalism but qualified by attention to the subtleties of the verse and prose, and revisionist in its approach to both established and unfamiliar repertoire. Moreover, with its substantial reorganization of the text and additional lines written by John Barton, *The Revenger's Tragedy* had adopted the dramaturgical tactics of *The Wars of the Roses* (1963), in which a trilogy had been fashioned out of the three *Henry VI* plays and *Richard III*, with cutting and reordering of scenes and the addition of pastiche dialogue.[10] In 1968, at the age of twenty-seven, Nunn became Hall's successor as artistic director, a post he held until 1986.

In 1989 the RSC's parting gift in retrospective celebration of his tenure was an intimate staging of *Othello* at the original, 'tin shed' incarnation of The Other Place, opened formally in 1974. *The Revenger's Tragedy* had asserted his ability to command the resources of a stage suited to spectacle. The 1989 *Othello* – discussed in Chapter 4 – exemplified another important dimension of his work, the penchant for telling use of domestic detail. Stanley Wells reflected in *Shakespeare Survey* that 'a fully written account of this production would read like a Victorian novel'.[11] Nunn's *Othello*, transferred effectively to television after a short run in London at the Young Vic, was not the first production to explore the play as a domestic tragedy, but the proximity of the audience in the small theatre – seating in any of its configurations no more than 160 – enabled Nunn and the actors to achieve nuances of character without the temptation (or perceived responsibility) to create large-scale public scenes or a storm on a scale considered appropriate for *Othello* on the company's main stage. Colin Chambers suggests that Nunn's work at The Other Place, which before *Othello* had included *Macbeth* (1976), *The Alchemist* (1977) and *Three Sisters* (1979), had 'unlocked him as a director and resulted in a string of notable productions in both the RSC's large and small spaces'.[12] By the time of his departure he had overseen the inauguration of two theatres in addition to The Other Place. The Barbican Centre superseded the Aldwych as the RSC's London base in 1981, but with theatre spaces that were an awkward fit for productions originating in Stratford. The literally underground venue aptly named The Pit was to take over from The Warehouse as an equivalent of The Other Place. At Stratford there was a much happier innovation: the

Swan, with a thrust stage surrounded on three sides by stalls seats and galleries, opened in 1986. A triumph of private philanthropy in a time of funding restrictions, it promised a kind of experience that the two other Stratford theatres could not provide, and was originally designated as a home for plays by Shakespeare's contemporaries. (It opened with *The Two Noble Kinsmen*, a play at least only *partly* by Shakespeare.)

One theme of this book is the dynamic relationship between Nunn's directing of Shakespeare in two of these spaces – he has not directed Shakespeare at the Swan – as well as their equivalents at the Barbican and at the National Theatre. It was at the RSC that Nunn achieved his greatest influence as a director of Shakespeare's plays. In many respects, his work there is representative of an approach with international as well as national significance, particularly with its emphasis on textual analysis and the speaking of the plays' language. For better or worse, the British – arguably, English – model of partially state-subsidized theatre supports directorial initiative and vision, but has rarely been accused of indulging them to the extent of some of the European theatres whose funding has long been the envy of British companies. The preference this has fostered among a considerable proportion of the RSC's audiences since the 1960s has been for productions with ideas, but not governed by a Big Idea, and featuring well-trained actors speaking most of the play's lines in more or less the right order: neither an old-fashioned star-dominated 'actor's theatre', nor a 'director's theatre'. In acting terms, this has evolved into a corresponding fusion of realism and respect for the formal qualities of the non-realist in dramatic writing of the early modern period. Working within this broadly pragmatic tradition, and beyond sharing passionately its insistence on the primacy of the text, Nunn has never identified himself with, still less formulated, particular theories of rehearsal and performance practice. Although these can be documented through interviews he has given and the commentary of critics, such statements have never been a preoccupation with him. At the time of writing there have been no manifestos or critical interventions to compare with those of Peter Brook or even the equivalent of Peter Hall's *Shakespeare's Advice to the Players* (2010).

Consequently, Nunn's influence on Shakespearean performance has to be identified in the productions and their reception. In discussing his directorship of theatre companies, the distinction between 'director' (in the rehearsal room and on stage) and 'Director' (in the office and the boardroom) is important. Nunn has been innovative, especially at the RSC, in shaping repertoire, building teams and formulating artistic policy, but has been perceived as lacking the relish for the less amenable aspects of administration that one senses in Hall's published diaries of his time at the National, even during the trying period of construction and strained industrial relations.[13]

Stratford and the legacy of Peter Hall

When Nunn took over from Peter Hall as the RSC's artistic director – Hall's title had been 'managing director' – he inherited (in Sally Beauman's words) 'a structure that had been invented at speed, that was already breaking apart at the seams, and that urgently needed change'.[14] It was facing a major financial crisis, effectively the prospect of bankruptcy, as well as the problems of resolving the financial, contractual and artistic consequences of the establishment of a London base at the Aldwych Theatre.[15] Programmes for Stratford productions during the late 1960s announced that the RSC was 'formed round a group of artists under long term contract', so that 'by working constantly together in a varied repertoire the company aim[ed] to be a flexible ensemble with a distinctive character'. The Aldwych repertoire, 'consisting mainly, though by no means wholly, of modern works', provided 'a bridge ... between Shakespeare and modern theatre so that each reflects something of the other's attitudes and techniques'.[16] Nevertheless, Hall's vision of an ensemble supported by extended contracts had proved untenable beyond the span of a season in Stratford and the transfer of at least some of the productions to London. The company's identity among the theatre-going public was now that of a revitalized, stable artistic organization with what would later be labelled an established 'brand', but its financial crises had become an almost annual event. Nunn later described the theatre's situation in the late 1960s as being 'as secure as a ride on a condemned big dipper'.[17] (In 2001, with a similar sense of the absurdly precarious, he would compare his new job as Director of the National Theatre to 'juggling plates, while riding a unicycle, on a tightrope, over Niagara Falls'.)[18]

In 1959 Peter Brook had cited the Stratford company – not yet the RSC – in arguing for subsidy that would free experiment from box-office anxieties: 'The theatre that covers its costs is the true theatre with its edges knocked off. Where has there been the most experimenting in the English theatre in the past ten years? At Stratford-upon-Avon.'[19] Eleven years later, as he worked with the company's available actors on *A Midsummer Night's Dream*, Brook's feelings about the RSC were less cordial. The journalist David Selbourne, who observed rehearsals, reports his complaints that the cast and the company itself were 'uninventive', referring with 'thinly concealed sarcasm' to its being 'supposedly the best Shakespearean company in the world'.

The exhilaration that comes from finding unlimited creative potential in a theatrical troupe was, he said, 'rarely present'. The essential prerequisite for developing such creativity was 'to take the promising actors' and give them 'a strongly-led, consistent and imaginatively-intensive training'. The leadership, the imagination and the training were all lacking in the company. The rest of the season's work, he said, was in consequence 'terrible'.[20]

This was said privately and partway through the process that produced a *Dream* that became iconic as an example of the triumph of 'the empty space', an ensemble work incorporating physical and vocal skills that would later be the focus of Brook's International Centre for Theatre Research at the Bouffes du Nord in Paris. Ironically, it was hailed by Peter Ansorge in *Plays and Players* as 'certainly a landmark for the RSC – a culmination of Trevor Nunn's attempts with the later plays to find a democratic principle in Shakespeare, as source of celebration directly influencing audiences in the seventies'. There was a downside to this exhilaration: 'Exactly how a company follows up a production like this must be one of the less consoling issues raised by the *Dream* – the most accessible of Peter Brook's theatrical experiments.'[21]

Whether or not it was a 'culmination' of Nunn's policies, the *Dream* had raised the company's game. Its significance for the RSC's seasons in the early 1970s will be discussed further in Chapter 1. In terms of the company's ethos and organization, it is a reminder of the troubled relationship with experiment and innovation that had characterized the RSC since its earliest days. As for the 'democratic' aspect of Nunn's work, in an interview with John Heilpern in 1968 the new artistic director claimed that 'the direction of the company [had] always worked democratically, but with the right amount of benevolent autocracy. It has to be that way.' Nunn explained that Hall had been prevented by other responsibilities from the greater contact he had wished for with the acting company. Now the appointment of an 'administrative director', would make it possible for Nunn to be 'leading the company from among the actors, which is just as it should be'.[22] Whether this would in the event be more than a gesture towards the fashion for collectivism is open to debate, but Nunn's personal style, and even his appearance (hair style, casual wear) were very different from those of his predecessor and very much in accord with what was considered 'trendy' in the late 1960s. Colin Chambers observes that despite his reputation for 'a particular piece of affable manipulation' known as being 'Trevved' – a warm embrace that could be a means of evading necessary explanation or even a simple answer to a question – Nunn inspired loyalty. He impressed by his 'sharp intelligence, impish sense of humour and apparently inexhaustible ability to talk at length without respite for breath or rumination'.[23]

In changing the Stratford enterprise from a summer festival season with companies assembled round visiting stars to a year-round programme with London revivals, work by living dramatists and a commitment to at least the makings of a semi-permanent ensemble, Hall had benefitted from Arts Council support to complement the box-office. The system of three-year contracts, with an option to take out a year to work elsewhere, instituted in 1960, was proving untenable. (A move to a two-year basis for actors' employment was one of Nunn's earliest administrative changes.) Hall had also created an organization that needed other means of support from a number of sources: transfers to the RSC's London base or, in partnership with commercial producers, to commercial theatres; exploiting successful productions through television and, if possible, film; and finding ways of replicating the success of *The Wars of the Roses*. The last of these imperatives resulted in a series of reincarnations over the years of the concept of the history play cycle.

The new climate in arts policy and finance through the ensuing decades called for the development of what would now be classed as 'outreach' in performances designed to tour to schools and locations without a full-scale theatre venue, and in due course to the need for Christmas shows that would generate income beyond that possible from leasing out the Stratford main stage to visiting companies. In these respects, the company's profile began to resemble that of many regional theatres, making it all the more urgent to assert a coherent artistic identity. In the course of the century's final decades, financial income, if not cultural kudos, would be sought in productions that arguably had little to do with its core values. The two-part adaptation of *Nicholas Nickleby* (1979) exemplified important aspects of the RSC's commitment to story-telling and ensemble work in ways not always possible in the full-scale Shakespeare productions, but *Les Misérables* (1985) was less easily justified as appropriate for the company, even though this co-production with the impresario Cameron Mackintosh proved an invaluable source of revenue. In 1987 the recently-appointed successor to Nunn, Terry Hands, described the musical as part of the company's 'self-help' scheme, sustaining it in the face of an £800,000 shortfall resulting from the year's standstill grant from the Arts Council and the government's failure to follow through with the £5.2 million recommended in 1985 by Clive Priestley's very positive report on the company's work, governance and finance.[24]

Challenges from left of field

Such transfers and co-productions were not necessarily inappropriate in themselves, but they would generate hostility towards both Hall at the National and Nunn at the RSC. Accusations in the press in 1986 that scheduling had been rigged, resources diverted and contractual deals fixed in the favour of the Directors were countered by the threat of legal action and withdrawn, but they reflected tensions and enmities within both organizations.[25] They also chimed with the anti-establishment feeling that fuelled anger among regional as well as 'alternative' companies at what was seen as the too disproportionate share of available funding allotted to the two 'nationals'. A summary of what the RSC was *not* when Nunn took over and what it did *not* do during his directorship provides a necessary background to his work with the company.

It had not been easy to justify the RSC's claim to centrality in the cultural Establishment, while at the same time striving for acknowledgement as a source of innovation. A complicating factor was the pressure of other forces in the theatre, ranging from avant-garde experiment to differently constituted classical ensembles. The ensemble principle was a frequently proclaimed element of Hall's intentions in forming a company rather than assembling a series of casts for annual festival seasons. In this he was following an ambition shared by many directors and actors in the 1950s and early 1960s, identified by William Gaskill as his own prime motivation in 1963 for joining Laurence Olivier at the National Theatre, where he 'was going to be in on the making of an ensemble':

> The idea of an ensemble haunted all our dreams: it was something that happened only in Europe where they could afford actors under long-term contracts, adequate rehearsal time, and the possibility of developing new methods of acting, direction and design.[26]

Examples of innovative, avant-garde companies from the early years of the century and established, subsidized theatres elsewhere in Europe – especially the Berliner Ensemble – were inspiring, but the vital element of subsidy could not be taken for granted, especially as Arts Council funding was reviewed on an annual basis, a recurring cliff-hanger that could jeopardize long-term planning. As Claire Cochrane observes in her survey of theatrical culture and finance in general in twentieth-century Britain, 'by the 1960s ... the concept of the company as an ensemble of actors dedicated to long-term sustained intense creative experimentation had acquired an additional aura as an idealized construct quite detached from its primary economic base'.[27] As well as the tension between the RSC and the National, a problem compounded in the 1970s and 1980s by plot and counter-plot for and against merger, there was the threat to the RSC's esteem constituted by the independent companies whose relative poverty was compensated by their freedom to innovate.

By now the *Zeitgeist* was relocating, commandeered by more consistently politicized companies, mostly with left-wing and issue-driven agendas and offering a challenge to the kinds of performance skill and approach to 'classic' texts nurtured at Stratford. Catherine Itzin's *Stages in the Revolution* (1980) took 1968, the year of not-quite-revolutions, as its starting point for a survey of the proliferating left-wing theatre groups. It is doubtful whether this 'heyday of agitprop' was really a sign that 'the working class was awakening and struggling', in quite the terms (or numbers) favoured by the theatrical activists, but the cumulative energy and variety of performance modes impacted on the mainstream.[28] Among the various labels attached to the new theatre groups, 'fringe' and 'alternative' seemed to emerge as the most inclusive and appropriately combative.[29] Roland Rees, co-founder of one of the earliest self-identifying fringe groups, Foco Novo, recalled the social as well as artistic change earlier in the decade, represented by what had first become 'the Fringe' and was now challenging the mainstream for the allegiance of young theatre-makers and, by extension, their audiences:

> It was a period when many who would ordinarily never have found their way into theatre chose it as a path of expression. Students from Art Schools and with musical backgrounds, saw attractive opportunities in performance. Mainstream theatre was about specialization of skills. The New Theatre ... wanted performers to be able to offer mime, juggling, acrobatics and the ability to play musical instruments; the desire was to fuse the variety of a single performer's expertise within a show.[30]

Simply by virtue of its building-related charter, the RSC was vulnerable to the challenges of this 'New Theatre', which, as Rees noted, was 'not building based but primarily in origin a touring phenomenon'.[31] Moreover, for the National or the RSC the cherished but rarely achieved semi-permanent ensemble was mainly a matter of recruiting actors for a range of productions of different kinds under different directors. By contrast, the kind of ensemble favoured by the Fringe was one of like-minded artists, together because they shared artistic and/or political aims. Charles Marowitz, co-founder of The Place in London, radical reviser of works by Shakespeare and other playwrights, and aggressively contrarian in his approach to the Establishment, defined experimental theatre as dependent on 'the establishment of little clans of artistic dissent which attract their own audience and do their own work'.[32] Clans of this kind were not part of the RSC's scheme of things.

Above all, size mattered. Whether or not they were touring, the new companies favoured small venues, especially those not originally conceived as theatres. Found spaces were in vogue, for ideological as well as practical reasons. Sally Beauman concludes her summary of the challenges to the RSC in the 1970s with the reflection that, given its commitment to large-scale work for the Royal Shakespeare Theatre itself, over the next ten years not only 'underfunding, inflation, rising seat prices and VAT' would be threats, but also 'the new and automatic suspicion of any theatre that seated more than two hundred people'.[33]

On this level, the development of the RSC's small-scale theatres in Stratford and London was a move towards reclaiming important artistic kudos. Colin Chambers, in his 1980 book *Other Spaces: New Theatre and the RSC*, wrote that 'social philosophy was in harmony with the artistic values of the most effective productions' at The Other Place (from 1973) and The Warehouse (from 1977).[34] More important than audience numbers over a season, necessarily minute in comparison with the Stratford main house or the Aldwych, was the small spaces' contribution to RSC 'culture', identified by Chambers as 'keeping the Company to its own standards with resilience in the face of a weak, mixed economy'.[35] (The economy in question was 'mixed' in its reliance on box-office as well as subsidy.) The attractions of these theatres included, as well as their increased (indeed, enforced) intimacy between audience and actors: the ability to stage repertoire that would not pay its way at the Royal Shakespeared Theatre (RST) or the Aldwych; the freedom to commission new writing; and the potential for revisiting familiar texts without the kind of stage-filling sets required in the large proscenium house. Parasitic in the best sense, in that it was supported by the technical and other resources of the main house, The Other Place, perhaps more by accident than design, was nearer to Brook's ideal of a theatre that did not need to cover its costs. By the mid-1980s, the situation of small-scale companies had changed. Graham Saunders observes that, after the publication of its report *The Glory of the Garden* (1984), the Arts Council was 'encouraging and, more frequently, coercing small-scale companies to adopt the same working practices employed in mainstream theatre'. The requirement to appoint full-time administrators and artistic directors 'broke with the earlier model of collectivism, since the artistic director now held overall responsibility for policy decisions'.[36] The mechanisms of financial support and accountability were drawing the professedly radical Fringe and the RSC's relatively radical wing closer together, but the RSC would never be identified fully with experiment, activism or collectivism. There would be no repetition of the 1963–4 'Theatre of Cruelty' season. Individual projects and productions might point towards these values, but the company's remit lay elsewhere. From the mid-1970s the claim to be innovative, as distinct from 'experimental' in the avant-garde sense, was staked by some notable developments: annual small-scale tours; a residency in Newcastle-upon-Tyne, when the Stratford season's main-stage repertoire, plus additional events would be staged; and the establishment of The Warehouse as a London equivalent of The Other Place.

Although compact, mobile and collectivist theatre groups were the principal seeding ground for experiment and activism, the most effective challenge to the RSC's predominance came from another direction. Companies with a 'classical' repertoire and comparable artistic principles came and went over the decades – Prospect, Compass, Renaissance and others. The Glasgow Citizens Theatre (aka The Citz) had become a leader in the difficult task of bringing the large-scale visions of the European avant-garde to audiences paying low prices, while monthly advertisements in *Plays and Players* proclaimed the theatre's transgressive, confrontational style with images of urban deprivation, camp decadence, and motifs from such older theatrical traditions as *Commedia dell' Arte* and Vitruvian scene design. Confrontation was often expressed in terms of hostility towards the subsidized companies South of the Border. Giles Havergal, one of the triumvirate of directors, laid claim to belonging in spirit to 'mainland Europe' and scorned the text-oriented approach of the RSC and the National Theatre: 'they are intellect-, not emotion-oriented; their productions approach you through your knowledge of A-level English, and the acting is full of psychological realism which tends to mean a lot of actors just standing very still and gazing at you very firmly'.[37] In the progressive theatre world of the 1970s, 'academic' was one of the strongest insults that could be directed against a rival company and its productions. But the most significant counter to the RSC's hegemony was offered by a precariously funded large-scale touring company whose name was in itself a challenge.

Founded in 1986, the English Shakespeare Company (ESC), directed by Michael Bogdanov and Michael Pennington, challenged the RSC on its own artistic territory by touring productions of the history plays in two cycles that together spanned the reigns from Richard II to Richard III. Created for large proscenium-arch theatres, touring internationally and eventually captured on commercial video, these productions were 'ensemble' in the full sense of a company (in fact, a series of companies) that shared principal and secondary roles, and a rough-and-ready but stylish aesthetic that generated vital audience engagement. In variations of modern and eclectic dress, and with aggressive reference to contemporary politics, these were in contrast to the RSC's approach to the material. At Stratford from the 1960s to 1980s the modern relevance of the histories was inferred rather than explicit, while costuming remained 'in period' – although definitions of period costume were negotiable.

Bogdanov's Stratford modern-dress productions of *The Taming of the Shrew* (1978) and *Romeo and Juliet* (1986) had a free-wheeling iconoclastic verve that seemed anomalous in the RSC context, but they were keyed to a thorough analysis of the texts and their significance. As well as his talent as an actor, Pennington brought his dedication to expressive, forceful and subtle speech to the ESC. This was another direct challenge to the RSC's claims to set standards. During the setting-up of the new company Pennington went to an RSC production at the Barbican. The most passionate verse of the lovers had been cut 'to suit the rationalist tone of the production'. The combined effect of emotional detachment and interpretive overload was ruinous: 'Actors loaded with metaphor despaired of their lines and did elaborate gestures of illustration.' As the evening 'stretched on' Pennington resolved that 'If this company of ours gets going ... it will be the best bloody verse-speaking outfit in the country ... Our style of playing will be accurate and fastidious, but it will come from urgent need.' The actors would be lit 'from above and the side as you see them in life' and the set would 'make the imaginary forces work, and not show off'.[38]

The ESC's large-scale touring closed down in 1994 after the withdrawal of Arts Council funding: its national and international touring and its education department had subsisted on a combination of sponsorship, box-office and grants, but when the last of these failed, the company could no longer survive. In his 'End Piece' in the final issue of the company's newsletter, Bogdanov reminded supporters of its policy 'to portray Shakespeare not as an enduring classicist but as a writer of our and future times, an egalitarian with deeply held political convictions'. His parting shot at the RSC encapsulates the Left's objections to the Stratford enterprise, whose productions 'over the past 30 years' had been 'concerned principally with the idea of an essential human goodness and the desirability of order, a view inevitably hostile to political action'.[39] Unlike other 'classical' companies of the period, the ESC existed as a direct challenge to the company Nunn was still leading, an opposition all the more effective for not being limited to small-scale productions in small-scale venues.

Cambridge, the Leavisite ethos and the question of 'house style'

Nunn's approach to Shakespeare had its own kind of radicalism, and these explicit or implicit critiques should be balanced by considering the positive aspects of Hall's legacy and Nunn's development of it. A newspaper article from the first year of Nunn's artistic directorship indicates the strengths and weakness of the RSC. Hazarding a definition of 'The Stratford Style' in his *Times* review of Nunn's 1968 production of *Much Ado About Nothing*, Irving Wardle suggested that staging and design were characterized by 'continuity of action, and an emphasis on sculptural, rather than pictorial, settings'.[40] Despite the fact that its members might 'come and go', the acting company was 'treated as an ensemble instrument whose members [were] usually called upon to give some proof of their skills in physical team-work'. The style was supported by 'a foundation of scholarship, undertaken to supply a human link between the Elizabethans and ourselves', and at its root lay 'the assumption that man is a social animal and Shakespeare the pre-eminent dramatist of society'. The season's productions of *Troilus and Cressida* and *The Merry Wives of Windsor*, directed by John Barton and Terry Hands respectively, 'were determinedly social', the former 'exhibiting a sick society', the latter 'a society in good health'. So far, so good, but the skills that created a coherent image of a society were not those appropriate to performing 'big melodramatic episodes at their own worth' and the company was under-equipped for 'plays demanding sublimity or music'. Nunn is quoted as admitting that the establishment of a 'house style' made it difficult to bring in outside directors. Wardle concludes his article with the warning that 'until Mr. Nunn either brings in outsiders to bend the rules or acquires the nerve to do so himself, his regime will remain what it has been until now, a caretaker administration'.

Wardle's reference to scholarship points to two important elements of Nunn's approach: attention to the texture as well as literal meaning of the texts, and a focus on creating a sense of the past that was more than decorative. The former was addressed through rigorous work on speech, complemented by an understanding of its relationship with physicality and movement. The latter was reflected in the way the social groupings within the plays were conceived, conveyed not only in the performances themselves but also in the way characters were listed in the programme. (In the case of *The Merry Wives*, Falstaff and his cronies were identified as 'from London', Parson Evans 'from Wales', and so on.) Like many directors, Nunn has habitually required his actors to do their homework, so that they 'own' an understanding of a production's historical and social milieu. Harriet Walter describes the research undertaken by the company for the 1981 Barbican production of the *Henry IV* plays: 'Every area was covered in an effort to match the epic scope of Shakespeare's play.' The company 'researched in twos and threes, and then had to stand up in front of everyone and spout out our findings – a terrifying ordeal for actors, but a great device for trust-building'.[41] (This practice also ensures that a given period setting is not simply grafted onto the individual's performance, but is an integral part of it.) The social emphasis, with its mildly political associations, complements the sense of social responsibility that Nunn proclaimed in 1973:

> I want to be concerned with a theatre that is determined to reach beyond the barriers of income, I want an avowed and committed popular theatre. I want a socially concerned theatre. A politically aware theatre. In reality not in name.[42]

In effect, he was making a pitch for the company's kinship with the Fringe, but without being aligned with specific political agendas. In 1997, when he was introduced to the staff of the National Theatre as Richard Eyre's successor, Nunn made similar commitment to a theatre that was 'to do with social and political responsibilities'. His 'watchword at the start of [his] journey' on the South Bank would be E. M. Forster's 'Only Connect,' an aim that as he spoke shaded off into an almost New Age vagueness: 'If we can only connect with each other, connect the individual with the community ... connect our souls with our bodies, our dreams with our endeavours, connect by looking into each other's eyes.'[43] This was the kind of rhetoric that no one could object to on such an occasion, but the words would have to be justified by contractual and organizational deeds as well as artistic work in the rehearsal rooms and before audiences. There is no doubting Nunn's good faith, but in the running of both organizations the broadly liberal aims would be put to the test. Nevertheless, the more immediate impact of the interest in 'society' would be manifest in productions by Nunn and the directors he chose to work with and for him.

It would also manifest itself in work with the actors, suggesting that team-building in the rehearsal room was more congenial – and its results more secure – than at the corresponding level of administration. An article, 'All for Nunn', from 1967 on 'the Company's new whizz-kid, aged twenty-seven' quotes the director's own account of work on *The Taming of the Shrew*:

> Nunn's a great believer in togetherness. He likes his company to show team spirit. 'When we rehearsed *The Taming of the Shrew* we started off with ten minutes of tossing a fluffy ball around. But this was simply to get actors to open their eyes at ten o'clock in the morning. We followed it up with lots of other exercises, all designed to make them work together as a team.'[44]

Another interviewer was told that 'to ensure authenticity [Nunn's] cast have been busy learning to juggle, tumble and sing and acquire all the professional attributes of an Elizabethan company on tour' to present the *Shrew* as a play-within-a-play.[45] The implication of both 1967 articles is that this kind of behaviour is very much part of the 'new' spirit at the theatre, one in keeping with a less formal culture. The sub-editor of 'All for Nunn' clearly thought so, captioning a photograph 'Trevor Nunn: togetherness is a fluffy ball'. Comparisons of the director's appearance with that of the Beatles, at least in their original guise, were of a piece with this. At the same time the seriousness of Nunn's approach was stressed. Like Hall, he would be appointed as artistic director in his late twenties but, unlike him, Nunn had not already established an international and West End reputation. He did share the academic and theatrical background of Cambridge (Figure 1).

FIGURE 1 *In the rehearsal room: Trevor Nunn directing Susan Fleetwood (Regan) (left) and Sheila Allen (Goneril) in* King Lear *(Royal Shakespeare Theatre, 1968). Photo by Reg Wilson © RSC.*

The significance of this has been traced in the treatment of the texts, and the influence of the Cambridge literary critic F. R. Leavis has often been identified in the approach of Hall, Barton and Nunn. Peter Hall reflected in 1978 that Leavis 'somehow inculcated a feeling that art was to do with better standards of life and better behaviour' and even claimed that 'all the textual seriousness at the basis of Trevor's work and mine comes from Leavis, and there is a vast band of us'. Nevertheless, it was 'comical to think that Leavis hated the theatre and never went to it'.[46] The *Times* review of *The Taming of the Shrew* (1967) noted that 'Mr. Nunn talks with that attention to textual detail that is the hallmark of the post-Leavis generation of ex-Cambridge producers'.[47] In 1971 the *Sunday Times* reported Nunn's acknowledgement of Leavis's influence during his time as an undergraduate at Downing College: 'I sat at his feet. That's why I instinctively believe in the possibility of ultimate standards.'[48] Looking back in 1997 on his early years with the RSC Nunn was more specific regarding these standards:

> I have always been what is known as a Leavisite – certainly I have always wanted to proceed in the way the critic F. R. Leavis described, which is, roughly, to say that of course there is a way of defining value, excellence, and the way is to ask the question 'this is so, isn't it?' and to expect the reply 'Yes, but' I felt that I was being asked by Peter Hall and his achievements with the RSC 'This is so, isn't it?' and I wanted to reply 'Yes, but'.[49]

By all accounts, even the most sympathetic, Leavis himself was unlikely to respond positively to anyone else's 'Yes, but'. Ronald Hayman suggests that the habit of lecturing had fortified his 'unSocratic dominance of tutorial conversations'.[50] Nevertheless, as Hayman recalls, 'Leavis was liberating because he made us feel that nothing mattered except the arrangement of the words on the page, but that mattered enormously because the partnership between writer and reader could be creative.' His insistence on the seriousness of this kind of close reading 'made us want to emulate him in bringing memory, imagination, sensitivity, moral judgment and taste to bear on the attitudes, ideas and feelings expressed in the words'.[51]

Nunn told Joan Bakewell in 1977 that Leavis gave 'readings from Dickens that were extraordinarily histrionic', but 'constantly said he had no faith in theatre, and people working in the theatre [were] bound to be superficial'.[52] Another student taught by him at Downing doubted 'that many actors could have spoken the lines he analysed so acutely in a way that satisfied him', and observed that Leavis 'was interested in complexities of linguistic organisation in Shakespeare which may well have been difficult to convey and which were likely to remain hidden to the average playgoer who only heard them spoken'.[53] Peter Hall later claimed that 'the primary building block of the RSC was the verse and the text, speaking it trippingly on the tongue, speaking it wittily, not singing it, not being pompous, meaning what you said, and therefore exposing the dialectic of the scene'. Doing this would 'expose the political truth of the scene and ... Shakespeare's skepticism about the nature of power'.[54] The break with self-conscious musicality did not altogether remove emotion from the company's speaking. Rather, a compromise was achieved between attention to the formal qualities of the verse and prose and the expression of emotional energy to be found alongside the 'analytical' quality.

In these matters another decisive influence on Hall, Barton and Nunn came from another Cambridge lecturer, George ('Dadie') Rylands. He had published little in the way of criticism, but his insistence on the techniques of verse speaking was felt in the Marlowe Society and other Cambridge student theatre activity. Reportedly, Hall once summed up the balance of Cambridge influences succinctly: 'the idea was to think like F.R. Leavis and speak like George Rylands'.[55] At the same time, the Rylands approach had limitations. As Michael Cordner points out, 'what was perceived as the professional stage's maltreatment of Shakespeare had generated its own puritanism which threatened to reduce performance to a form of recitation'.⁵⁶ The RSC's renewed attention to speech was effectively a compromise between such formalist discipline and the demands of imaginative characterization in the post-Stanislavskian world that Rylands had never valued or inhabited. The development of this aspect of the company's work was enhanced by Nunn's appointment of Cicely Berry as part-time voice consultant in 1969, and as head of a newly created Voice Department in 1970.

In a retrospective evaluation of Hall's directorship at the time of his departure from the RSC, Simon Trussler warned that 'the company's tendency [had] been to over-elaborate a basically simple and austere dramatic statement. A determination to elucidate meaning has sometimes served to obscure it, by allowing dramatic rhythm to be dictated by the explication of language rather than its sense. A style which espoused bareness has bred its own baroque'.[57] Interviewed by David Addenbrooke for his book on the 'Peter Hall Years' of the company, Hall insisted that the 'style' was not the result of his 'early concentration on verse speaking', but came from '"doing" – and a group of people and a particular way of regarding the plays'. It lay in 'the realization that there is a rhythm to each speech and a rhythm to each play – find it! Don't put naturalistic crap within the speech – and don't put music and scenic effects within the play'.[58] Hall's insistence here on the plays' poetic unity, an echo of the Leavis approach, suggests one of the ways in which the plays would be taken seriously both by him and his successor.

Reviewers hazarded definitions of a distinctive 'Nunn style' from an early stage in his career. The *Times* review of *The Taming of the Shrew* already quoted suggested that 'his work so far has shown a notable eye for detail and a very assured control over mood and atmosphere', citing 'the balance he achieved in the Tourneur play between all-out tragedy and black, bilious comedy'.[59] Quite how this marked him out already from other Stratford directors is not made clear. In 1977 Jim Hiley reported that 'Nunn refuses point blank ... to talk in terms of a house style': 'When I took over [Nunn recalled] I was content for people to talk about an RSC style, but I've never been able to identify it, still less promote it.' He also refused to accept the notion of 'artistic policy', insisting that 'our output is our policy'.[60] Nevertheless, in some respects Nunn's implicit response to Hall – the 'Yes, but' – amounted to a qualification of the tendencies pointed to by Trussler. What he sought for the productions was a redefined 'style' whose attributes will be traced in the chapters that follow, but it should be noted here that in the first years of his tenure the new approach included a degree of austerity in staging – identifiable in aspects of the *Revenger's Tragedy* production for all its flamboyance – that also responded to the straitened financial situation he had inherited.

Beyond the RSC

By the end of the 1970s it was clear that the RSC had expanded its activities to a degree that called for a readjustment of its managerial structure: the imminent opening of the Barbican Centre – in the event delayed until 1982 – prompted the appointment in 1978 of Terry Hands as joint artistic director. When Nunn stepped down in 1986 he left his successor with what Chambers describes as 'an almighty mess', in terms of the financial situation and new problems that were due in part to the success of the newly-opened Swan.[61] Finding a home for its productions proved impossible within the Barbican Centre, and the new Stratford theatre made considerable demands on resources. A mess of this kind, and the responsibility of dealing with it, were persistent features of handovers between artistic directors: the chalice would contain at least a fair dose of poison. Under Nunn's directorship there had been many remarkable productions, beneficial innovations in company policy, and initiatives such as The Other Place had enriched and consolidated the RSC's work and extended its range. At the same time, economic forces beyond the control of any arts organization, which continued throughout the coming decade, frustrated the ability to create a company along the lines envisaged by Hall, his associates and his successor. It was a sign of the times that in 1985, in his 'Afterword' to *Flashback*, Micheline Steinberg's pictorial history of the Stratford theatres and the RSC, Nunn insisted that this retrospect was representative of the company's continuity, identifiable in the loyal associate directors and designers, and in 'a group of actors whose loyalty to and sacrifice for the ensemble has been inspirational'. Having invoked once more the ensemble ideal, he could not resist ending with a plea for funding: 'because the RSC has a sense of history and a sense of purpose, it must be recorded in this volume that if the provision of subsidy to the theatre in this country is, in the minds of government, to be gradually eliminated, the book recording the next period of our work will be brief and sad and shameful'.[62]

As he entered a freelance phase of his career, Nunn was at the top of his game. Although he had directed many other kinds of production, in his time at the RSC Nunn was perceived primarily as a leading director of Shakespeare. Between 1967 and 1986 he had directed or co-directed eighteen plays by Shakespeare for the company. (He would return later as a guest director: *Measure for Measure* coupled with *The Blue Angel*, which opened the 'new' Other Place in 1991, and *King Lear* with *The Seagull* in 2007.) Between his departure from the RSC and his appointment as artistic director of the National Theatre in September 1997, the perception of his professional profile altered: he concentrated on musicals, many of them with Andrew Lloyd Webber as composer and Gillian Lynne as choreographer. On leave from the RSC, he had already directed *Cats* (1981) and *Starlight Express* (1984). After the RSC co-production of *Les Misérables* (1985) came West End productions of the Lloyd Webber musicals *Chess* (1986), *Aspects of Love* (1989) and *Sunset Boulevard* (1993). Not all were internationally successful, and for many critics – if not for the public – his association with the composer was a mixed blessing: Frank Rich in the *New York Times* described his work on the Broadway version of *Chess* as not so much 'injecting passion into a play ... as adding a branch store to an international conglomerate'.[63]

Nunn has always insisted that there is no contradiction between his work on Shakespeare and directing musicals, including those he directed for the National Theatre. In his 2011 *Guardian* interview, Andrew Dickson asked why 'a director who could achieve so much with so little' would 'want to expand into musicals?' Nunn's reply emphasized the kinship between the kinds of work: 'The first proper theatre I saw was pantomime. My theatregoing was always a mixture, going to see classical plays and seeing shows in town. I've never seen any dividing line, and I don't think Shakespeare saw one.' Setting aside the consideration that except in the form of court masques the Elizabethan never had the chance to make the comparison, Nunn's point holds that for a director 'the skills involved in working with a musical score and lyrics, people who act, sing and dance, are every bit as particular as the skills required in putting on a Shakespeare play'.[64]

Like many such encounters, Dickson's interview has a clear subtext of reproach, which surfaces later when he asks impertinently (and without getting an answer) how much money Nunn has made from this freelancing. The emphasis in his question is on the small-scale Shakespeare production rather than Nunn's main-stage work, setting up a false dichotomy, but one that recurs not only in general articles about the director but also in the reception of his Shakespeare productions. After the mid-1980s, reviews often accuse Nunn, with varying degrees of justification, of wanting to turn a play into a musical. In terms of the RSC's productions, Colin Chambers points out, impressed by the higher technical standards of productions on Broadway, Nunn 'introduced in 1981 a policy of enhancing physical presentation as a means of changing that situation and keeping the RSC's big stage work popular'. This was 'an apparent reversal of the anti-decorative, actor-based approach associated with the RSC's best work, as well as a response both to the minimalism of previous seasons and to the growing assertion by designers of their presence and contribution'.[65] (The growing influence of designers would be one source of discontent among the RSC's acting company in the 1980s.)

The continuity between Nunn's main-stage Shakespeare productions and the musicals has in fact been a two-way process. Like many other directors who have made the crossover, he has brought to the musicals the intimacy and attention to detail associated with his Shakespeare productions, in both large and small venues, while several (though arguably not all) of his Shakespeare productions have benefitted from the energy and scale of the musicals. The fact that he has directed *Porgy and Bess* not only in an operatic version at Glyndbourne in 1986, but also in the West End in 2006 in its 'musical' form with spoken dialogue, shows a similar flexibility of approach. Like Peter Hall, though, whose 1973 National Theatre production of *The Tempest* suffered from the influence of his experience of baroque opera, in some cases the attention to detail in musicals became fussiness, while the 'musical' treatment of the Shakespeare stagings distracted from more important matters. At the National impetus was given to Nunn's leanings towards the great Broadway shows by the need to generate revenue, both at the theatre itself and in transfers, and to occupy the Olivier stage profitably. *Oklahoma!* (1998), *My Fair Lady* (2001), *South Pacific* (2001–2) and *Anything Goes* (2002–3) were acclaimed and successful in themselves: all had West End transfers and *Oklahoma!* was filmed for television. The theatrical (or cultural) politics of devoting resources to them was another matter, although 'crossover' ventures into popular theatre of this kind had long since become a commonplace – and lucrative – element of programming in not-for-profit theatres and opera houses in Europe and America. At the National Theatre itself, *Guys and Dolls* had been planned for the 1970 season but abandoned on account of Olivier's illness: after a series of musicals in the intervening years, it was directed by Richard Eyre in 1982 and revived in 1997.[66] Musicals were an accepted as well as profitable element of strength in the company's portfolio of theatrical genres, but Nunn's last Shakespeare production for the National Theatre (NT), *Love's Labour's Lost* (2003), was regarded in some quarters as a sign of his being seduced yet again by the opportunity for musical spectacle. By now, the accusation had become a critical cliché.

In taking over the National, Nunn at least did not have to concern himself with a legacy of 'House Style' of the kind associated with the RSC. He was now also free, in organizing schedules as well as in his personal choices, from the RSC's obligation to keep the works of Shakespeare at the centre of their annual seasons. In this light, the relatively small number of Shakespeare plays directed by Nunn at the National is less significant. But administration was of course a major element of the new job. It was claimed that his hunger for directing (and especially rehearsal) took time and energy from coping with the other burdens devolving on the theatre's Director. Daniel Rosenthal notes that a recurring note in Board minutes – 'the Director left the meeting to attend rehearsals' – was indicative of the cause for concern.[67]

In the years since his departure from the National, Nunn has worked again as a freelance, and although he was the 'artistic director' of two seasons of plays at the Haymarket Theatre in London, he has not had managerial responsibilities on the scale of the directorship of the two major English 'nationals'. At the Old Vic he directed *Hamlet* (2004) and *Richard II* (2005); in 2007 he returned to the RSC for *King Lear*, paired with *The Seagull* at the temporary Courtyard Theatre; the Haymarket season included *The Tempest* (2011); and in 2015 he staged a revival of the 1963 RSC adaptation *The Wars of the Roses*, regarded as a homage to his early mentors, Hall and Barton. In 2016 Nunn directed *Pericles*, his first Shakespeare production with a cast entirely made up of American actors, for the Theatre for a New Audience in New York. 'Mr. Nunn believes in doing whatever he can to get a story across', the *New York Times'* Alexis Soloski reported, under the headline

'Trevor Nunn, British Shakespeare Master, Tries Something New: Directing Americans'.

> His style, which seeks out the immediate, the accessible, the real in any text, has hardly changed since his student days. (Neither, it seems has his look: a denim shirt paired with denim trousers, hair and beard still straggly and still dark.) He works closely and collaboratively with his actors, but his first duty is always to the story.[68]

Nunn's approach to rehearsals has, as this report suggests, been consistent, and its combination of rigour, sensitivity and pragmatism emerges clearly from comments by the actors with whom he has worked.

Accounts of his rehearsals suggest that although Nunn has used improvisation strategically, this has not been a dominant element of the preparation. Close textual work has been supported by searching discussion of the context of the plays and, as appropriate, by improvisation of one kind or another. Cicely Berry, comparing the methods of the directors she encountered when she joined the RSC in 1970, describes John Barton's meticulous analysis of the text and Terry Hands' way of 'getting the sweep of the play right from the beginning'. Nunn, she writes, 'went into great detail with character and character relationships – not Method as we know it, but he rehearsed quietly and with great intimacy, getting the actor to feel personal contact with the character by bringing his/her own personal experiences to bear'.[69] Andrew Lloyd Webber describes Nunn on the first day of a workshop for the musical *Starlight Express* (1984) asking 'our bemused cast' to describe their first memory of a train journey, a process that lasted 'two hours of cathartic revelations'.[70] Although some actors have felt frustrated by the conflict of the sometimes lengthy process of 'tablework' with their desire to 'put the play on its feet', many have found it beneficial to lay the groundwork so carefully, and the supportive and thoughtful quality of his attention to the task in hand has been valued. Actors have felt that they –

and the play – have been respected. In 2010 Nunn wrote what is in effect a brief retrospective summary of this aspect of his own work in his 'Preface' to Julian Curry's *Shakespeare on Stage*. The actors interviewed about productions ranging from the 1960s to the date of publication 'were all working through a period of enormous and exciting change in approaches to Shakespeare'. The 'age of rhetorical delivery' had given way to 'the discovery, particularly aided by the influence of small-theatre intimate productions, that Shakespeare was at times an astonishingly naturalistic dramatist'. The 'voice beautiful' had been superseded by 'the search for and presentation of meaning above all, and in consequence, to the ceaseless search for the underlying thought'.[71]

When he took over as artistic director of the Royal Shakespeare Company, Nunn would have been vividly aware of the financial and organizational challenges that have been outlined above. The competing agendas of the fringe corresponded to a considerable extent with his personal attitudes, and he already had first-hand experience of the RSC's need to balance artistic innovation with fulfillment of the terms of the theatre's charter. Planning each Stratford season involved coordinating casting across several major productions, which sometimes entailed delicate negotiations between their directors, and overseeing the allocation of material resources and personnel. These would have to be addressed with a view to transfers to London and touring commitments, with the added complication of offering a fair number of plays that had proved dependable at the box-office while avoiding or at least mitigating the relegation of others to small-scale productions and limited runs. From the thirty-seven plays in the canon the company needed to stage five or six productions in the main house each year: as Nunn explained in an interview, 'to present the plays of Shakespeare relevantly, but also to present them (roughly) once every five or six years is contradictory'.[72] An artistic director would have to square more than one circle at once or, to use an analogy with a once-popular puzzle, 'solve' the Rubik's Cube on a daily basis – and then start over again at least a year in advance for the next season. This would be in addition to directing at least some of the season's plays and in some cases assisting colleagues on their own productions.

All this was familiar as the lot of an artistic director of any major theatre company, but one aspect of the legacy Nunn inherited would be less tractable to managerial skill and artistic vision: the building itself, and the stage where an artistic director would be expected to lead by example. If only for financial reasons, this remained the case even after the opening of The Other Place in 1975 and the Swan in 1986. Consequently, achieving an overall vision for the company, as well as in approaching individual plays, would be bound up with the quest for another goal, that of creating a financially viable space in which audiences and actors would share performances, as the mantra became, 'in the same room together'. Like his quest for ensemble and zest for the meticulous realization of the words of the texts in psychological and emotional terms, an important element of his work with Shakespeare has been his response to the challenges of the different plays and a range of performance spaces.

With the exception of Chapter 3, the organization of the chapters that follow is chronological. Chapter 1 examines Nunn's Shakespearean work during the first four years of his tenure as Director of the RSC, during which he engaged, often with great success, with the constrictions of the Royal Shakespeare Theatre itself. His most notable productions between 1968 and 1972 were *The Winter's Tale* (1969) and the season of Roman plays in 1972, for which the theatre was radically reconfigured. (After this season, the alterations to the stage itself were largely abandoned.) Chapter 2 includes discussion of his *Romeo and Juliet* and *The Comedy of Errors* on the 'Elizabethan' structure created for the 1976 season, his first Stratford *Macbeth* in 1974, a 'semi-operatic' *As You Like It* in 1977, and *All's Well that Ends Well* (1981) – the last of these being a major departure in theatrical interpretation of the play.

One of the recurring elements of Nunn's productions throughout these seasons was his desire to combine detailed exploration of the plays in psychological terms with an appropriately expressive and attractive design and staging. Another was the desire to achieve a performance space in which audience and actors would at the very least be 'in one room'. Since 1975, Nunn had been excited by the potential of 'chamber theatre' in The Other Place. In Chapter 3 his Shakespeare productions there and in its successor are examined: his third version of *Macbeth* (1976), *Othello* (1989) and *Measure for Measure* (1981). Chapter 4 discusses three productions during his directorship of the National Theatre (*The Merchant of Venice* and *Troilus and Cressida* in 1999 and *Love's Labour's Lost* in 2003) and three of his subsequent productions: *Hamlet* and *Richard II* at the Old Vic (2004 and 2005 respectively) and *King Lear* for the RSC in 2007.

1

The Main Stage at Stratford, 1968–72

Ever since the opening in 1932 of the Shakespeare Memorial Theatre (as it was known until Peter Hall renamed it in 1962), actors and directors had been struggling with a theatre that was handsomely executed and furnished as a public building but ineptly designed for the putting on of plays. Not only was it yet another proscenium-arch house, it was also poorly designed even within the chosen configuration of stage and auditorium. The overall effect was to enforce a separation of audience and performance, as the seating faced the stage in rows parallel to the front of the stage, with blank side walls; and the dress circle and gallery (subsequently designated as a balcony) receded from the stage in a manner that challenged actors with the prospect of gazing into a void above and beyond the stalls. In addition to this fundamental flaw, the acoustics were eccentric and the sightlines from many parts of the house were poor.

In 1960 Peter Hall had commissioned plans from the stage designer and architect Sean Kenny for a radical rebuilding to create a thrust stage with a 2,000-seat auditorium configured as an amphitheatre, but it was clear that the removal of the proscenium arch would take away structural support from the stage house and, critically, cause the fly tower to collapse: the compromise was the creation of a wedge-shaped forestage and a 1-in-18 rake to project the performance as far forward as possible.[1] Alterations to the masking around the proscenium opening and the space on either side of it served to mitigate the effect of a picture frame, but the basic architectural space, 7.23 metres (23' 9") high and 9.06 metres (29' 9") wide at the curtain line, remained problematic. In subsequent years further alterations were made, notably an extension to the front of the original gallery and adding side boxes and by various reconfigurations of the forestage. But a forestage could never be taken far forward without losing visibility from the balcony, and only a limited number of seats in the stalls could be repositioned to allow for spectators to be placed alongside it.

Despite all its limitations, this remained the theatre that would have to provide the main revenue of each season. One of Christopher Morley's first actions on his appointment as Head of Design in 1968 was to devise a new, box-like masking for both Stratford and the Aldwych to surround the central acting area behind the arch. This was a 'grey box', as close to neutrality as possible, that would help to facilitate quick changeovers from matinée to evening. Among possible future developments, Morley told an interviewer for *Flourish*, the house magazine distributed to the RSC's mailing list (or 'club'), perhaps the company 'should be considering the area over the stage not to be a place where scenery is flown but to restrict it to lighting equipment'. As the area above the stage in Shakespeare 'must always be associated with "the heavens and the elements"', it should be possible by this means to achieve 'lighting in the truly Shakespearean sense'.[2] The desire to achieve a degree of flexibility in the use of the space, and an increased freedom from the older pictorial conventions, were accompanied by a revision in the kind of stage picture offered. The basic set for Nunn's production of *Much Ado About Nothing* in the 1968 season illustrates this: within the grey box 'a translucent gauze box' was formed. Morley described this as 'a device to emphasize, by its use with lighting, the ever-changing light and shade of a charming Elizabethan society'.

Between 1968 and 1971 most productions on this stage, including those by other directors and designers, occupied the space created by this strategy, although not all made use of an inner box within that delimited by the masking. Nunn's productions during this period were *King Lear* and *Much Ado About Nothing* (1968), *Henry VIII* and *The Winter's Tale* (1969), and *Hamlet* (1970). The solid lateral walls of the white box for Brook's 1970 *Dream*, designed by Sally Jacobs, extended across the curtain line, with vertical slots to accommodate the legally required safety curtain. It is arguable that Morley's example influenced or at least facilitated this famous 'empty space', if only in the sense that his thinking was inspired by the same ideas as Brook's.[3] (The important distinction is that Nunn and Morley put things into the space, while Brook emptied it, at least of extra scenic elements and furnishings.) The significant break with the 'box' strategy came in the 1972 season of four Roman plays (plus a revival of *The Comedy of Errors* from 1962), for which machinery was installed to support a complex of stairs and platforms. This was a spectacular stage in its own right, flexible in a different sense from that offered in 1968. After 1972 this staging was not seen again, and the next substantial rethink produced a pseudo-Elizabethan wooden stage that would serve for all the plays in the 1976 season, this time without any coherent theme in the programming of the repertoire.

Although other adjustments would be made in the course of the next three decades, this was the last attempt at radical structural alterations to the stage before the major demolition and rebuilding of both auditorium and stage in 2007–10. After *Romeo and Juliet* (co-directed with Barry Kyle), *The Comedy of Errors* and *King Lear* (co-directed with Barry Kyle and John Barton) on the season's 'Elizabethan' stage in 1976, Nunn directed only two main-stage productions at Stratford before his departure to become a freelance in 1986: *As You Like It* (1977) and *All's Well That Ends Well* (1981). The first of these transferred to the Aldwych in 1978 and the second to the Barbican in 1982. He also directed the two parts of *Henry IV* for the Barbican's opening season in June 1981, but these were not shown in Stratford. His focus as a director of

Shakespeare during his tenure as head of the company was thus predominantly on its main-stage productions. In doing so he took on the challenges and opportunities afforded through its various permutations, notably through his collaboration with two designers, Christopher Morley and John Napier.

Before the Romans: Variations on the 'box'

Morley's account of the 'grey box' and its use in the 1968 *Much Ado About Nothing* has already been cited: Nunn was not the only director working with it, but it is his productions between his appointment and the radical reconstruction of the stage in 1972 that reflected most fully the range of possibilities it afforded. Morley's set for *The Taming of the Shrew* in 1967 was 'a masterpiece of ingenuity and design', displaying the exterior and interior of the inn where strolling players performed the comedy for Christopher Sly, but was so positioned that the presence of Sly and his companions as onstage 'spectators' obstructed the view from parts of the auditorium, a mistake that seems not to have been rectified when the play transferred to London late in the summer.[4] *Much Ado About Nothing* opened with a masked dumb-show that reminded some reviewers of *The Revenger's Tragedy*, but it was more notable for an aspect of Nunn's direction that would be more fully revealed in some of his subsequent work on the comedies. Irving Wardle describes the 'players' in *The Taming of the Shrew* as being 'prone to form up into rings and chorus lines to the accompaniment of a scratch wind ensemble'.[5] Whereas Wardle hailed 'an intricate variation on the Shakespearean theme of false appearances, and the interchangeability of dream and reality', identifying a serious thematic intention consonant with Nunn's reputation as a Leavisite, Harold Hobson vented his disgust at the antics of 'a crowd of greasy, noisy, dirty country louts playing about on the dunghill of [a] deliberately proletarian production'.[6] Nevertheless, Hobson was won over by the emergence in the second half of the evening of 'dawning tenderness' between Janet Suzman's Katherine and Michael Williams's Petruchio. At Katherine's declaration of obedience 'a great stillness fell upon the stage audience; these louts and layabouts were moved to a bemused silence'. Hobson ended what began as a hostile review, infused with social and political prejudice, with the surprising declaration that this was the best production of the play he had ever seen. Nunn's strategy in framing the play was not in itself innovative, but the balance of critical opinion seems to suggest a desire on his part to make the strolling players less than respectable, and to push the collective antic disposition even further than some reviewers could accept, at least until the shift into seriousness at the end.

The first of Nunn's two productions in his first season as artistic director showed the potential of the open stage within the new masking. They also gave a fuller sense of his interpretive approach in establishing an onstage world corresponding to a view of each play and the range of his technical skill as a director. *King Lear*, the season's opening production in April 1968, began with an effect reminiscent of *The Revenger's Tragedy*, against a dark background but this time in gold rather than silver. Rosemary Say in the *Sunday Telegraph* captured the impact of the court's entrance after the brief conversation between Gloucester, Kent and Edmund:

> An entry of soldiers as stiff and precise as guardsmen on sentry duty; a group of courtiers sombre against a pitch dark background save for the metallic gleam of their cloaks as they turn their backs on the audience; a flaming crown perched high and fantastic; a sweep of collective obeisance, and an old man is revealed, huddled on his throne, waiting impatiently for the coming ritual ... In front of him lies a giant, many handled sword to remind the audience that these are pagan times; the indeterminate clothes show that we are in the world of myth and legend.[7]

For their declarations of love, Regan and Goneril sat to each side of him with Cordelia at the centre, forming a tableau of sinister splendour with the sword stretched out in front of them, its point towards the audience. All wore robes of gold-painted netting, and the pattern of the gold crown worn by the king, with its high spikes, was continued in the smaller crowns worn by all three sisters. The grouping seemed to exemplify the societal organization described by Nunn in one of the programme's extracts from his talk 'at rehearsal', where he reflected that 'Lear's action is irrational, it is virtually a denial of reason, and so the perfect pyramid, which is only held together by reason, tumbles and collapses, and each individual thereafter is stumbling in anarchy'.[8] This was an arresting example of what J. C. Trewin identified as Nunn's 'surprising gifts for theatrical atmospherics and significant movement'.[9] Other critics recognized the intention of what Herbert Kretzmer in the *Daily Express* called 'this dark, stark and thunderous production', played out on 'an empty stage bare of any adornment except light and props'.[10] The hunting of a boar, wrote Harold Hobson, 'in which the baited animal seeks in vain to escape from the ring of cruel spears held by Lear's gentlemen', was in itself 'a thrilling piece of theatre'.[11] The battle was suggested in 'slow motion mime, with silver lances moving in the half-light as though seen in a nightmare',[12] and like the storm scenes appeared to be integral to the more general world picture that Sheila Bannock described in the *Stratford-upon-Avon Herald*: 'the stage represent[ed] both Lear's terrestrial realm and the region of his imaginative experience. It is peopled, as the mind is, with dimly perceived figures patterned with signs and portents.'[13]

The comparisons with *The Revenger's Tragedy* suggest that in *King Lear* Nunn established his credentials as a director capable of taking on a tragedy central to the Shakespearean canon, deploying the same command of spectacle on a set no longer borrowed from another production. He was also unavoidably challenging comparison with the austerity of Brook's 1962 production. Whether this was in fact (as Trewin claimed with evident relief) 'a major tragedy put directly upon the stage and allowed to speak for itself with its traditional meaning' is another matter. Nunn may not have had 'any revolutionary theories to support', but the contrast with Brook's confrontational avoidance of glamour was in itself indicative of an informed approach to the play and to the means by which it might be expressed – not at all the unmediated access to 'a major tragedy' hailed by Trewin.

Robert Speaight found the performance 'well-balanced rather than inspired', praising the actors – in particular Eric Porter's formidably aged king: 'Here was kingship incarnate, and Mr. Porter had in every wrinkle in his face what Kent recognized as authority.'[14] In the *New Statesman,* Philip French described the effect when the 'tent' was opened to reveal Lear 'bald, frail, old, and lit like a Rembrandt patriarch', conjuring up 'a coherent spiritual and social order ... with at its head a tired, remote man convincingly ready to be unburdened and crawl towards death'. (Porter was in fact thirty-nine, but appeared to be nearer eighty.) French found the 'excellent, beautifully spoken performance ... a sustained intellectual achievement and powerfully moving'.[15] Speaight's response to the company's speaking of the text was sympathetic but not uncritical, for example in his comment that Alan Howard was

> a most persuasive Edgar, letting us see an alert intelligence behind an apparent gullibility – an intelligence which would have been just as clear without so arduous a labouring of the text'. Porter 'understood – what Peter Brook so perversely ignored – that the passion of the part must be sustained by a rhythm which is plain for those who have ears to hear.[16]

Trewin, who had contrasted the production's rich and ceremonious opening with Brook's 'Beckettian treatment of the tragedy in a world of decay', compared Porter's performance with that of Randall Ayrton at Stratford in 1937, in its sense of 'a crumbling crag, a similar agonized pathos'. What Irving Wardle described as 'the shadow of the Brook-Scofield *Lear*' could not be avoided, and a number of reviewers shared his opinion that this was 'a workmanlike addition to the repertory presented in the familiar bare Stratford style' that offered 'no new way of looking at the play' and came 'nowhere near touching sublimity'.[17] Hobson found Porter 'admirable' in the scenes of anger, but possessing 'scarcely any touch of beauty or of pathos' in the later scenes of the play.

Among the critical and historical material that had become customary, the programme included extensive quotation from Trevor Nunn's comments 'at rehearsal' that supported not only his general thinking about the play, but also some specific elements of the production, notably the first scene's demonstration of the hierarchical order and the stripping of Lear in the storm, exhibiting in literal terms the vulnerability of the king's naked body. The text (Folio version 3.4.102–3) suggests that Lear starts to remove his clothes but is prevented from doing so, but here Edgar's near-nakedness was complemented by that of the king. There was also a lengthy quotation from the fashionable psychiatric theorist R. D. Laing on psychotic experience: 'No one who has not experienced how insubstantial the pageant of external reality can be, how it may fade, can fully realize the sublime and grotesque presences that can replace it, or that can exist alongside it.'[18] The literal as well as emotional or psychic denuding of Lear seemed to be a stage in the kind of experience Laing describes.

The season ended with *Much Ado About Nothing*, which demonstrated the potential of the basic design outlined in Morley's *Flourish* interview for evoking a world very different from that of tragedy. In the *Observer*, Ronald Bryden gave a lyrical description of the 'high, bare Jacobean chamber through whose translucent panels filters the dappled light of dim diamond panes, summer orchards, or moonshine in leafy village streets'. It was 'peopled by Elizabethans: pigeon-chested courtiers in plump trunks and hose, rice-powdered women with frizzy halos of curls'. Bryden identified a 'warmth and coherence' that 'show[ed] up sharply the bogusness' of Zeffirelli's attempt at the National Theatre in 1965 'to impose these from the outside like so much Neapolitan icing'.[19] Other reviewers found less warmth in what they perceived as a distinctly sombre set, regarding it as consistent with the production's approach to comedy. Irving Wardle in *The Times* described 'an anonymous plastic hangar, into which trundle Christopher Morley's heavyweight properties – a civic monument, a group of fossilized bushes – none of which establish any strong sense of locale'. The *Stratford-upon-Avon Herald*'s headline, '*Much Ado* in a set like a huge vault', and subheading, 'The Mood is Darker', reflected the reviewer's complaint that there was 'gaiety in this Messina but no fun', while Harold Hobson in the *Sunday Times* was not the only critic to reach for Shaw's 'view of the chief characters as people who might indeed get one invitation into decent society but would assuredly never obtain a second'.[20] For Hobson, the central emphasis of Nunn's direction of the church scene (4.2) had become the rejection of Hero rather than Beatrice's 'Kill Claudio'. As Claudio, Bernard Lloyd 'sets about this with a venom that makes the episode, which is anyway one of the most disgusting in Shakespeare, the penetrating point of the evening'. The Friar (Julian Curry) was 'the only one gentleman in the rabble', while Alan Howard's Benedick was 'without agility and fancy'. Both Howard and Janet Suzman, as Beatrice, had 'not been directed so as to evoke laughter or grace'. The significance of 'grace' for Hobson is evident in his assertion that the production was 'a coherent whole, a sardonic view of secular life as dark and dull, with just the merest flash of suggestion that there is salvation in the Church'.

Complaints of this kind were symptomatic of the desire to identify a 'Trevor Nunn approach', and at the same time to define yet again a distinctive 'RSC style'. Frank Marcus commented that the company 'continu[ed] to uphold their allegiance to the three V's: Vigour, Volume, and Virility' at the expense of the 'subtlety, poetry, and maturity' demanded by the play. Harking back to his *Taming of the Shrew* in the previous season, Marcus reflected that Nunn was 'temperamentally, much more at home in the crude rough and tumble of Petruchio and his Kate' and Alan Howard 'looked rather puzzled most of the time' and lacked 'Benedick's sly relish', while 'Janet

Suzman's great gifts were sadly wasted: her Beatrice is an aggressive governess'.[21] Even when a reviewer's response to the actor's performances differed from those quoted above – as in Gareth Lloyd Evans's praise for the 'wit and grace' of Benedick as played by Howard, an actor 'who commands attention by a kind of controlled eccentricity' – the overall impression is of an ensemble as well as its director finding its way.[22] One aspect of this was the nurturing of talents such as those of Howard and Suzman: another was the formulation – not necessarily voiced as such – of an approach to the character of a play's society as well as its individuals. 'The plot', wrote Bryden in the *Observer*, 'with its fairy-tale resurrections and kitchen-fire sex warfare, grows out of its society and time.' Even Milton Shulman's dismissal of the Messinans as 'little people reveling in cheap and mean emotions' suggests a coherent if unwelcome approach to the play, and identifies a distinct intention on Nunn's part, to 'follow a psychologically coherent line through the confusions of an action that can only be reconciled by accepting the changes from comedy to melodrama at full theatrical value'.[23] Despite its heavy reliance on music 'the production somehow lack[ed] its own harmony', but Wardle was nonetheless discerning a motive for Nunn's exploration of its passions. In his retrospective article on the 'Stratford Style' he reflected that the company was 'well equipped for plays in which no one man is much better than his fellows', but was 'under-equipped for plays demanding sublimity or music'.[24]

One aspect of the *Much Ado* production seemed to be already a Nunn trademark akin to the comic elaboration of the 'frame' in his *Taming of the Shrew*: the energy and spectacle of such moments as the arrival of Don Pedro and his companions at the masked ball, 'a court masque in mottled scarlet, all dancing torches and leering silver visors'.[25] Peter Roberts, wondering in *Plays and Players* which productions from the 1968 Stratford season would be chosen for transfer to London, noted that *Much Ado* had picked up after 'a shaky first night' and included in his appraisal a suggestion regarding another aspect of Nunn's work in the church scene, 'where his practical staging rises to the height of his directorial ideas. I shall not easily forget this Beatrice and Benedick alone among a maze of pews inching their way to make physical contact in a chapel that seems the emptier for having been so recently the scene of such brutal drama.'[26]

Another element of the new direction taken in Stratford was reflected in comments by J. C. Trewin in 1968 in *Flourish* to the effect that the company seemed to be favouring young actors who lacked the desire to 'give' and 'fling the door wide' that he identified in the previous generation of stars: 'It is curious, for there are many current actors of spirit and intelligence. Can it be that they and their directors – who so often have the final word – are intent upon interpreting a play to us rather than letting us experience it?'[27] In *Shakespeare Survey*, Gareth Lloyd Evans took up the suggestion, citing the programme notes of the 1969 season's productions as evidence for an '"academic" spirit which, both for much good and some ill, has penetrated Shakespearian productions'. The new directors – Nunn, Terry Hands, David Jones and even John Barton ('successfully making good with the new dispensation') – 'will turn the bazaars and museums of scholarly exegesis upside down to find a good bargain'.[28] Trewin returned to the theme in the Spring, 1971 issue of *Flourish*, wishing for productions with 'a plain text, spoken richly without self-consciousness; for unobtrusive decoration (rather more than an over-size bathroom or a large box); and, if possible, an absence of the director's programme notes.' Harold Hobson had joined the attack in the Spring 1969 issue, accusing the company of being 'anti-British and anti-greatness' in, respectively, the choice of new work in its Aldwych repertoire and the treatment of its actors. Claiming that 'the Industrial Revolution stamped out of the working class any originality, and creativeness that it might display in its processes of earning its living', he asserted that this was what the Royal Shakespeare Company was 'doing to its actors and actresses, under the dictation of the director of whatever play they [were] appearing in'. On the facing page Nunn responded, drawing a distinction between the kind of spontaneous, ephemeral effects that (he suggested) characterized Hobson's definition of 'greatness' and defending the ensemble principle: 'My job demands that I create an environment when something "great" (and subjectively I yearn for something "great" every bit as much as Mr. Hobson) can happen, but I am not interested in what is "great" in spite of the play, the dramatist, the intention, the cumulative pattern of what is being communicated.' Glancing at the reactionary political tone of Hobson's article, Nunn insisted that there was 'nothing democratic or egalitarian' about the ensemble, which served 'the whole experience' and was 'prepared to sacrifice the individual moment if meaning or intention is endangered'. The difference between this and the star system was that 'the actor is asked to serve the play, the play is not allowed to serve the actor'.[29]

As a statement of principle, Nunn's article amounted to a manifesto not only for the ensemble ideal, but also for the importance of 'interpretation', adding a term – 'cumulative pattern' – that reflected his background in a combination of the 'close reading' practised in the 'New Criticism' of the 1950s and 1960s and the moral earnestness of Leavis. The 1969 season offered an overview of the late Romances, with *The Winter's Tale, Pericles* and *Henry VIII. Cymbeline* was absent, as was *The Tempest* (produced in 1970 under Barton's direction). Though Barton's elegiac *Twelfth Night* might be claimed as sharing the 'romance' atmosphere identifiable in the later plays, the same could not be said of *The Merry Wives of Windsor*, revived from the 1968 season. Like Peter Hall's repertoire of comedies in 1960, this was presented as one of the themed seasons that, together with the series of history plays, would become a company standby, a means of including seldom-seen works alongside familiar plays by benefitting from their box-office support. Morley's overall design concept for all except *Twelfth Night* was a development of the 'box', reinforcing the sense of interpretive consistency that irked some reviewers but satisfied others. This seemed an exciting sign of the company's modernity and seriousness to many of those who, as students, had been imbued with the same attitudes as Nunn and his team. His production of *The Winter's Tale* was the most significant and effective embodiment of this engagement, capturing the spirit of the times while reasserting the play's centrality in the canon.

The ten critical commentaries excerpted in the programme for the production (in addition to contextual and historical material) resemble a reading list for an undergraduate course of the 1960s on the Romances, including Northrop Frye, Frank Kermode, D. A. Traversi, S. L. Bethell, C. L. Barber – and, of course, F. R. Leavis. Nunn's own contribution, citing Hamlet's speech 'What a piece of work is a man', characterized the Romances as 'not naturalistic', and reconciling 'the paradox of man', the coexistence of 'the beast' and the 'angel'.

> They are parables, they work both as fables and allegories. Leontes is in a destructive nightmare, 'performed' in a 'wide gap of time'. Spring breaks through the grip of winter, love returns, enabling Leontes to awake his faith and be redeemed. Shakespeare absolves the gods of our failures; the responsibility is in us, the faith demanded is faith in ourselves.[30]

The plays 'speak to a time in need of moral certainty' but there is none of the sense, proposed in a notorious essay by Lytton Strachey, of a playwright 'exhausted by his tragedies and turning to escapism'.[31] Nunn's final sentence reflects his own belief in the social and moral significance of art, effectively presenting Shakespeare as a Leavisite: 'As always he was interpreting life to his audience and at the same time offering a challenge.'

'We live in an age that's increasingly uncertain where evil ends and sickness begins.' Under the headline 'Leontes Syndrome?' Benedict Nightingale's review in the *New Statesman* opened with a reference to the most striking element of Nunn's approach, the use of a drastic change in lighting and stroboscopic flickering to signal Leontes' madness in his quasi-hallucinatory imagining of Hermione's dalliance with

Polixenes. Nightingale objected that even if there was such a thing as the 'Leontes Syndrome', this was not 'a reading that enriche[d] the play', as it took from Leontes his 'responsibility for his actions and his fate'.[32] R. D. Laing had been quoted in the *King Lear* programme, but no such reference to him appears in that for *The Winter's Tale*, and although Nunn may have applied his ideas to the delusions of Leontes, it was some variation on Freudian psychology that critics inferred from the production's emphasis on childhood experience – its first scenes unfolded in a nursery, with a large white rocking-horse. Nightingale wondered whether the 'sound of a music-box, the preponderance of toys on stage, the puppyishness of the principals' who were 'cavorting innocently', suggested 'something infantile in their antics'. The initial scenes characterized the play as a family drama, with no obvious indication that these were royal personages: they inhabited a world and wore clothes that suggested the well-to-do occupants of a fashionably minimalist household. But the production's other emphases commanded equal attention from the critics: a hippyish age of innocence in the Bohemia scenes, and the suggestion of kinship with the other Romances. Woolfenden's score included use of the sitar, an instrument associated with the fashionable enthusiasm for Indian mysticism and familiar from George Harrison's 'Within You Without You' from the Beatles' album *Sgt Pepper's Lonely Hearts Club Band* (1967).

As the house lights dimmed to the sound of sitar music, a prologue in which the distinctive, amplified voice of Time (Alton Kumalo) was heard speaking the lines from the chorus speech that begins 4.1:

> I that please some, try all, both joy and terror
> Of good and bad, that makes and unfolds error,
> Now take upon me, in the name of Time,
> To use my wings. (1–4)[33]

Leontes, his arms and legs outstretched in imitation of Leonardo's representation of Man as the centre of a circle, rotated in a plexiglass box under strobe lighting. (The season's production of *Pericles*, directed by Terry Hands, began with a gauze drop curtain showing the Leonardo image.) The figure in the box reappeared in miniature form as one of the toys in the nursery where Hermione – heavily pregnant – and Polixenes, together with Mamillius and Leontes, presented the picture of a happy family with a long-absent friend. An outsize, white rocking-horse, a humming top and a kaleidoscope, with white cubes (toy boxes) completed the picture (Figure 2). The flickering light returned with Leontes's fit of jealousy, along with amplified

FIGURE 2 The Winter's Tale *(Royal Shakespeare Theatre, 1969)*, *Act 1, Scene 1: Hermione (Judi Dench), Mamillius (Jeremy Richardson) Leontes (Barrie Ingham) and Polixenes (Richard Pasco) in the nursery.* Photo by Reg Wilson © RSC.

heart-beats and a distorted jingle of 'Jack and Jill', seemingly from the music-box, as the intimacies he imagined were seen in slow-motion. 'It was almost as though the audience is taken on a trip into another dimension of awareness', wrote Herbert Kretzmer in the *Daily Express*, using language associated with psychotropic drugs.[34] If this was a 'trip', it was one in which the audience shared the visions, as the stroboscopic and slow-motion effect returned when Antigonus met his fate at the claws of the bear, and the 'magic' effect of the plexiglass box was used in the final scene when Hermione's statue was displayed. The Leonardo image suggested the emblematic nature of what was about to happen, a sign of the human condition rather than simply an individual's psychosis: it was the kind of generalization outlined in Nunn's comments on Hamlet's speech. The costumes for Leontes' court were identified by Philip Hope-Wallace in his *Guardian* review of the Aldwych transfer as '"Kate Greenaway" clothes' consistent with the nursery setting.[35] They blended early Victorian and modern fashion, sufficiently fantastic to avoid evoking more than a hint of specific period, but at the same time consistent with a society in which a jealous royal patriarch might credibly enforce his will. As Patricia Tatspaugh points out in her study of Stratford productions of the play, 'the set and the seemingly innocent toys had begun to take on a darker significance'.[36] As the scene progressed, the set's white box seemed to trap Leontes, as though the kaleidoscope (through which he and his son looked) suggested distorted vision, and the humming top's sound was amplified as his jealous delusion took hold. In the trial scene, the news of Mamillius' death produced an apparent stroke in Leontes, a 'bright idea' that Robert Speaight (in *Shakespeare Quarterly*) thought appropriate, with the reservation that the physical impairment was accompanied by an impediment in his speech 'just at the moment when the clearing of Leontes' mind and the cleansing of his soul are indicated by a new-found freedom in the verse'.[37] The sinister music-box tune recurred at the end of 2.1 as Antigonus picked up the teddy bear Mamillius had dropped, growled at it and hit it on the head.[38]

After the interval and the appearance of Time, now in the 'glass' box, the sense of participation in a healing festivity was reinforced by the audience's experience of the sudden release into the world of contemporary counterculture afforded by the appearance of Autolycus (Derek Smith) with a coiffure to out-hair *Hair*, dressing-up box trousers and shirt, and what Kretzmer characterized as the 'exuberant lurches and twangs of Guy Woolfenden's modern beat score'.[39] The current fashion of sleeveless sheepskin coats helped to make Florizel's disguise as a shepherd credible, Perdita's flowing gown and bare feet evoked London's King's Road (like Carnaby Street, then a parade ground for the latest trends) as well as the central figure of Botticelli's *Primavera*, and 'the stage fill[ed] with long haired men and leggy girls'.[40]

The notion that innocence in a war-torn world could be regained by progression – or regression – to a freer, less inhibited self-expression in music and dance was a key aim of the counterculture, typified and to a degree sanitized in *Hair*, the 'American tribal Love-Rock Musical', that had arrived in the West End in September 1968. The clown's announcement that twelve of the locals had 'made themselves all men of hair' for their 'gallimaufry of gambols' (4.4.333) suddenly seemed very appropriate. LOVE – often spelled out thus in capitals – was a recurrent theme in popular art and culture, notably as something to be 'made' in place of war. Betrayed by their supposedly mature and worldly-wise elders, the young might usefully express themselves in sexual freedom and general benevolence in a refusal to accept the social responsibilities insisted on by their parents' generation. (Pandarus' reference to 'the generation of love' in *Troilus and Cressida* [3.1.126] took on a new resonance that audiences were quick to catch.) One of the 'background' programme excerpts, by the cultural critic Stuart Hall, defined Love 'in the Hippie alphabet' as 'something wider and more inclusive than sex', its 'widening circle of inferences' culminating in 'the all-embracing love for mankind, naïve and vulnerable in its apparent simplicity, but transformed, in Hippie philosophy, into a sort of silent power'.[41] This *Winter's Tale* presented the notion of a new generation curing society of the ills done by their elders, with the image of an alternative community – albeit more of a partying world than some kind of ashram – that would somehow embody this therapeutic effect, at least by implication. It should be admitted that the notion of Hippies as truly innocent was not universally shared, either in society at large or among the reviewers. Robert Speaight objected on the grounds of realism: 'You cannot produce the pastoral fourth act ... with any hope of success unless you are prepared to take peasants as naturally and seriously, as realistically and also as unromantically, as Shakespeare took them'. The 'sensuality' of the rural community was 'healthy, whereas the one certain thing about the Hippies is that they are sick; Autolycus had a good number of shady wares in his basket, but "pot" was not among them'.[42]

Although this time there was no specific reference to Laing by Nunn, the production was to some extent shadowed by the psychiatrist's basic proposition that mental illness could be cured by the means advocated in the 'antipsychiatry' movement in which he had become a guru. Roy Porter summarizes its 'varied and controversial' tenets: 'mental illness was not an objective behavioural or biomechanical reality but either a negative label or strategy for coping in a mad world; madness had a truth of its own; and psychosis could be a healing process and, hence, should not be pharmacologically suppressed'. The common factor was a 'critique of the asylum' and, in Laing's words, 'Madness need not be all breakdown. It may be a break-through. It is potential liberation as well as enslavement and existential death'.[43] The 1969 *Winter's Tale* did not make any connection between the 'recuperative community' of the Bohemia scenes and the healing of Leontes – although he is the person most in need of a cure, he does not travel there – but by association the awakening of 'faith' in the play's final scene was the result of this kind of experience, emphasized by Judi Dench's doubling the roles of Hermione and Perdita. Her photograph as the daughter, dancing at the sheep-shearing feast, in her 'Botticelli' dress, was used on posters (and on the sleeve of the recording of songs from the show) with the Old Shepherd's line 'Thou metst with things dying, I with things new-born' (3.3.110–11). In the sheep-shearing, Nunn told Peter Ansorge in *Plays and Players*, 'we tried to make an entertainment within the centre of the play which would actually have the value of an awakening, to make everyone in the audience suddenly come alive'.[44] For many of us, to have passed through this healing experience, even by witnessing it as an audience, was deeply moving. In the final scene, the characters 'touching hands in a silent circle of reunion' (Wardle) suggested the restoration of harmony in a world that had been traumatized and fragmented.

Ideas of this kind, circulating in responses to the production as well as being directly expressed within it, are signs of the company's engagement with the Zeitgeist, perhaps on a level that could be dismissed by some, in the parlance of the time, as mere 'trendiness', but undeniably with a renewal of the mission to assert the contemporary resonance and relevance of the plays. Despite the absence of *The Tempest* and *Cymbeline* and the somewhat tendentious inclusion of *Henry VIII* as a 'Romance', which limited the season's effectiveness as a statement about 'late' Shakespeare, the RSC was now established as a theatrical complement to and reflection of thinking in the literary-critical sphere. Nunn himself, moreover, was becoming identifiable as an *auteur*, a director whose artistic development could be traced and assessed, even when he worked as one of a group of co-directors in the team he had assembled. Not only had 'letting the play speak for itself', favoured by Trewin and others, ceased to be an option, its very validity as a concept was in question.

In his *Observer* review, Ronald Bryden suggested that Morley's 'bare white box' fulfilled the director's intention in 'thread[ing] together the disparate elements of Shakespeare's rambling romance – Victorian melodrama, pop musical, low vaudeville and high, icy poetry – on a line of consistent intelligence and sweet design'.[45] Beyond the production's striking visual enactment of the thematic patterns of the play, it impressed through the effectiveness of the performances – particularly those of Judi Dench, Barrie Ingham and Richard Pasco as Hermione/Perdita, Leontes and Polixenes. There were many incidental felicities, signs (in Nightingale's words) that 'Nunn has his ear close to the text'. The verse speaking was 'scrupulous' and Judi Dench achieved 'a dignified splendour in her defiance of her husband' that showed she had 'clearly pondered Hermione's "I am not prone to weeping, as our sex commonly are."' John Barber observed that a consequence of the light and sound effects used to illustrate Leontes' delusions might have been 'to deprive the actors of their subtler methods for conveying states of mind', but in this case 'they conspired with Mr. Ingham to create a hard-eyed intellectual Leontes, a distracted introvert in the grip of a neurosis'. Lloyd Evans, in *Shakespeare Survey*, understood the psychological reasoning behind the performance, and observed that Paulina (Brenda Bruce) became 'the main agent in the healing process', prompting the grieving king to 'talk out' his illness. Unfortunately, Ingham achieved 'meaning without melody, exposition without characterization', while Judi Dench gave 'a moving display of her characteristically vulnerable style of movement and facial expression, but falter[ed] at the details of character, nuances of meaning'. Both seemed 'engulfed by interpretation'. Critical comment on all the various special effects ranged from downright approval to complaints of directorial heavy-handedness. Bryden read the stroboscope as 'a perfect symbol' with 'light and dark, either in itself offering a coherent view of the world, alternating in scrambled, bewildering energy'. J.W. Lambert found this, and such other touches of stylization as Hermione's 'slow-motion faint' in the trial scene as she advanced towards her husband with her arms outstretched imploringly and the courtiers moved in slow-motion towards her, part of a pattern of 'things unnecessarily spelt out', given that 'in Shakespeare's own day the explanatory dumb-show had become a bit of a joke'.[46]

The Winter's Tale was a considerable achievement, bringing the play into contact with the mindset of the time as an example of distinctively modern theatre. Arguably, Nunn's production was influential on the play's standing in the repertoire: Roger Warren observed in 1990 that, on the evidence of the number of revivals since 1969, 'a play that was rarely performed has now been firmly re-established in the repertoire'.[47] It further established Nunn as adventurous in his approach to the plays, meticulous in using the theatre's resources to express interpretation grounded in the text and able (with the support of designer, composer and choreographer) to respond to the contemporary appetite for both psychological realism and musical theatre. It toured abroad before arriving at the Aldwych in August 1970 with minor changes of cast, most notably Elizabeth Spriggs taking over from Brenda Bruce as Paulina. But the reservations of some critics, not just those who yearned for some kind of 'plain unvarnished' Shakespeare, were significant.

Of the productions of plays that fully qualified as 'Romances', *The Winter's Tale* was the most successful. *Henry VIII*, which opened in October, was altogether less convincing in its claims to the label. The element of 'things new born' invoked at its conclusion had to be heavily qualified by the depiction of devious political dealings in a reign that was less than happy and a monarch whose cruelty was of a different order from that of Leontes. However troubled Donald Sinden's Henry might seem, the character was selfish and manipulative, politically driven rather than the victim of some kind of psychosis. The production nevertheless began with an assertion of its kinship with the others, with Leonardo's image on a scrim, but ended, not with the published play's epilogue but with Henry alone on stage in a spotlight after the cast, clad in white for the christening, had advanced towards the audience chanting 'Peace, Plenty, Love, Truth' from the stage and whispered the same words from the aisles at the side of the stalls. (Words from 5.4.47–8, but omitting 'terror' from the 'servants' inherited by the successor of 'this chosen infant'.) This was an attempt, wrote Philip Hope-Wallace in the *Guardian*, 'at forcing us into audience participation'.[48] In the *Observer*, Ronald Bryden described it as 'a sonorous white hippy mass', but Henry's isolation as he wandered into the darkness holding the baby Elizabeth left a question mark over Cranmer's prophecy.[49] The Brechtian device of placards announcing the events of each scene in tabloid press headlines such as 'Queen in Labour' had already suggested qualification to the play's credentials as a romance rather than simply a late (and co-authored) work. Was it the 'romantic' view of history as leading towards Elizabeth's reign that was being scrutinized? Benedict Nightingale, under the title 'Forget History' in the *New Statesman*, observed that although the play had been revived 'at such times of mindless pomp as our own Queen's coronation', Nunn had attempted to adapt it for 'a less gullible atmosphere' with a coda that was 'hardly emphatic enough to eradicate the impression of distorted, sentimentalized history that's been left behind'.[50] Hope-Wallace praised 'strong, simple and unforced acting' with 'bravura where needed, but no phoney sentiment' from a cast that included Peggy Ashcroft as Katharine of Aragon, Donald Sinden as the king and Brewster Mason as Wolsey. At the Aldwych the 'Brechtian' titles had been removed, but the impression was still a 'sombre and rather ponderous' revival, with its emphasis 'firmly on the grinding harshness of the Tudor monarch's court'.[51] Although the director attempted to lighten the mood with such details as Cranmer playing football with 'sportive choirboys while awaiting a summons to an ecclesiastical court', for Michael Billington the overall effect remained 'the image of a dark, semi-totalitarian society into which light suddenly intrudes at the end'.[52] Barbara Hodgdon, examining 'closure and contradiction' in the history plays and their performance, suggests that the final moments invited audiences' to examine their own social text, their own 'succession', at the end of one decade and beginning of another.[53]

Despite his overall approval of *The Winter's Tale*, Ronald Bryden had wondered 'whether, for all his skill and enormous invention, Nunn [was] really the sort of director who gives actors the freedom to flower in their own way'. *Hamlet*, in the 1970 Stratford season, seemed like an answer to this cautionary opinion, while pursuing once more the theme of aberrant psychology in a notably distracted Prince. In an interview with Peter Ansorge, Nunn declared that in most of its work the company was now 'concerned with the human personalities of a king and queen rather then with their public roles'. The 'chamber setting' he and Morley had developed supported this by 'establish[ing] that the most important object on the stage is the actor. It has to work within the scale of the individual actor – to make his words, thoughts, fantasies and language seem important'.[54] Nunn contrasted his *Hamlet* with Hall's 1965 production, and his own lack of interest in politics – in interpreting the plays and in terms of running the company – with his predecessor's approach to both.

Like *The Winter's Tale*, *Hamlet* was presented as a family drama with little emphasis on regality or establishing a sense of 'real' politics. The chamber of the set confined the action to a white space that was not so much empty as chilly and oddly antiseptic. Peter Thomson, in *Shakespeare Survey*, noted that the 'off-white boards of the stage floor leading up to four off-white screens across the back wall and broken intermittently with off white furnishings' confirmed Nunn's explanation in *Plays and Players* that he wanted 'something believably Scandinavian in terms of climate and practicality' that would also represent a court 'in celebration rather than mourning'.[55] The court was dressed richly with enough fur for a cold climate, in the kind of modified period mode now familiar at Stratford, Elizabethan in outline and cut but modern in materials – 'clothes' rather than 'costumes' – so that the production offered a revision of what might be thought of as 'traditional' Shakespeare. In contrast to the gleaming white of the rest of the court, Hamlet wore a shabby black suit, 'stained by use and wrongly or inadequately buttoned'.[56]

In 'Nunn's *Hamlet*: a Report from the Kitchen', Ronald Bryden in the *Observer* identified the interpretation as 'a

Laingian *Hamlet*', although nothing had been said about the psychiatrist in a talk given by the director to the cast: Hamlet's madness was not feigned, but 'a Laingian escape from a society built on lunatic deceptions into the lonely sanity of private truth'.[57] Reporting on his experience of the rare privilege of being admitted to a rehearsal, the critic described the 'labour of self discovery and exposure' behind Howard's performance. In the fourth week of rehearsal, Howard was still playing Hamlet 'as a glittering, sardonic concealer of his genuine feelings, the most adept Machiavellian in a Machiavellian court'. Bryden observed how the actor gradually discarded this, seeming younger as he progressed:

> It was as if he was stripping from himself not only years, but the defensive armour, the competence to hide the child in the adult, which they had brought. The jeering glances, the sharp small-toothed smiles diminished. In their place emerged a dark, smouldering stare of misery, a sudden, dismayed fall of the mouth, like a child who has been slapped.

This 'slow, painful mining of themselves for the emotions we normally hide' was the actors' 'real work'. The combination in Nunn's approach of historical insight and the quest for a connection to twentieth-century psychological theories is evident in an interview Howard gave to *Plays and Players* in February 1971. The actor recalled that Nunn 'had attached great importance to Hamlet's university education at Wittenberg', returning from the Lutheran university to Catholic Denmark 'impregnated by the "new philosophy"' and 'with the protestant idea of individual responsibility in his mind'. Quite why his father, a 'stern, austere Catholic king', had sent him to Wittenberg was 'never resolved'. Perhaps he suspected Claudius and wanted to hide 'what was going on' from his son? As for the relationship between Hamlet and Ophelia, after a 'long discussion' Nunn thought that she and Hamlet had not slept together, but Howard and Helen Mirren both decided they had, 'but probably in secret, a short slot [*sic*], bringing an added tension to their relationship'. Central to Howard's interpretation was the notion that Hamlet 'could only face the situation he was in by being an actor', and the 'relevance' of the character to the modern world as lying in his 'doubts about the values of the world in which he is living'. Unable to reconcile what he has so far learnt with what he sees around him, Hamlet loses 'his absolute' and 'the development of his personality is affected'.[58]

Reviewers concurred with the general impression that Howard's Prince was (as John Barber put it) 'genuinely demented ... a manic-depressive before fate laid its terrible burden on his frail shoulders', with a 'fixed eye, dusty clothes, dishevilled hair and unshaven look'.[59] In *Plays and Players,* Peter Roberts warned that Howard's Hamlet would not satisfy those who 'repair to Stratford in search of a Prince Charming', but predicted that 'those who recognize in Hamlet an intelligent and not insensitive neurotic making a desperate and ultimately successful bid to come to terms with himself' would 'find something of what they are looking for'.[60] Peter Thomson noted that the division the long evening into three acts supported a narrative development: the first part 'carries Hamlet to breaking point in confrontation with his father's ghost'; the second includes 'the shifts between real and performed madness'; and the third 'completes the story after Hamlet has recovered his self control'.[61]

In what Roberts thought 'an interesting deployment of the Pirandello-like concern with the nature of illusion and reality', the players were the only characters not dressed in black or white. They brought with them 'a visual hint of hippiedom' and performed 'in a stylised manner reminiscent of Oriental theatre'.[62] Their effect on Hamlet was pivotal, providing both a new means of expression for his anguish and a means of disguise in the form of a monk's robe from the troupe's wardrobe. Even Claudius, who barged onto their stage to stop *The Murder of Gonzago,* seemed to be affected beyond mere shock of possible exposure: for his prayer he knelt on the spot where the play's king had died. By hiding behind the curtains of their portable stage at the end of 3.3, Hamlet overheard

Claudius' plans to send him to England, then donned the monk's robe to creep up behind the praying king. Still wearing it, he dragged Polonius from behind the arras and stabbed him in a frenzied attack, harangued his mother in the same father-confessor guise and subsequently escaped from his pursuers by joining a file of chanting monks. When he was brought before Claudius, the king stripped him of his robe, leaving him in his black briefs. Hamlet was then held up so that Claudius could punch him viciously in the stomach. There was more than a hint of a Christ figure here, and Thomson was not alone in wondering whether 'this stripping ... was intended to be the beginning of his recovery'. Comparison of this moment with the literal stripping of Lear in Nunn's 1968 production, as well as the figurative 'stripping' of Leontes, suggests at least a common, perhaps specifically Laingian, image for the passage through madness. Hobson, discerning a reference to Genet's *The Balcony* in the disguise, took this as a sign that Hamlet was 'in the grip of erotic fancies' and speculated that by the end of his interrogation 'he has got what is necessary to the satisfaction of his needs: a bloody murder, and the subjection of his body to physical torment', and observed that 'Thereafter until the end of the play, Hamlet is calm, joyous and fulfilled'. Eccentric as Hobson's reading may have been – he even managed to drag in a claim that Nunn intended a reference in Hamlet's 'perversions' to those of 'student radicals' – it was to a degree licensed by the emphasis on Hamlet's 'distraction'.

Where Hall's production had ironically juxtaposed Hamlet's dying words with Fortinbras's men hammering at the doors, breaking them open and entering in a display of military force, Nunn had Fortinbras arrive with only one attendant soldier. Claudius (David Waller) was every inch the 'bloat king' of Hamlet's complaint and the Queen (Brenda Bruce) was what the Victorians would call 'no better than she should be', affectionate with her son but doting on the sensualist she had clearly been happy to marry. There were innovative touches of direction, such as Ophelia (Helen Mirren) dressed in black for her 'mad scene' and playing a lute in accord with the First

Quarto's stage direction, but there were none of the large-scale directorial gestures of *The Winter's Tale*.

'Variable geometry' and the 1972 'Romans' season

Nunn did not direct any new productions at Stratford in 1971, but preparations were being made for another thematic season and the extensive reconstruction of the stage that was to support the sense of its coherence as an exploration of the Roman plays. After the relative austerity and openness of staging within the 'box' in its various permutations, this was, to say the least, surprising. Rapidity of transition from scene to scene was to be provided by means utterly foreign to the original stagecraft of the plays, and the architectural effects seemed rather to pay homage to the scenography of Adolphe Appia at the turn of the century and the more recent work of the Czech director and designer Josef Svoboda, who had developed a theory of non-naturalistic design that would be responsive to the ebb and flow of nature and dramatic action in its mobility and active manipulation of the theatrical space. 'I don't want a static picture', he told an interviewer, 'but something that evolves, that has movement, not necessarily physical movement, of course, but a setting that is dynamic, capable of expressing changing relationships, feelings, moods, perhaps only by lighting, during the course of the action'.[63] Like Svoboda's most radical designs, the new Stratford stage would define the stage's playing area by redefining the whole of the architectural space itself. An account in *Tabs*, the magazine of the theatre lighting company Rank Strand Electric, began with a concise summary of this 'variable geometry':

> The four plays employ the same basic but very variable set, including a perspective engagement of the observer, extending from 5 m in front of the proscenium and continuing

through what was a proscenium arch, for a further 9m. The size, shape and character of this focal area is determined by the combined disposition of several features, including four periactoid towers, various portable props and flown pieces, articulated flown borders, and the configuration of the new and enlarged mechanized stage.[64]

The stage was now 12.2 metres (40 ft) deep, with a width of 11.3 metres (37 ft) at the front and 5.63 metres (18 ft) at the back. It could be tilted to a rake of 1-in-4, bringing the front edge down almost to the level of the first row of stalls. In the auditorium side balcony seats and slips (standing places behind them) had been added, cantilevered out from the 22-inch thick walls, with the front of the structures clad in white material to complement the stage itself.[65]

The new stage represented what Sally Beauman characterizes as 'not just a break with the principles Nunn had been at pains to establish, but a defiant reversal of them'.[66] Although indeed an unashamed exploitation of the theatre's suitability for the 'perspective engagement of the spectator', it also highlighted some of its limitations even in that respect. The trapezoid shape of the main acting area, with its narrowest side far upstage, reinforced the persistent acoustic problems, so that most of the dialogue was placed near or in front of the proscenium line, while the mobility of the floor units often impeded the desired fluidity of action: it was not unusual, especially in the first production (*Coriolanus*) to see signs of the actors' anxiety to ensure that there would be a floor in the right place for their next move, especially at the end of scenes. As the season went on, use of the possible mechanical effects diminished, and *Titus Andronicus*, the last play to join the repertoire, used only the upstage elevator and the central downstage trap. The simple three-tiered raked platform of Clifford Williams's production of *The Comedy of Errors*, revived from 1962, was placed centrally on a stage set at a moderate rake. The new stage was not funded as extravagantly as was widely reported at the time – some £25,000 rather than £250,000. (Beauman points out that this was 'roughly equal to a four-production budget combined'.[67]) Nevertheless, there was an element of extravagance in that no equivalent could be provided at the Aldwych. This was in fact a blessing, as on transfer to London the productions became leaner and in some respects more powerful than they had been in Stratford. With what turned out to be an over-optimistic glance towards the future, the programme for *Coriolanus* claimed that the new developments were 'designed to bring the Stratford auditorium nearer to the "one room" relationship between actor and audience planned for the RSC's new London theatre now being built by the City in the Barbican (where the company are to move from the Aldwych).' In the RSC's 1978 *Yearbook*, James Sargant, the RSC's administrator for the Barbican, described its auditorium: the stage would lie 'in front of rather than behind the arch' and that acting area would be 'at the focus of every seat in the house', which was wider and shallower than the Royal Shakespeare Theatre, with balconies that 'papered' the walls with spectators rather than setting them at a distance.[68]

In an interview with Margaret Tierney in *Plays and Players*, Nunn and Morley explained their thinking more fully, with an insistence that they were not 'trying to get back to the precise conditions of Shakespeare's staging' but wished 'to serve more of his original intentions, creating more of the relationship between human beings on a stage that he originally had in mind'. This had to be done, of course, within the confines of the Stratford theatre's permanent architecture. The 'white box' and 'grey box' seasons had been part of a quest for 'a chamber permanence in which the plays could happen, and in which the focus would be properly on the actors, their relationship with the spoken word'. The new stage, Nunn explained, 'can appear to be small, intimate, domestic. Then at the press of a button it can appear immense and epic'.[69]

Reviewing *Coriolanus*, the opening play in the season, Irving Wardle praised the 'marvellous box of tricks' and hazarded the opinion that 'in its present hands there seems no danger of its being used as a toy'.[70] Robert Speaight, in

Shakespeare Quarterly, welcomed the season's productions as 'full of beauty and surprise', reflecting that 'the eye has been somewhat starved at Stratford in recent years, and this change is enormously for the better'.[71] The use of the new stage for all the plays was an important contribution to the coherence of the season. To critics of the whole master-plan, the disparity between the plays remained a reminder of the contrast between the 1972 season and the history sequences in 1963–5. *Julius Caesar* had at least a direct narrative and thematic connection with *Antony and Cleopatra*. *Titus Andronicus*, latest in the chronology of Rome but earliest in terms of the playwright's career, closed the season and seemed like a play from another era and was given a markedly different visual treatment.

Given the configuration and dimensions of the new stage, the dominant impression was inevitably 'immense and epic', an effect enhanced by the spectacular dumb-shows that preceded all four tragedies. *Coriolanus* began with a procession celebrating the power of patrician Rome, with plebeians kicked out of the way and two boys held up beneath an oversize sculpture of a wolf to represent the emblem of Romulus and Remus. As if to demonstrate the stage machinery from the outset, the forestage tilted down to the floor of the stalls, a disconcerting experience for those in the front row, who would in any case find that when it was returned to its full height their view of the upstage area was partially obscured. Except for the night scenes, notably those in which the Volscians gathered downstage around a fire, the lighting in *Coriolanus* was bright, which tended to enhance the dominance of the scenic space.

As the house lights dimmed for *Julius Caesar* a red carpet unrolled down the raked stage, pulled taut when it reached the lip of the forestage, red banners dropped from the flies, and, to deafening drumbeats, Caesar entered at the head of a massed entry. Brutus crowned him with a laurel and there was a shout of 'Caesar!' accompanied by raised-arm salutes. The world now seemed a darker place, bright for its public scenes in Rome, but otherwise more tenebrous if only on account of the night scenes of the storm and the meeting of the conspirators, the murder of

Cinna the Poet, and Brutus' tent at Philippi. *Antony and Cleopatra* opened with a procession of masked figures holding symbols of the Egyptian gods, with Antony and Cleopatra presented as Isis and Osiris. The lighting retained the clinical harshness of the public scenes of *Julius Caesar* for Rome, but the Egyptian court was set in a space suffused with warm light. In Rome the stage was sparsely furnished, with the upstage vista cut off by a wall-sized map of the Empire. The most impressive use of the stage machinery was the creation of Cleopatra's monument: for the exterior the central upstage lift and a flight of six steps rose from the stage floor to meet a backward-sloping panel with an open doorway lowered from the flies, while a small rostrum was placed in front of the resulting platform. (This created a promontory that accommodated the sight lines from the upper reaches of the auditorium for the appearance of Cleopatra, Charmian and Iras and facilitated the business of raising the dying Antony aloft.) For the interior the small rostrum was replaced with steps and the flown panel, secured to the platform at the rear, was then tilted forward to form the ceiling.[72]

Coriolanus gave the season an uncertain start, owing partly to the distractions of the excessively mobile set, which found few enthusiastic defenders. Hobson, one of the least sympathetic and most vehement complainers, wrote that the theatre's new machinery now had 'a series of epileptic tricks to show off'. An 'expensive toy' had been given to Nunn, and he might as well be allowed 'to fool around with it as much as he pleases', since the Arts Council's charter would not allow it to 'fob him off with a model train, which he could have taken home and played with to his heart's content'.[73] As Caius Marcius, Ian Hogg was choleric and athletic but hardly – by any definition – heroic. He possessed 'a psychotic zest' that carried him through the action 'with blood-thirsty sportsmanship'.[74] Frank Marcus in the Sunday *Telegraph* described him as 'hotheaded rather than noble and headstrong rather than arrogant. He wore his Oedipus complex like a laurel wreath'.[75] Hobson complained that although the actor had 'memorably snarled his way through minor parts in other productions', as Coriolanus 'all his rebarbativeness [had] left him' and he had 'no arrogance, no pride, and very little voice'. In *Plays and Players* Frank Cox was one of the few reviewers to find depth in Hogg's performance, noting the progression from 'a sinewy lion-cub, a born fighter and slayer of men, arrogant simply because of his muscular superiority' to 'a spoilt child ... a misfit, a liability to the Senate which backs him', but ultimately revealing 'a sensitivity ... which is the more terrible for being unexpected'.[76] J.C. Trewin described Hogg as 'steadily intelligent as the obdurate child' although he missed 'what I once called the flint-flashed snap', and Robert Speaight regretted the casting of 'an actor who in personality, voice, movement, and physique, was everything Coriolanus was not', which 'did a grave injustice to the play'.[77]

Apart from the deployment of the mobile stage and the performance of the protagonist, particular attention was attracted by the treatment of the plebeians and the Volsces. 'Although the production does not go the full Brechtian hog on their behalf', wrote Wardle, the plebeians were 'individualized, given real work to do and legitimate grievances to express, and led by an eminently respect-worthy pair of Tribunes'. Frank Cox described the shift from the opening procession to the play's first scene, 'achieved with an hydraulic ease with which frequenters of any of the modern opera houses of Europe will find unremarkable' – Cox was one of the few truly enthusiastic admirers of the new stage – 'and we are in the public place in Rome, a teeming work centre hung with a framework of stinking, blackened leather and skins, strung with ropes and peopled not with the usual faceless extras but with individuals, carpenters, butchers, masons, crippled beggars and so on'. This was 'a whole level of society, and, in a nutshell, a statement of what is to be Nunn's approach'.

The Volsces, in a strenuous and misguided attempt to distinguish them as strikingly as possible from their Roman adversaries, were given an exotic, tribal identity, impressive in itself but making little sense of the play's opposition between regimes similarly constituted (both with senates, after all) and with similar goals. In their feathered headdresses and black leather briefs and strapped torsos, they seemed to have wandered in from a production of *The Royal Hunt of the Sun* as (in Wardle's description) 'they surg[ed] on hissing and yelping to the accompaniment of gongs' to gather round the flames that sprang from small rostrum rising out of the forestage. As Tullus Aufidius, Patrick Stewart 'wore a mandarin moustache and a superb black ponytail, and spoke with an unemotional oriental lilt', but (wrote Peter Thomson) 'there was something haywire about the Volsces. No others spoke like Stewart', while the servingmen 'were traditional stage cockneys' and the senators and lords 'were prone to enigmatic stillness'. Although Stewart's 'feline grace' of movement seemed appropriate for the 'bisexuality' of his greeting to Coriolanus in 4.5, the concept of the Volsces as tribal 'contributed nothing to defining the political conflicts on which the Roman scenes were made to pivot'.[78] Wardle was not alone in feeling that Stewart's Aufidius, 'sensuous and almost lachrymose in his relationship to his great rival', came over as 'a deliberately exotic creature rather than a believable warrior of even the most primitive tribe'. Having dubbed the director 'Cecil B. de Nunn', on the strength of his 'urge to impress us', Frank Marcus suggested the Volsces would have 'brought tears of joy' to eyes of the great Hollywood director. Nunn had deployed every available technical means of support for the fight scenes, including strobe lighting to support the quasi-cinematic effect of slow-motion, but there was no resemblance to the manner of stylization famously adopted in the Berliner Ensemble's *Coriolan*. This was probably just as well, as the attempt to reproduce it in the National Theatre's 1971 production of Shakespeare's play at the Old Vic – co-directed by directors from the Ensemble – had produced the unhappy effect in the assault on Corioles of actors chasing the massive city gate round the revolving stage. The combats in the RSC's *Coriolanus* and the other plays were in the serviceable mode familiar since *The Wars of the Roses*, with smoke, the deliberate clashing of swords and sometimes too-evident avoidance of actual contact.

In *Julius Caesar* the stage was less active than in *Coriolanus*: Irving Wardle took this as a strategy on Morley's part, 'to convey architectural stability and the forces of disruption'.[79] A row of statues descended from the flies, resting on the raised steps behind the forestage, to form the scene for the Senate; a rostrum for the funeral orations was pushed far enough downstage to allow them to be directed towards the audience, although allowing scant room for the rather sparse onstage crowd; and the central trapezoid acting area was tilted to make a steeply-raked hill for the final battle scenes. A single bare-branched tree indicated Brutus' orchard, and during the second interval a tent was pitched for the 'quarrel scene'. The only eccentric feature was a gigantic statue of Caesar, mounted on a wheeled platform as if in preparation for storage or transit, which was seen in the dictator's private quarters and then reappeared, suffused with red light, to represent his ghost in 4.2, before being trundled upstage to preside over the battle. (Wardle thought it reminiscent of the Commendatore's statue in *Don Giovanni*.) 'Caesarism' was equated in the programme with more recent experience of dictatorial and fascistic regimes. In performance the message was reinforced by the triumphal opening, the images of the man himself (who was lent a sinister intelligence by Mark Dignam), and the presence of a squad of black-clad bodyguards (who proved singularly ineffective in the assassination). But the statue was an image too far. Symbol or not, in the tent scene it was a clumsy substitute for a more eerie kind of haunting, a rare sign of directorial mistrust in the audience's ability to register that Julius Caesar was 'mighty still' in the final reckoning. The common people, less politically acute than their predecessors in *Coriolanus*, were a dangerous force: the jesting carpenter of the play's first scene became the bloodthirsty leader of the pack that murdered Cinna the Poet. This was not a problem if one accepted the season as an exercise in 'compare and contrast' or simply an exploration of Shakespeare's continuing interest in Roman history, rather than a demonstration of his development as a political dramatist. It was also inadequate as a comment on Roman history: Wardle pointed out that 'the plays hardly support the idea of civic development unless development means the debauchery of the population'.

Brutus (John Wood) presented the kind of complex characterization that had become one of Nunn's specialities. John Mortimer, in the *Observer*, identified him as 'the intellectual revolutionary, whose calm smile is the result, not of happiness, for he is never happy, but of having solved life as if it were a proposition of logic or a mathematical equation'. The soliloquy, 'It must be by his death' (1.3.10–33), came 'with an especial chill from a man whose faith in his power of reasoning is quite unshakeable'.[80] On occasion, Wardle observed, he was 'prone to sudden attacks of fury, rounding with screams of exasperation on his servant and his wife', and John Barber thought that these 'sudden blasts of passion' suggested 'a man who has leapt onto the monstrous chariot of conspiracy after agonising self-doubt, and is stoically determined to ride to the end'.[81] In the tent scene Brutus responded to the outburst of temper from Cassius (Patrick Stewart) with icy calm. Cassius had overturned furniture, swept the papers from the table and flung himself to his knees with 'There is my dagger / Here my naked breast' (4.2.154–5), holding himself in readiness for a blow. Brutus went round the tent picking up the scattered documents, speaking 'Sheathe your dagger. / Be angry when you will; it shall have scope' with studied calmness (161–2). The intrusion of the 'Poet' – a soldier in drag, determined to cheer the generals up with a bit of satire – caused Brutus to flare up and strike the intruder. When he told the astonished Cassius about Portia's death, Brutus sobbed quietly, prompting his comrade's realization, 'How scaped I killing when I crossed you so?' (202). The two accounts of Portia's suicide (199–208 and 240–5) were both included, and to add to the enigma of Brutus' personality, there was a suggestion (Peter Thomson thought it 'not a firm one') in his handling of his papers that 'he had read the information only just before he announced it'.[82] After Messala's report of her death, Cassius' 'I have as much of this in art as you, / But yet my nature could not bear it so' thus seemed spoken in admiration for Brutus' ability to maintain the stoical front in the presence of his subordinates.

Peter Ansorge identified the hand of Nunn (rather than his co-directors) in this element of the play, with Wood locating 'a schizophrenic quality' in a character who 'wants to kill Caesar in cold blood, has to rush into his allies during the assassination to prevent a total bloodbath' and then administers the *coup de grace* with a knife to an artery, 'finishing the job like a surgeon performing a mercy killing'.[83] The appalled silence following the murder, and the shedding of considerable quantities of blood, 'more eloquent than words', thought Speaight, would be 'for many in the audience ... a topical rebuke to violence'. (Although, he added ruefully, 'To some, no doubt, it was an encouragement'.)[84] Brutus' subsequent failure to show emotion in his funeral speech, contrasting sharply with the display of feeling on the part of Antony (Richard Johnson), was all the more effective – and clearly self-destructive – given the evidence elsewhere of the emotions he suppressed. It was in this that the production achieved its greatest success, rather than the familiar political message that would-be dictators are dangerous but opposing them by force may have terrible consequences. The final moments found the 'swarthy, black-bearded, black-haired Antony in uneasy alliance with a blond, pink-skinned, clean-shaven Octavius' (Corin Redgrave).[85] His laconic assent to Antony's praise of the dead conspirator – 'According to his virtue let us use him' (5.5.74) showed a dangerous and unyielding detachment, and in the final lines, 'Let's away / To part the glories of this happy day' (79–80), a momentary pause before 'happy' suggested an uneasy truce and the seeds of the conflict to come.

In many respects *Antony and Cleopatra* was the most successful of the season's plays. It derived a sense of coherence from carrying forward the narrative from *Julius Caesar*, a greater sureness of hand in using the resources of the stage, and the opportunity for actors and director to focus on a compelling and sophisticated erotic relationship. Michael Billington thought that it benefitted greatly from its position in the season 'in that personal emotion is placed squarely against a political background'.[86] It also gained from the dynamic, keen-minded and alluring Cleopatra of Janet Suzman. After the variously formidable, stoic and self-denying women of the other plays, Cleopatra was especially welcome. So was the environment of Egypt. Charles Lewsen in *The Times* contrasted the clear sky that 'gleamed' over Rome with 'the mottled heaven [that] looked down upon the changeable world of Cleopatra, whose every mood was framed with a different environment'.

> Beneath canopies of midnight blue or orange the Queen lay on divans or cushions; or, dreaming of angling for Antony in the river, on a great keyhole-shaped bed. While the stark black and white of the Romans' clothes was modified only by a formal purple, Cleopatra's court disported themselves in pinks, mauves and oranges [Figure 3].[87]

FIGURE 3 Antony and Cleopatra *(Royal Shakespeare Theatre, 1972)*: *Cleopatra (Janet Suzman) tended by her entourage. Photo by Reg Wilson © RSC.*

Why would anyone except an Octavius want to spend time in the cold – and coldly lit – Roman world of the other plays when Egypt was literally warmer? A sense of duty would be a factor, vividly present in the military envoys watching the opening parade with some disgust – they had a fine example of 'this dotage of our General's' to prompt them. After all, this was a world where queens and generals reclined on couches, cushions and rugs, fanned by eunuchs and tended by handmaidens. It was already clear that Johnson's Antony, in whose oration at Caesar's funeral genuine emotion had impressed as much as political guile, would be convincing in his readiness to 'let Rome in Tiber melt, and the wide arch / Of the ranged empire fall' (1.1.34–5). Robert Speaight observed that 'there was a soft centre in Mr. Johnson's Antony, but no trace of the actor's craving for unmerited sympathy'.[88]

Both Suzman and Johnson possessed the vitality and vocal technique that could command the theatre, combined with a subtlety of expression. Johnson's beard and hair suggested the 'grizzled' warrior but the overall impression was of lovers more youthful than many reviewers expected: to Benedict Nightingale they seemed on the first encounter to be 'attractive, exuberant and irresponsible overgrown adolescents who must learn the danger of self-indulgent play'. This was 'a conception which, to say no more, gives those playing the parts the opportunity to change and develop as the evening proceeds'.[89] The lovers' first scene was played out in full view of the court and the black-armoured envoys from Rome, suggesting to Margaret Tierney that the pair were 'monumental actors, who need the presence of an audience'.[90] (They acted out the erotic horseplay referred to in 2.5.23–4: she 'put her tires and mantles on him' and 'wore his sword Phillipan'.) Suzman was 'the Shaw Cleopatra becoming the Shakespeare Cleopatra', but Nightingale conjures up a modern woman especially attractive to a male reviewer, keeping up with the latest feminist texts – Germaine Greer's enormously influential book was published in 1970 – and open to amorous adventures on her own terms:

> Possibly, she does not love the 'old ruffian' as much as she did: certainly, she is increasingly interested in manipulating him. She lies there, casually leaning on an elbow, her hand cupped beneath her chin, looking formidable and even masculine, the Ptolemaic equivalent of your modern emancipated woman. You would expect to catch her reading *The Female Eunuch* rather than dallying with male ones – and, possibly, eyeing you over the book with a look at once flirtatious, challenging and slightly sarcastic.

Reservations were expressed about the quality reflected in Nightingale's comment that 'the bias of Miss Suzman's Cleopatra is always towards intelligence and cunning'. J. W Lambert found her 'a woman with a mind alert to the worldly advantages of switching loyalties yet furiously at the mercy of desperate caprice, rising to her death even though driven to it by vanity'.[91] These verdicts suggest something of the abundant if not infinite variety encompassed by the performance, though there were dissidents. John Barber regretted the absence of anything to suggest 'a woman half-blasted by a too-arduous life, who has had too many children by too many lovers', and the 'tarnished glamour' he expected from the play.[92] More representative was Michael Billington's applause for the production's achievement of the 'authentic Shakespearian double vision' that 'hero and heroine are simultaneously ageing libertine and decaying queen and great lovers who through passion triumph over death'. The diversity of responses is indicative of diverse expectations and, for that matter, of shifting attitudes to women as well as to the play. Intriguingly, the prompt copies show the omission of two passages in 1.2, in which Enobarbus is dismissive of women: his comment on Cleopatra's 'dying' when she is told of Antony's departure, 'Under a compelling occasion let women die' (1.2.144–51), and his reaction to the news of Fulvia's death, 'When it pleaseth their deities to take the wife of a man from him' (169–77).[93] Barber seemed to be taking the 'Roman', or Octavian, view of both the play and its women, while Billington sided with the conflicted but admiring Enobarbus. In any case, there was nothing 'decaying' about Suzman's Cleopatra, whose wistfully remembered salad days must have been enjoyed at a very early age.

Peter Thomson describes the 'mastery of the comic line' in the 'pause, then a half-smile, and then the confession which she made erotic, "My salad days, / When I was green in judgment"' (1.5.76–7). Lewsen observed that in the final act, when 'looking at Octavius' proffered hand, she clearly compare[d] it with the hand of Antony'. Her dying speeches 'were informed by the same concern for the beautifully perfected'. Johnson marked the differences in Antony's posture in the play's contrasted worlds: 'In Rome he stood straight, and spoke decisively, as in the quelling of Octavius at "I am not married, Caesar" [2.2.130]. In Egypt he was slightly stooped, self-consciously ageing, the vacillating Antony divided against himself'.[94] This was not at all surprising in itself, as the scene on Pompey's galley had shown Octavius to be (in Thomson's words) 'a killjoy and a lubricious puritan', the kind of man who would 'enter Egypt in the hope of finding blue films to confiscate'. The foil to this Roman perspective was provided by Patrick Stewart's Enobarbus, 'a grizzled old sweat who has given his life to imperial wars [and] also has the voice of true feeling',[95] but showing 'a dangerous, steely gleam behind the heartiness, melting effectively into his description of Cleopatra in her barge'.[96] The speech was 'perfectly delivered', thought Speaight, with Enobarbus speaking 'more to himself than to the audience or his interlocutors – a memory, not an aria'.[97] After his 'I will tell you' (2.2.197) its lyricism transcended and implicitly chastised the desire for scandal shown by Agrippa and Maecenas.

Overall, the play's text was cut very sparingly. This was a long performance: with 15-minute intervals at Stratford after

2.7 (Pompey's barge) and 4.3 (Antony's soldiers hear 'music i'th'air'). After previews, the scene (3.1) in which Ventidius brings back the body of Pacorus from Parthia, was cut – it was partially restored at the Aldwych – and the final running times were 1 hour, 10 minutes for the first part, 45 minutes for the second, and 1 hour for the third, giving a total of 3 hours 25 minutes including intervals.

Titus Andronicus entered the repertoire on 18 October and played for comparatively few performances. The brevity of the run reflected the fact that, although Peter Brook's 1955 Stratford production, with Olivier as Titus and Vivien Leigh as Lavinia, had done much to reestablish its theatrical potential, it was still the least bankable of the Roman plays. (Its stock was raised considerably by Deborah Warner's 1987 production in the Swan.) Like the other plays, it began with a 'period-defining tableau', in Irving Wardle's phrase, this time 'showing a black-habited throng paying court to a bloated imperial waxwork that reclines on a litter clutching the ultimate symbol of carnal indulgence – a bunch of grapes'. More attempts followed 'to impose a *dolce vita* atmosphere on the comfortless world of the play', an element Nunn had 'handled more fittingly' in *The Revenger's Tragedy*.[98] Peter Thomson felt that this image of decadence was 'over-enforced from the start' and obscured Titus' fatal error in supporting Saturninus, as 'the play describes not the continuance of established decadence, but the overthrow of virtue until its promised restoration through Lucius Andronicus'.[99] Federico Fellini's *Satyricon* – which the company had been shown as part of their preparation – was invoked both onstage and by the inclusion of a production still in the programme. Harold Hobson described 'a debauchery scene [the opening of 4.2] whose bulging-breasted, big-thighed women' were 'enough to put one off orgies for the rest of one's life'.[100] Benedict Nightingale considered the 'red-haired whores, the transvestism, the tumbling, sprawling and noisy eating' acceptable as part of Nunn's 'determination to find something luxurious and overblown' in the play's 'cataloguing of improbable revenge', with characters who 'seem lacking in sensuality' and verse that 'far from being sated and relaxed, hops stiffly and gawkily along, as if on crutches'.[101]

Hobson found Colin Blakely's Titus 'a rough and shaggy bear, with whose brutality and misfortunes one has no sympathy', and Nightingale suggested that this 'peppery, bustling Titus, with his grizzled pate and leather jerkin, pushing and pummeling others like a distraught goatherd organizing his flock', could not be blamed for 'the hollowness of his climaxes'. He reserved his praise for John Wood as Saturninus:

> To Shakespeare, this character is a stage villain: Mr. Wood finds not only malice in it, but urbanity, irony, pettishness, narcissism, hysteria, and even a strange infantilism, as when he responds to disaster by relapsing into baby-talk. At one point, he appears with golden arrow and armour, a scrawny cupid, smirking priggishly at his sycophants; at a still queerer one, he slithers across the stage and sinks his teeth into the calf of a courtier.

Hobson observed that he 'neatly deflat[ed] other people's rhetoric'. Wardle found his performance 'spellbinding to watch', veering from 'the chatty cadences of modern English' to 'spitting fury' and 'linking blood-drenched inhumanity with domestic realism'. Nevertheless, he insisted that the character was merely 'a poisonous gadfly at the margin of the action whose main weight falls crushingly on Titus'. Peter Thomson listed more of the emperor's (or actor's?) excesses: 'The marriage to Tamora became the pretext for an inserted skipping entrance in a fancy cloak'. After his wedding night 'the hunting horns found out his hangover, and he slapped his cheeks ringingly to rouse himself'. Thomson relished the inventiveness of Wood's performance, while registering his 'uneasiness about so demonstrative a Saturninus'.[102]

Titus, Thomson suggested, was 'a man more suited to the containment of passion than to its expression' for whom 'the events of the play were literally unspeakable'. To begin with 'his anger, like his pride [was] physical rather than verbal'. But then there were usually people 'near enough to hear what he quietly says', and after the 'first tumultuous scene, when Saturninus has led Tamora off' he spoke the line 'Titus, when wert thou wont to walk alone...' (1.1.339) 'in bemused awareness of an astonishing reversal'.[103] Nightingale noted that the actor marked the progression of Titus 'as if with hammer blows: wrenching expression from even the barest lines', so that 'To be dishonoured. By my sons. In Rome' (1.1.382) became three sentences 'as a crescendo of priorities'. Although his delivery, 'often relying on stabbing words, and variations between stoic briskness and the cry of an old abandoned child, reache[d] its limits before the end', the 'speed of playing' compensated for this. When the severed heads of his sons arrived, 'Lavinia (Janet Suzman) who has previously shrunk from human contact, turns and kisses her father'. This was a 'marvellous detail, at once deeply felt and marking a decisive point in the events'. Michael Billington wrote that Lavinia became 'a pitiable, hunched grotesque crawling out of the darkness like a wounded animal', a comment that reflects the literal darkness of the background against which the events played themselves out. Guy Woolfenden's score contributed the 'growl and scream of brass backstage and the thunder of percussion' as a soundscape that expressed the presence of tigers in this wilderness Rome had become.[104]

It was these acting choices, rather than the elaborately 'decadent' element in itself or the production's relatively muted but unstylized acts of violence, that conveyed the underlying emphasis on the psychological effect of the heinous state of Rome and the crimes committed there. The low standing of the play in the 1970s is reflected in the reviews, with Hobson warning that 'the director of an entertainment like this is necessarily in a dilemma: he must choose between being disgusting or dull', Nightingale referring to 'a fatuous, beastly play', and Wardle admitting that he had expected that 'the season would come a cropper' with a script 'whose Senecan atrocities are worlds removed from the death's-head sensuality of the Jacobeans' – implicitly, that is, from *The Revenger's Tragedy*.

The programme for *Titus Andronicus* contained fewer references to critical commentary than those for the other Roman plays, possibly because few positive statements would have been found.[105] The focus was on historical context, and the lengthy quotations from Edward Gibbon included part of his account of the spectacularly decadent emperor Elagabalus. This emphasis on 'Decline and Fall' was interesting in itself as a pre-emptive strike in defence of the production's depiction of orgiastic excess, but more significant was a two-page article by Nunn, 'Shakespeare and Rome', reflecting on the plays as illustrating the path to the situation where 'the worst a Roman could fear [had] become a reality', and Rome had become 'a "wilderness of tigers," ruled by a sadist, his Gothic [*sic*] empress and her Moorish paramour'. This was effectively a reiteration of the rationale for the season, implicitly (if not expressly) an answer to the critics who had questioned its coherence. 'Thinking about Rome was the only way an Elizabethan had of thinking about civilization', with topics unavailable in the treatment of the antecedents of the Tudor regime: 'much of unity of Shakespeare's histories came from the limitations under which he wrote them. Tudor policy framed his argument', with its focus on the 'primal sin of regicide' and its consequences. 'The matter of Rome, less certain about good and evil, offered greater freedom'.[106] The final paragraph of the essay turned to *Titus Andronicus*, which, Nunn claimed, was 'the most prophetic today'. The preceding plays in the season raised issues regarding civilization and the direction it should take, but now civilization itself was in question. Aaron was its 'most articulate questioner ... dedicated to the destruction of society which degrades him – to assert the beauty of his blackness he will tear down Rome itself'. Titus, representative of the old virtues, had become 'the new outsider, rebuked and mocked'.

> Shakespeare's Elizabethan nightmare has become ours. The questions his other three Roman plays pose seem the more prophetic and urgent. How should we govern ourselves? What do we believe in? Can we afford to compromise

morally for political expedience? Must 'the time of universal peace' mean subjection to a monolithic imperial civilization? Above all, have we time for answers, or are we already in the convulsion which heralds a fall greater than Rome's?

This seems to reflect the widespread feeling that any euphoria generated during the 1960s was over.

Contextual material in the *Coriolanus* programme had included a one-page essay on the ways in which 'the Elizabethan attitude to Rome reflected their horror of civil disorder', with references to John Ball, leader of the Peasants' Revolt in the fourteenth century, and Gerrard Winstanley, the seventeenth-century Leveller. Among the other quotations dotted in much smaller type around the programme were comments on industrial relations from the Prime Minister Edward Heath and a *Sunday Times* editorial from February 1972, arising from the major dispute over pay and conditions in the still-nationalized coal industry that flared up in January and February 1972 between the National Union of Miners and the Conservative government. These constituted the only explicit connection offered between the play and current events, which had included the declaration of a state of emergency by the Conservative government. (As it happened, the installation of the new stage at Stratford had been delayed by power cuts: rather than rehearse on it when they arrived in Stratford, the *Coriolanus* company were obliged to make the best of the theatre's rehearsal room.)[107] It is difficult to resist the contention by Carol Chiilngton Rutter that Nunn's strategy, while acknowledging in interviews the pressure of contemporary events, was one of evasion.[108] In the light of this, it was remarkable that the programme contained no references to or quotations from Bertolt Brecht. The Berliner Ensemble's production of his version of the play had been seen in London in 1956, but was absent from the brief 'stage history'. In 1970 at the Aldwych, David Jones had directed an RSC production of *The Plebeians Rehearse the Uprising* by Günter Grass, which dramatizes the response of a theatre's director (unmistakably identifiable as Brecht at the Berliner Ensemble) to the 1953 workers' uprising in East Berlin during his company's rehearsal of what is clearly Brecht's version of Shakespeare's play.[109] Nevertheless, during the 1972 season, apart from a paragraph quoting his 'imaginative reconstruction of the state of Rome in the year of Caesar's assassination' in the *Julius Caesar* programme, on the evidence of its publications Brecht did not figure in the company's reckoning with the Romans.

In this respect, Nunn's sense of politics did not chime with the left-wing radicalism of the time, still less with any variety of Marxist hard line, but rather with liberal concerns about democracy and the rule of law. Peter Holland points out that in his *Coriolan* Brecht was 'fascinated by the ways in which the people might learn their political power'.[110] In Nunn's (Roman) world-view, the emphasis was on the individual's relation to the state in its different stages of development, and above all on the problems of heroic and principled action. Even if the Brechtian rewriting itself or the insights it might offer are not accepted as indispensable to work on the play, Robert Ormsby's summing-up seems appropriate: 'the impetus for the ... season was politically vague'.[111] Against this one should set the view expressed by Peter Thomson, that the productions evinced 'too much insistence on continuity in the visual presentation, and an alertness to political analogy that drew too much of the plays' weight with it and became [the Stratford] season's particular distortion'.[112]

In an interview published in 1973, Nunn reiterated his views on the significance of the plays for the dramatist, and the plan for the 'new marvelously flexible stage' to be 'permanently available to the company' after the 1972 season. As has been noted, practice did not quite match the theory, with the two opening productions obliged to rehearse without access to the stage after the company's arrival. The weeks of rehearsals in the Floral Street rehearsal space behind Covent Garden had been 'golden': 'Free to let the plays find their own shapes, we improvised all around them: sensitivity exercises, physical exercises in release and coordination, exercises based on parallel modern instances of political violence and Goya's war etchings'. Voice work with Kristen Linklater inspired exploration of the language, as 'slowly, painfully, lying on the floor or slumped in corners, actors would let the words resonate inside them, and then ooze or spill out of them with a life of their own'.[113] A run-through of *Coriolanus* 'ranged unpremeditated all over the rehearsal rooms, upstairs and downstairs and even out among the lorries and squashed vegetables of Floral Street'. (Covent Garden was still the site of the fruit and flower market.) This was 'the more strenuous of the two productions, physical, energetic and anarchic'. *Julius Caesar,* rehearsed in the evenings, emerged as 'more reflective and deliberate, gaining a stillness and economy resulting from our tiredness after the day's exertions'. The conspiracy scene was rehearsed in total darkness, and in one 'long, disturbingly messy' improvisation of the assassination the guards, asked why they had not intervened, said that 'none of them had dared to interrupt the famous, excited statesmen arguing over the dictator's body with waving, bloody arms'. (Thus anticipating one of the queries raised by reviewers when the production opened.)[114]

It is evident from this interview that references to Shakespeare's nightmare in the programme for *Titus Andronicus* corresponded to Nunn's approach during rehearsals for a play whose 'idiom was cruder and wilder, like popular sensation journalism' after the 'achieved poetry'. He had misgivings about the relaxation and warmth found in the rehearsals for *Antony and Cleopatra,* feeling that this had made the performance 'bland'. It is hard to resist the inference that after the rigours of rehearsing and playing the other productions, and having now settled down in Stratford for the summer, the acting company were simply having too much of a good time. If this was the case, *Titus Andronicus* would be a shock to the system, as the company now improvised dreams of violence, orgy, rape, 'torture and wish-fulfillment' and even 'dreams of dreams'. More than the other productions 'it detached itself from the stage and became a series of pure acted sequences'. Nunn felt that a 'firmer historical approach would have fitted it more neatly into the season', but insisted that this would have been contrary to the exploratory freedom he had sought. He was disappointed by 'the number of critics who lacked the space or the inclination to see the season as a whole and discuss it as a project'.[115]

In the event, the transfer to London prompted reviewers to take this longer view, with shorter intervals between the opening nights of the productions and the opportunity to see at least two of them on one day. The reworking of the plays for the smaller stage of the Aldwych refined the expression of the project's aims – and its political and historical emphasis – while one important change of cast, with Nicol Williamson taking over as Caius Martius in *Coriolanus*, affirmed the focus of heroism and its dilemmas. *Coriolanus* now began, not with the procession and the she-wolf, but with a tableau of the arming of Coriolanus, 'looking rather like a professional strong man', thought Trewin, who added 'Rightly, for the play (in maybe a too-easy simplification) is the tragedy of an obdurate man's pride'.[116] In *Plays and Players*, Alan Brien, who was seeing the productions for the first time, described the effect in more martial terms:

> We see him first (indeed he is the first sight we see) spotlit in centre stage, rather skinny and skeletal, too tall for his width, rather like a gingery, shivering, Dutch Christ, being armed for combat. Naked he appears as dangerous and invulnerable as the horn of a snail. But once the shell is on, he is transformed. It is a striking, unexpected vision of the martial champion in the eye of his period. (Olivier in a similar pose looked like a pocket Hercules.)[117]

The tableau 'carri[ed] within it a very modern truth'. This was 'a one-man panzer division'. Williamson was 'massive and uncompromising'.[118] 'Present him with an inferior, and he's all growl, sneer and spit', wrote Benedict Nightingale, 'the most innocent phrase becomes massively sarcastic'. Confronted with an equal, 'violence is never far beneath the surface'.[119] John Barber hailed the fact that 'a guest actor, in a troupe which has lately disdained stars, made a nonsense of that whole policy – at least, for the Shakespeare heights'. The 'contempt for the rabble' was powerful, but Williamson 'seiz[ed] every opportunity to create a hero instead of the usual immature, shouting oaf', with 'the soldier's modesty, his embarrassment over the fuss they make of him after a victory'.

> His courtesy, his tenderness to his son, his zest for a brave deed, and the constancy of his temper, all speak of a noble mind, and so make his fall tragic. It is a great performance not only because it is well played: it has been thought out with intense intelligence.[120]

Nightingale was especially impressed by the pause before his capitulation to Volumnia's plea that he should not attack Rome:

> She finishes, and Williamson stands with his back to her, his face fraught for 30 seconds ... 40 ... 50 ... 60. Then he puts out his hand ... 70 seconds ... 80 ... 90. And 'mother, mother, what have you done?' comes with a pucker and a sob, painful to perceive: the mailed fist opens to reveal, of all things, a baby's rattle.

Alan Brien reported the line as 'Mother ... what ... have you ... DONE?' with each word given 'like a pint of blood'.[121]

As Barber noted, the casting of Williamson, who did not appear in the other productions, cut across the company's ensemble policy. Otherwise, with a few alterations that may reflect the usual adjustments and departures attending transfers after the Stratford season, the company identity was maintained. Patrick Stewart's role as Aufidius was taken over by Oscar James, with the consequence that the 'tribal' but effectively white-skinned Volscians were led by a black actor, while Stewart now appeared as Aaron in *Titus Andronicus* –

possibly the last time the role would be played in blackface in a major revival of the play. Janet Suzman was replaced by Judy Geeson as Lavinia and Margaret Tyzack by Margaret Whiting as Tamora. John Barber, in a review titled (possibly by a sub-editor) 'Tactless Comic Touch in Saga of Murder', praised Whiting for understanding that 'rodomontade must be declaimed with huge, high exaggeration' and reported that 'she speaks musically and attitudinizes superbly, a stained-glass freak with emblematic gestures as preposterous as her earrings at the hunt'. Wood's Saturninus was 'also twice life-size, and his axe-sharp face and gliding walk [had] a true heraldic artificiality and menace', while Blakeley 'perform[ed] prodigies with wailings and explosions of grief' but could not make Titus a Lear: 'These characters are not pathetic; they exult in their grief'.[122] Other reviews do not suggest the degree of exaggeration described by Barber, or that there had been a significant change in interpretation, indeed Brien thought that Wood made the emperor 'a mad sadist all too believable when we think of Caligula and Nero'.[123] Nightingale observed that both his performances were 'much less ravelled' and 'intricate' than at Stratford. As Saturninus, Wood no longer sank his teeth into a courtier's leg, but Nightingale regretted the absence of the 'overt symptoms of self-absorption and self-love that seeped from his spinsterish smirk and bobbing Adam's apple' in his Brutus in *Julius Caesar*.

The scripts of all three productions underwent alterations to suit a stage less adapted to the grander scenic and processional gestures of the Stratford performances, and Morley's new setting reverted to a familiar version of the 'box' in its various incarnations, which Wardle welcomed as contributing to the greater sense of a unity of vision across the plays:

> [Morley's] stage is now a bare chamber, surrounded by metal galleries and mechanized only by a ponderous mobile bridge which comes fully into action only in the final play. It is a dark, austere arena, erupting into instantaneous bursts of detailed realism and brilliant colour (like the skin-

festooned market place, or the great sails that unfurl over Cleopatra's court), but always returning to itself.

The effect was strengthened by Woolfenden's music, 'drums, and a brazen hiss as of the sharpening of a thousand swords; and the use of the set itself as a percussion instrument at the moment of pandemonium that punctuates each production'.[124]

Changes in directorial strategy included the use of stroboscopic lighting for the storm and in a slow-motion effect for an 'action replay' of Julius Caesar's assassination, and the substitution of what Wardle characterized as 'a chorus of masked Senecan elders' for the 'dolce vita revels' in *Titus Andronicus*. After the 'plain statement' of the 'strong, clear production' of *Julius Caesar* at the matinée he attended, Trewin welcomed the 'gorgeous rhetoric' and Nunn's 'swift-flowing treatment of those myriad scenes' in *Antony and Cleopatra*. Individual performances seem to have been developed and refined, as might be expected in the course of the Stratford season after the press nights – in some cases eighteen months ago – and the re-rehearsal for London.

The completion of the Stratford and London runs of the Roman plays prompted new evaluations of Nunn's work as director and the state of the company after four years of his artistic directorship. Peter Thomson considered his work as director in relation to the arguments about 'directors' theatre' that had been raised by John Russell Brown and others, and the claim that the over-determination in advance of the work to be done by actors seriously limited the potential of the plays. Thomson was at pains to avoid suggesting that Nunn had pre-determined what his actors would do – 'his rehearsals are freer than Peter Hall's for example' – but felt that he had 'decided what will be meant by what they do'. Nunn admitted to his productions 'nothing that he could not paraphrase', but it was Thomson's view that 'his theatricality is an overlay on a disparately unadorned interpretation of the text'. A consequence of this was that 'his attempts to realize his responses theatrically' were 'more wayward than the responses themselves'. Only the measured, thoughtful tone of Thomson's argument, and his evident desire to *enjoy* performances, mitigated what might have been a damning conclusion, that these 'wayward' attempts 'seem sometimes imposed rather than inherent, an expensive gift-wrapping on an unpretentious gift'.[125]

To have overseen the productions of the 1972 season, and – albeit with a team of associate directors – to have directed or co-directed them on a day-to-day basis, were remarkable achievements, and Nunn had risen to the challenge of presenting all of them with vitality, panache and intellectual rigour. These were exciting and intellectually stimulating productions, especially for those who, like me, were seeing the plays in the theatre for the first time. It is too easy to dismiss them as 'Shakespeare-plus-Relevance': many of us were enthralled by the sense of a connection with the concerns of our own time, the focus on psychological realism, and the at times visceral excitement afforded by the spectacle and supported by the power of Woolfenden's music. The cooler response of experienced reviewers, including expert colleagues, and the more rigorous effect of historical perspective (or possibly mature consideration) may qualify this experience, but it should not discount it. Nunn and the company were working in an exciting way – by no means the only possible one – with plays whose differences from each other seemed to be more fully revealed, whatever the season might lack in a wished-for coherence or sense of development in the playwright's view of his material.

Once they were thoroughly 'played in' they proved consistent with Frank Marcus's identification of 'the three V's: Vigour, Volume, and Virility' as hallmarks of RSC style in his notice of the 1968 *Much Ado About Nothing*. The reproach that these were achieved at the expense of the 'subtlety, poetry, and maturity' no longer seemed valid, at least as a characterization of some company policy. In *The Winter's Tale*, Nunn had sought a means of expressing psychological realism that encompassed what I have identified as 'large-scale theatrical gesture', in a paradoxical combination of a literal 'chamber' presentation and the use of the resources of a large stage. In the context of a 'themed' season, and admittedly with varying degrees of success, the 1972 productions seemed to confirm this as Nunn's approach. During his Stratford tenure, other directors found their own ways of dealing with the opportunities and responsibilities of the large stage. Colin Chambers' assessment of the 'Romans' experience in terms of the company and the director himself strikes an appropriate balance: 'As a director, his two main impulses – the human scale of the actor and the social swirl of humanity – were not always reconciled, yet he created moments of great power that displayed these two qualities separately as well as some when both were in harmony'.[126]

2

The Main Stage at Stratford: After the Romans

The restaging of the Roman plays at the Aldwych in 1973, and the successful adaptation of *Antony and Cleopatra* to television, with the action placed against 'neutral' and subtly lit studio backing, underlined the fact that a journey had been taken into and then out of the theatre of spectacle, at least in so far as the treatment of the stage's architecture was concerned. Although the full panoply of Stratford's new stage machinery did not reappear after the 1972 season, the main cross-stage elevators were sometimes used, and smaller traps could be created by opening up the panels above the steel grid supporting the stage floor. In the 1974 season the Stratford stage was once again a raked platform surrounded by masking on three sides, within which the sets for individual productions were placed.

1973–5: Scenic austerity and emblematic staging

Nunn did not direct any of the Shakespeare productions at Stratford in 1973. His first production of *Macbeth* played in the 1974 season, and transferred in a reworked version to the Aldwych, where he also directed *Hedda Gabler* with Glenda Jackson in the title role. A decisive move in his direction of the company, now facing renewed financial pressure in the straitened economic circumstances of the early 1970s, was the opening of The Other Place, in 1973. An even more radical revision of *Macbeth*, effectively his definitive staging of the play, opened there in 1976 and was subsequently shown in London at the Warehouse and adapted for television. The revivals and revisions offered Nunn the equivalent of the opportunities provided in heavily subsidized European companies by the long gestation period of productions through extended rehearsals and subsequent retention in repertoire, though without their permanent or semi-permanent acting companies.

Thus, between 1974 and 1976, *Macbeth* evolved in the context of the company's development of smaller performance spaces alongside its continuing engagement with the responsibility to put on large-scale productions in the Royal Shakespeare Theatre. Its different versions also represented the shifting balance between the articulation of a 'concept' with an emphasis on grand design statements, and renewed attention to psychological complexity in character and situation. In this respect it can be compared with John Barton's *Richard II*, which had originated in a simple and in most respects conventional staging seen in the 1971 season alongside Buzz Goodbody's briskly parodic *King John*. (This was a Stratford showing for the final touring productions of Theatregoround.) In the 1973 Stratford season, Barton achieved a stylized main house staging with a platform raised and lowered on escalator-like lateral rails – Richard descended to stage level as from the walls of Flint Castle, spreading his gold-lined cloak wide to embody 'glist'ring Phaeton, / Wanting the manage of unruly jades' (3.3.178–9).[1] At the Aldwych, where the machinery was no longer practicable, the production was, so to speak, more firmly grounded, but retained many stylizing elements of the interpretation: the symbolic use of mirror, crown, book and robe and a golden mask that became a death's head in the final moment when the 'new' king was crowned and the actors who had played Richard and Bolingbroke stood alongside a masked figure evoking Richard's prison meditation on death and the monarch. The performance began with Ian Richardson and Richard Pasco, who shared Richard and Bolingbroke, seeming to decide who was to play which role, then one or the other of them was handed the large book by an actor resembling Shakespeare. The correspondence between usurper and usurped was emphasized when Bolingbroke, disguised as a groom, visited Richard in prison, handing him a wooden model of his horse Barbary. When Bolingbroke threw back his hood to reveal himself the pair faced each other as the actors has done in the opening mime, now holding between them the frame of the mirror broken in the deposition scene (4.1). The interpretation was rooted in ideas of role-playing and the 'player king', expounded in a programme essay by Anne Barton.[2] Michael Billington admired 'its combination of expressive ritual with the genuinely free emotional rein it gives to its actors'.[3]

The emblematic framework and the use of a dumb-show – reflecting Barton's interest in pre-Elizabethan presentational techniques – were by now familiar trademarks of the RSC, but his textual alterations went further than those of his colleagues. The most important of these was the addition of a soliloquy for Bolingbroke, adapted from *Henry IV, Part Two*: 'How many thousands of my poorest subjects / Are at this hour asleep!'[4] The perils of taking this tactic too far were apparent in Barton's 1974 *King John*, where the director's wholesale revision and rewriting drew on two earlier plays, *The Troublesome Reign of King John* (1591) and *King Johan* (1539), with presentational staging that recalled the stagecraft of Tudor morality plays. There are two coronation scenes in Shakespeare's play, but Barton included no fewer than six, and his additional lines included crudely straightforward allusions to the politics of the mid-1970s.[5] As Robert Smallwood remarked, 'Mr. Barton had to rewrite *King John* in order to make it say the things he wanted it to say.'[6]

Few RSC scripts were as radically revised as Barton's, but the presentation of political and social assumptions underlying the plays had become a hallmark of RSC productions since *The Wars of the Roses* and was a feature of all three versions of Nunn's *Macbeth*. John Russell Brown's critique and manifesto, *Free Shakespeare*, published in 1974, took the company's productions since 1968 to task as manifestations of an over-determined, design-dominated style that disenfranchised the actor and simplified the play. The 'selected realism' of the mid-1960s had given way to 'overt statement about the play's "themes," the ideas that the director had observed in the play and chosen to bring into prominence'. Brown identified the colour-coding of costumes and the 'outsized nursery toys', and other prominently featured props of the 1969 *Winter's Tale* as examples of the pervasive and controlling presence of '"keys" or dominant "images" for each scene'.[7] There was a challenge to the quasi-academic (or indeed Leavisite) assumptions in the work of Nunn and his colleagues in Brown's rhetorical question as to whether the plays were 'best performed when actors and audiences submit to a simple overall conception and point of view arrived at by the director after private study of the text?'[8] The publication of *Free Shakespeare* coincided fortuitously with a notable example on Nunn's part of the kind of over-determined production under attack.

Michael Coveney's *Plays and Players* review of the 1974 Stratford *Macbeth* placed it in the context of Keith Hack's ornate deconstruction of *Measure for Measure* and Peter Gill's austere *Twelfth Night*, attributing them respectively to the directors' usual affiliations: Hack with the Glasgow Citizens Company, Gill with the Royal Court. In *Macbeth* it was 'sobering indeed to see the RSC themselves plodding through one of the shortest, fastest tragedies ever written, willfully disdaining any head-on confrontation with the bones of the text in favour of still more neo-Gothic effects and stagey, obfuscating ritualism'. Nunn had 'obviously expended all directorial energy on externalising the play's imagery in broader, more visual terms'.[9] The 'neo-Gothic' element was proclaimed in the opening dumb-show, described vividly by Robert Cushman in the *Observer*:

> As we enter the theatre we are faced by what appears to be an altar-table ... At the beginning of the play we watch the coronation of Duncan, a paradigm of order; a pair of white curtains close across the scene, and, in shadow-play, we watch destruction sicken. Some kind of horned being appears to be breaking up the ceremony with a gigantic inverted crucifix; silhouettes can be peculiarly horrific; it looks as though three figures are levitating from the debris, and, sure enough, when the curtains part, there are the witches, perched cosily on a giant chandelier. The conflict of good and evil established, we begin the play.[10]

As the production 'appear[ed] to be going on partly inside its hero's head and partly in church', Cushman felt that the 'theological emphasis' allowed Nicol Williamson as Macbeth to 'give full value' to the religious significance of 'passages that are generally skimped', but others complained that the director's emphasis on 'one strand of the poetic imagery' restricted 'the play's potential to shock and excite on many levels'.[11] The schematic use of costume, with sacerdotal robes and religious imagery, had the blind, priest-like Duncan in a white surplice, with a crown surmounted by a cross, and Macbeth exchanged a black cassock for red after his assumption of power. The murder of Banquo and the combat between Macbeth and Macduff were seen in shadows thrown against the white curtain, asserting a degree of coherence with the dark goings-on of the prologue, and in the final act Macbeth, isolated in his castle, was enthroned precariously on top of the table that had served for Duncan's 'coronation' and the banquet. A single chalice served for both, leading some reviewers to interpret the frame of the production as a black mass, punctuated in Guy Woolfenden's score by thunderous organ music and 'heavenly' choral episodes recorded by the choir of New College Oxford and distorted into a discordant parody.[12]

Michael Billington welcomed a framework that avoided the simple 'crime and punishment narrative' and intimated the gravity of the threat to 'social, moral and spiritual harmony' constituted by the usurpation: he prophesied that 'simplified and speeded up, it should ... be a fine production'.[13] At the Aldwych, shorn of some of its more elaborate devices – the witches no longer descended from the flies on a chandelier – the production's religious emphasis remained, but there was another, more important, constant: the central performances by Williamson and Mirren and (in Coveney's words) 'the sexual electricity generated between the unfortunate couple'.[14]

John Barber described Macbeth as 'a neurotic gradually losing control and allowing his imagination to drive him melancholy-mad', in 'a powerfully histrionic exhibition by an artist of enormous accomplishment'. Unfortunately, this was taken to excess:

> Visiting the witches for hard facts, he grovels on the ground in a drugged frenzy. Wild-eyed he ends razor-slashing his servants or hiding his head in a bag. The buried good in the man has disappeared. He cannot achieve a kingly front.[15]

Reviews of both the Stratford and the Aldwych versions reflect the power of Williamson's performance, and Coveney, who found the increase in tempo of the London version detrimental in most respects, thought Macbeth himself an exception: 'The performance bristled with vigorous intelligence and his hallucinatory behaviour at the Banquo-less feast was a memorable high spot.' The actor, 'quaking with apprehension ... fixed on the empty place at the head of the table with a physical conviction unthinkable had some blood-boltered mirage actually been represented'.[16] Frank Marcus in the *Sunday Telegraph* commented that 'Mr. Williamson's face was designed to register the sight of horrifying apparitions.'[17] There were suggestions that, as a consequence of the intensity of Williamson's performance, the isolation of husband from wife was too complete, though Coveney, reviewing the

Stratford performance, was impressed by the 'mutual reliance' that survived Macbeth's 'symptoms of frenzied anxiety and expressions of chilling doubt', so that in 'She should have died hereafter' (5.5.16–27) the actor was 'able to recapitulate their mutual reliance most movingly'. Harold Hobson suggested that 'the civilized, controlled, intelligent, and irresistible sexuality of Helen Mirren's Lady Macbeth' was a 'handicap' to the production, arguing somewhat eccentrically that she was so compelling that one wished the other characters would leave the stage to her alone: 'I really do regret that Shakespeare never knew Miss Mirren. We should then have had a different play.'[18]

1976: Neo-Elizabethan variations

In the Royal Shakespeare Theatre, the 1976 season offered a further permutation of the stage in a feat of what might be considered radical antiquarianism. The theatre's celebration in 1975 of its 'centenary'– a movable feast, given that this was the year of the inauguration of plans for the Memorial Theatre rather than an anniversary for the RSC itself – had been memorable for the spectacular impact of Terry Hands's production of *Henry V*. Although the watchword in this period of national economic crisis was frugality, Hands, who took sole responsibility as director for the 1975 Stratford repertoire, achieved a remarkable degree of spectacle combined with quasi-Brechtian theatrical self-consciousness. As the opening production, *Henry V* revealed Abd' Elkader Farrah's overall design for the season, 'not a set', writes Sally Beauman, 'but ... a black platform, bare of adornment, it jutted out towards the audience with all its working trimmings clearly visible'. The steeply raked stage resembled 'the deck of a great aircraft carrier'.[19] For the 1976 Stratford season, Farrah's innovative overall design was removed and the stage was converted by John Napier and Chris Dyer into a pseudo-Elizabethan permanent setting, using (it was proudly announced) recycled wood. Once again, a programme note explained the alterations with an emphasis on contact between audience and stage:

> The stage is 33 feet deep, 48 feet wide at its widest point and 17 feet at its narrowest. It extends 16 feet in front of the proscenium arch, giving maximum contact with the auditorium.

'Up to 74 spectators' could be seated on balconies at the back of the stage, but in the event these proved impractical, as actors could not avoid turning away from them for most of the performance. The additional facilities were a downstage 'grave' trap, an additional on-stage balcony 'supported on columns to the [audience's] left of the stage' and the provision of 'seven possible entries' for actors from the back and sides of the stage and through the auditorium.[20] As if to emphasize that this was not a slavish historical reconstruction, in addition to a reproduction of the De Witt drawing of the Swan, the *Romeo and Juliet* programme reproduced examples of imagined reconstructions of Elizabethan theatres from the nineteenth century, together with the engraving of a 'memory theatre' from 1619.

The new stage could also be seen as a combination of artistic policy and response to economic pressure. Nunn emphasized both in an article for the *Sunday Times*:

> This stage certainly isn't a reconstruction and makes no attempt to be nostalgic about past ages. Simply, with little money, it is the best we can do to express our belief in a theatre of imagination; actors on a bare platform, conjuring the audience with language and nothing else onto Prospero's island or that balcony in Verona; in short, a theatre that asks its audience also to work with the actors.[21]

Once again, there was the appeal to the 'wooden O', implicit here and explicit in statements by Hands and others before him. Nunn prefaced his article with a rejection of 'Free Shakespeare' and other 'essentially academic slogans', including the attack on 'director's theatre' – hardly a cause he would be expected to adopt – and elaborated on his desire to create 'a place for telling stories'. Napier told John Barber that the ambition was to 'create a small space with the potential to become anything, anywhere', insisting that 'It's the words that count ... and we want a sounding-board where language can resonate.'[22] In a survey of the company's work in *Plays and Players* Jim Hiley quoted the claim by Barry Kyle ('one of the RSC's younger directors' in the team assembled for the season) that after the 'enormous expenditure on stage machinery and effects' of the 1972 season, 'critical opinion and harsh reality in tandem forced the company to adopt an austerity which ... has been transformed into the house style Nunn denies exists'. Kyle welcomed a 'new simplicity' with the focus on the actors: 'directors' theatre is dead'.[23] This was as premature as many such reports, but the sentiment had been absorbed into the ethos of the RSC with Nunn's habitual mixture of pragmatism and artistic principle.

Hiley reported that after the construction of the 'Elizabethan' stage 'there was not a great deal of money to disguise it from play to play', but that the company could now afford 'decent rehearsal periods'. Michael Pennington, who played Mercutio in *Romeo and Juliet*, recalled Nunn's first words to the cast: 'He said it was all down to us, to us and the language. What better brief could an actor have? We had so much time that we were able to postpone decisions even when we were ready to make them. This meant that the text could really shine through.'[24] The programme included some of the cast's responses to a memo from the director, asking them to recall their first adult love affair (or kiss), to write down three things the phrase 'Renaissance Italy' evoked, and the 'most extremely violent thing you have done in your life'. Not everyone took this seriously – one of the 'three things' answers gave the names of a chain of shoe shops, Freeman, Hardy and Willis – and one answer seemed to bring together two of the ideas that would be dominant in the production: the 'most extremely violent' thing one actor claimed to have done was 'copulated'. A member of the company recently told me that he didn't remember all this, but that it must have been a company-building exercise on Nunn's part. It was also, like similar elements reported in some of Nunn's other rehearsals, a means of engaging the actors' imaginative connection with the themes of the play. In any case, publication in the programme was a way of asserting that vague notions of romantic love would be kept at arm's length, and that the RSC would be seen to have its finger on several pulses at once.

The text of *Romeo and Juliet* was full enough to cause the first-night performance to run for 3 hours 40 minutes – at least as timed by reviewers who could not resist complaining that the Chorus' reference to 'the two hours traffic of our stage' was misleading. (The twenty-minute intermission followed the marriage, separating it from the brawl in which Mercutio and Tybalt are killed and Romeo is banished.) Few of the alterations and omissions in the script of *Romeo and Juliet* had any notable interpretive significance: the most radical were linked to the decision to make the Chorus a denim-clad contemporary figure, whose role was extended after the prologue by retaining the prologue to the second act; giving him the four lines that begin the Friar's speech in 2.3 in Q1 and are spoken by Romeo in other texts (2.2.188–91, 'The grey-ey'd morn'); and reassigning the last four lines from the Prince's concluding speech (5.3.307–10). In Stratford the spectators seated in galleries at the back of the stage found themselves included in the injunction to 'Go hence and have more talk of these sad things.'

Other changes removed obscure references or repetitions of points of character or expression already established. In the final scene there was no reference to Tybalt's body being in the family vault, as this was the grave trap on the open stage: only Juliet could be accommodated. As is commonly the case, in the second half of the play, after the deaths of Mercutio and Tybalt and Romeo's banishment, cuts appear to be have been made in order to maintain the play's momentum. Nunn and Kyle adjusted the action of the final scene and cut a few expository lines, the most important being in the Friar's account of the chain of circumstances that led to the deaths of Romeo, Juliet and Paris (249–55). The effect was to keep the sense that events need to be explained to the assembled characters and that the Friar must be allowed to justify his actions.

On the unadorned stage, the production adopted a degree of self-denial that commanded respect but had its disadvantages. In the pursuit of quasi-Elizabethan directness of communication with the audience, lighting was confined 'within very narrow limits of dark and light, and keeping all the torches and lanterns in the play unlit'.[25] Michael Billington thought this a problem in 'a play where the relation between climate and action is crucial', so that 'instead of an Italianate daze of heat in which passion inevitably spins, the permanent set ... all too firmly anchors us in a cool, dry, indoor world'.[26] Felix Barker asked, 'Should the night balcony love scene be played in the unrelenting glare of simulated daylight?'[27] The key word here is 'simulated', the element of artifice that intervened between many reviewers and the qualities of 'realism, sincerity and simplicity' admired by Frank Marcus.[28] In Brook's *Dream*, the even, constant lighting through most of the play had been part of a scheme of abstraction (though not austerity) in the 'empty space' that projected the actors and their speaking of the text out towards the audience by throwing them into relief against a simple but by no means unsophisticated background. This *Romeo and Juliet*, on a stage designed to bring the audience closer to the actors and the text, distanced them with its artificial authenticity emphasized by the unlit torches and lanterns, and the gesture towards a 'wooden O' that could not be more than a wooden polygon with a few sides missing and a few hapless spectators marooned upstage.

Robert Cushman complained that 'for all its austerity, this [was] at heart a normally complicated RSC production, full of comings, goings and elaborate standings-still', and John Elsom in the *Listener* described it as characterized by 'an extroverted delight in snatching up Shakespeare's scenes and playing them to the hilt, without bothering with too much deep thought or justification'.²⁹ The 'normally complicated' busyness of the production was matched by a the frenetic energy in McKellen's Romeo, described by John Barber as 'a scampering, impish, long-necked adolescent'.³⁰ In the programme, McKellen referred to his anxiety that the character should not seem 'soppy' to a modern audience. Michael Coveney commented that in this 'wild, studiously vehement performance' Romeo was certainly not the 'flower of courtesy' as 'he retreat[ed] from any form of civil behaviour into giggly participation at the Capulets' ball'.³¹ Richard David describes him jumping on and off stools, popping up unexpectedly 'in various balconies' and finally making 'a jet landing from the staircase stage-left to snatch Juliet for their first meeting'. (This extravagant behaviour was 'reduced' in later performances.)³² In *The Times* Irving Wardle complained of 'a return to Ian McKellen's worst mannerisms, the alternation of slack-jawed uncoordination and spasms of headlong energy ... and imposed contortions of slurred and staccato speech intended to convey extreme emotions'.³³ A number of critics thought the physical and verbal hyperactivity were adopted to overcome the distance between the actor's age (he was 37) and that of the character, but that (as Kenneth Hurren wrote in the *Spectator*) in the pursuit of this he lost 'vital words rather more noticeably than vital years'.³⁴ Cushman observed that in the moment of his resolve to find poison and hurry back to Verona 'he defies the stars with a violent twist of his mouth, sounding like tragedy and looking like toothache'. More suggestive of a deeper purpose in the strategy of both actor and director is David Nathan's observation that the performance was 'directed inwardly, an examination of [Romeo's] emotional entrails as he flails about in an agony of introspection', resulting in 'an interesting study that totally ignores any romantic, poetic aspect'.³⁵ Romeo's energy was complemented by that of Mercutio (Michael Pennington), 'a volatile fantasist whose jokes are always apt to turn dangerous', he clowned throughout the combat with Tybalt, and leapt into his arms to kiss him, thus receiving his deathblow by accident. 'Even after that,' wrote Wardle,

'Mercutio the joker survives, finally dragged out fixing Romeo with a ghastly smile.'

As Juliet, Francesca Annis was 'infinitely still, vastly more mature' so that (Sheridan Morley suggested) in contrast to McKellen's 'leaping, Puckish figure' she 'seem[ed] at moments to be playing his mother'.[36] Richard David's description of Juliet's response to the Nurse's advice that she should marry Paris reflects both the quality of Annis' performance and an instance of the kind of psychologically suggestive detail characteristic of Nunn's work with his actors:

> This scene was a beautiful study in stillness. The Nurse's crooned advice appeared more diabolical in its very softness. Juliet's progressive awareness of the fiend behind the angelical disguise was marked by a series of significant withdrawals so that from nestling in the Nurse's lap she came to be completely separated from her on an isolated stool in the centre.[37]

David also provides one of the fullest descriptions of the *coup de théâtre* in the final scene, 'one of the most powerfully imagined effects of the production' (Figure 4).

> Romeo, having levered up the down-stage trap, emerges from it with Juliet in his arms and, as he speaks, moves very gently with her round upon the stage as if they were engaged in a dream dance, eventually sinking to the ground, Juliet on his knee, as he prepares to drink the potion. Just as he lifted up the phial, Juliet began to stir: a touch that is in fact contradicted by Friar Laurence's subsequent narrative, but that neatly emphasised the hairsbreadth chances that defeat the lovers at every point.[38]

Although in his final speech – and dying scream – McKellen's Romeo seemed to aim for anguish yet again, the 'near miss' was the truly memorable moment in the scene. Montague's anger remained in need of counselling (he kicked the dead Romeo),

FIGURE 4 Romeo and Juliet *(Royal Shakespeare Theatre, 1976)*: Romeo (Ian McKellen) embraces Juliet (Francesca Annis) *on the edge of the grave (Joe Cocks Studio Collection © Shakespeare Birthplace Trust)*.

which made the final explanations all the more necessary and also acted as a further counter-measure to sentimentality: once again a production was striving to evoke a violent, passionate social world, proclaimed in the programme's excerpts from historical sources as well as in the frenetic energy of the performance. This provided a context for the apparent waywardness of Romeo and Mercutio's satirical energy, which militated against any suggestion of picturesque fantasy in the 'Queen Mab' speech (1.4.53–95).

Most reviews described the press night performance, making it difficult to take account of developments over the season, but the London opening was welcomed (once again) as an example of a Stratford production benefitting from its own experience, and from the freedom from the original staging. The wooden 'O' was gone, energy had been channelled into performances of greater subtlety, and excesses trimmed. Michael Coveney, in the *Financial Times*, found McKellen's Romeo 'quick, intelligent and impressionable, forever finding fresh resonance and passion in his verse'.[39] Billington thought that Romeo's passion was now 'intelligently presented', and that Pennington's Mercutio, 'much in love with Romeo' had also 'shed his mannerisms while retaining his neuroticism'.[40]

Although directing credit was shared with Barry Kyle, *Romeo and Juliet* had emerged with the hallmarks of a Nunn production: a degree of showmanship that had initially been expressed in showiness; attention to the expression of, at times, extreme states of mind; the creation of a coherent social context; a desire to engage the audience, here through energy and 'bustle' on a newly configured stage; and the focus on expressive and realistic details of behaviour. By the time of the London transfer not only had adjustments in staging been worked out, but the actors had also accumulated experience individually and as a team both in the production itself, and through their other parts in the season. In particular, McKellen had played Leontes on the main stage and Macbeth at The Other Place.

The stage's austerity was disguised for the productions that followed *Romeo and Juliet* in the 1976 Stratford season: *Much Ado About Nothing*, *Troilus and Cressida*, *The Winter's Tale* and *The Comedy of Errors* all dispensed with the use of the upstage gallery for spectators, and the wooden structure was modified with hangings and scenic units of one kind or another. Lighting was returned to the habitual range and subtlety available. *The Winter's Tale*, directed by John Barton 'with Trevor Nunn', was set in a non-specific Scandinavian world, providing what Irving Wardle accepted as 'a strong framework for the play's rhythm: a long dark night followed by an unclouded summer'. Di Seymour's setting 'transfigure[d] the dauntingly permanent innyard' with 'a panoramic screen of diagrammatic folk images ... laced through the timber uprights, encircling the stage and lit either coldly from the front or warmly from behind', with a withered tree centre stage 'like a frozen flash of lightning ... representing the sterile mortality of the two kings, redeemed through their children's union'.[41] The precedent of Nunn's 1969 production was potentially encouraging and comparisons were inevitable, but Robert Cushman felt that the invented 'ritual games' – which included the celebration of Jul and appropriate behaviour when the oracle was brought into the trial scene engraved scrimshank-fashion on a horn – were such as to 'leave the audience cold'. This was 'dehydrated Shakespeare, the earnest taming of a Shakespeare play'. But Cushman, and critics who shared his reaction, found that individual performances redeemed the production, notably McKellen's Leontes, Barbara Leigh-Hunt's Paulina and the Autolycus of Michael Williams. Cushman wrote that 'As Leontes's lucidity goes, Mr. McKellen's increases, the course of each shaft of jealousy precisely plotted.'[42] Michael Billington identified the ability to register inner torment with startling physical and vocal precision that would later characterize the actor's Macbeth and once again reflected Nunn's habitual attention to extreme psychological states: 'Into an idyllic image of family life, he suddenly injects a wracked sexual anguish, spitting out words like "sluiced" and "bedswerver." And when his new-born daughter is deposited in his lap, he lifts his curled, white knuckled hands above his head as if fearing physical contamination.'[43]

The use of an altered lighting state to accompany Leontes' fits of jealousy recalled the similar – though more elaborate – device in the 1969 production, suggesting the influence if not the direct intervention of Nunn in this detail. With the season's directors working in pairs or teams – *King Lear* had three directors – reviewers sometimes attempted to distinguish between their contributions, not to mention the unfathomable question of the part played by the directors in the creation of a given actor's performance. John Barber 'groaned' at the beginning of *The Winter's Tale*: 'With John Barton as director, there is always a gimmick', and the shifting of Sicily to some point north of the Baltic did not augur well. 'But Trevor Nunn co-directs, and the result is a fine production of this beautiful work.'[44] He did not specify any elements of Nunn's influence.

Nunn was listed as co-director (the mysterious 'with' of the credits) of two other productions in the season but *The*

Comedy of Errors was attributed to him alone. This became a would-be musical comedy, set in the market place of a Greek seaside town, with a pavement café facing the door of the Ephesian household across the stage, and provided with racks of postcards and other adjuncts to tourism, 'the absolute epitome of a timeless Mediterranean tourist-trap'.[45] Comparison was challenged, for most reviewers and many other habitual playgoers, with Clifford Williams' production, first staged in 1962 to fill gap in the schedule caused by a delay to Brook's *King Lear* and revived in the 1972 'Romans' season.

This was the first manifestation of the director's engagement with the musical genre as such, and the forerunner of subsequent productions in which he amended and augmented Shakespearean comedy with music, song and dance beyond what was explicitly called for in the text. Nunn told an interviewer that it was necessary to find an approach that did not replicate that of the much-revived 1962 version. The play was 'a work of no intellectual pretensions', so that his task must be 'to honour its intention, which is primarily to entertain'. The answer was not simply cutting the 'doggerel sections' and jokes that were 'utterly impenetrable' now, but by 'working the difficult areas into songs'.[46] Critical response ranged from Anthony Everitt's gratitude in the *Birmingham Post* for 'one of the most sheerly delightful evenings at Stratford for many seasons' to unequivocal rejection.[47] In the *Observer*, Robert Cushman complained that in this 'half-cock musical', individual lines 'balloon into songs and dances after which we return to find the play exactly where we find it – except that we cannot quite remember where that was'.[48]

The music (Guy Woolfenden) and dancing (Gillian Lynne) were in expert hands, and even if the numbers seemed to be grafted onto the incidents rather than, as in the best musical theatre, furthering the action and character development through song and dance, *The Comedy of Errors* was also notable for the scope given to the actors. Judi Dench's Adriana was 'a peremptory odalisque, downing her terrified servants with flying trays and point-blank bursts from the soda syphon'. She was also able to deploy a comic modulation of her considerable gift for pathos as well as 'relapsing into voluptuous submission with her supposed husband'.[49] Her long harangue to him, after to his amazement she had 'wafted him' from her balcony – 'Ay, ay, Antipholus, look strange and frown' (2.2.110 etc.) – was a *tour de force* of comic indignation and pathos, responded to by Roger Rees with perfect timing: 'Plead you to me, fair dame?' It was not surprising that his resistance was overcome when Adriana melted at the end of the scene into explicitly seductive insistence that he should 'dine above' with her today. As Luciana, Francesca Annis wore wire-framed spectacles – that reliable indicator of feminine bookishness – and indeed immersed herself in her book in the midst of the frenzied goings-on in her sister's household. She literally read her sister a lecture from one of them, indicating on the page the instances that illustrated how 'headstrong liberty is lashed with woe' (2.1.15–25). There was even room for the time-honoured gag of Antipholus of Syracuse taking off her spectacles to reveal her beauty, only to put her at the mercy of her short-sightedness. The freshness of the acting *on* the lines, and the aptness of the business that supported this, made up for a good deal of the activity that often seemed to be levered in *between* the lines, though the acrobatic inventiveness of the physical performances by the Dromios, Michael Williams (Syracuse) and Nikolas Grace (Ephesus), was in itself impressive. Woolfenden's score and Lynne's choreography were skillfully adapted to a company not recruited from music theatre performers, but energy and good humour made up for the fact that this was only half-way to being a musical.

Yet again, the move to London reflected the company's experience of playing a show to enthusiastic audiences in Stratford after the critics had left town. Reviewing the production again when it transferred to the Aldwych, Cushman recanted: 'the comic pressure has been raised so high that song and dance are the only possible release'.[50] Michael Billington, underwhelmed in Stratford, now hailed 'one of the most joyous entertainments in town' and identified the root of this change of heart in a corresponding element in the performance, since 'the gags [were] now given a human context' and the accumulation of sight gags created 'the right sense of vertiginous bewilderment'.[51] Even at Stratford, despite the critics' reservations, audiences had responded enthusiastically, and the overall effect was one of joyous festivity, generated by enthusiasm and commitment on stage and shared generously. This was one way in which Nunn's frequently declared aim of breaking down barriers might be achieved on the main stage. It was an asset in the company's quest for moral and financial support from its audiences, and tapped into the desire for community and rejection of elitism that characterized most the work of many fringe companies.

The season ended with *King Lear*, co-directed by Barton, Nunn and Kyle. Jonathan Croall reports that 'Nunn was in overall charge, Barton looked after textual matters, and Kyle handled the Gloucester sub-plot'.[52] In an interview in *The Times*, Donald Sinden, whose reputation had been mainly as an actor in comedy, told John Higgins that he had imagined himself playing 'an epic Lear, pre-Saxon, even prehistorical ... much larger than life, almost like one of Wagner's gods in *The Ring*'. He had been obliged to reassess his ideas on discovering that the chosen milieu was that of the late nineteenth century, and distinctly domestic.[53] Many of the reviews evince a longing for the epic and elemental. Milton Shulman's, headlined 'Lear out of Step', in the *Evening Standard* was representative: in this setting the king was 'no longer a symbol of universal order and decay but a petulant small-minded dictator bordering on the fringes of senility and madness'.[54] Billington in the *Guardian* suggested that the loss of 'religious resonance' made him 'less King Lear than Archduke Lear', though Irving Wardle in *The Times* noted that Sinden's performance, 'stumping in like the aged Hindenburg, chewing a cigar and creakily lowering himself into his seat in absurd top boots', was more credible than the figure of legend referred to by the actor in his interview.[55] The consensus was that, while some details of characterization and business were effective others seemed extraneous – such as Goneril's speech impediment and Gloucester nursing his 'nightly cocoa' as he succumbed to Edmund's plotting.[56] A particular success was Michael Williams's Fool: he was as old as his master, and Wardle declared that he would not forget 'the sight of Lear helping the bald, infirm Michael Williams down [from a cart] to play his palsied routine on an improvised platform'.

In the storm scene the Fool brought the wind and rain effects to a sudden halt with a click of his fingers to deliver his prophecy (3.3.81–95). (Billington could not resist observing that this was a case of 'play stops rain'.) Michael Coveney in *Plays and Players* suggested that in the scene with Gloucester near Dover, Lear seemed to have taken his absence to develop 'what was, in the first place an alter ego, rambling dottily on with a little cane, half a tambourine and lapel facings identical to those previously worn by the Fool'.[57] Cornwall was 'an urbanely dominating grandee, affected with spasms of homicidal rage, who finally turn[ed] aside from the blinded Gloucester and react[ed] with a shriek of horror to the sight of his own wound'.[58] The production seemed to lack unity of purpose and effect, with its eclectic costuming, located but not firmly anchored in the long nineteenth century; a set that was at once symbolic, real and metatheatrical (the floor boards were removed for the storm scene to reveal gravel, and the wind and rain machinery was visible on stage); and a mixture of effective and unfocussed physical and emotional detail. Herbert Kretzmer accorded it respect as a 'sturdy, painstaking production'.[59] Coveney found it 'a selection of strong visual ideas, together with a sort of internal RSC sense of experimentation', not in itself a bad thing, because 'as a finale to the Stratford season, it emphasise[d] how open-ended and flexible had been the approach this year'. Barry Kyle reflected that the production, which had really been done in order to give Sinden the role, 'lacked a singularity of purpose' because of the 'dilution' occasioned by having three directors, and the result was 'a respectable show, but not an urgent one'.⁶⁰

1977–81: Back in the picture-frame

For the 1977 season the 'Elizabethan' stage was abandoned, and the main house reverted to a configuration that might be described as a modified picture-frame, retaining a wide forestage in front of the line defined by the fire curtain's unavoidable position behind the permanent architectural arch, but using once again the width and perspective depth of the main acting area. In John Napier's set for *The Merry Wives of Windsor*, the Elizabethan era returned but in a different form: a mellow autumnal scene with falling leaves and half-timbered houses, with mullioned windows and gables, that slid apart and opened to reveal detailed interiors. This was a view of Elizabethan England, peopled with authentically costumed figures, that seemed revolutionary by being surprisingly 'traditional' in a manner tourists might expect of the theatre in Shakespeare's town: rather than photographs of real Tudor houses, the programme used images of the realistic studio sets from John Mortimer's *Will Shakespeare,* broadcast by ATV in 1978. (Simulacra were thus enlisted in support of another simulacrum.) The production shared the attention to social and domestic detail (choirboys playing conkers, for example) and autumnal setting of Terry Hands's 1968 staging, and Roger Warren's claim that it 'amounted to little more than a refining and paring down' of that version echoed the comments of other reviewers.⁶¹ But Nunn offered a somewhat less benign view of the characters, notably Tim Spall's 'twitching, straw-haired neurotic' Simple and Ben Kingsley's Ford. The latter was clearly moving into a middle-class version of the Leontes territory: socially 'the Elizabethan equivalent of a used-car salesman', while Falstaff (John Woodvine) appeared 'in a greasy, sweaty nightshirt in his cramped, low-ceilinged inn-room', obviously on his uppers and in desperate need of money for more than mere recreational purposes.⁶² The play was clearly driven by the twin motives of money and revenge, but the comedy was there, sometimes expressed in exaggerated behavioural eccentricities and stage business, and the final scene at Herne's Oak became 'a song-and dance routine from which the three elopements of Anne [were] barely perceptible', identified by B.A. Young as an indulgence of Nunn's 'new-found love of music'.⁶³ In *As You Like It*, the last play in the season, this trait was even more evident.

The 1976 *Comedy of Errors* had been taken as symptomatic of an element of the RSC's strategy and a sign of duality in the director's own work. In his review of *As You Like It*, Michael Billington suggested that 'as productions in The Other Place get simpler, so there is a tendency to over-elaboration in the main-house Stratford Shakespeare', while Robert Cushman identified two Nunns. One was the 'showbiz Nunn', who 'turns as much of the show as possible into a musical', the other 'the alert and scholarly Nunn, combing the text to amplify the story'.⁶⁴ Once again, both aspects of the director's work were evident. The play was transformed into a pastiche baroque opera, with arias for Celia and Orlando, a sung prologue in which Hymen disputed with Fortune and Nature, the former represented not only by a singer but also by a statue that remained on stage throughout the court scenes; production numbers evolved from simple songs; an elaborated and musical wedding ceremony for Touchstone and Audrey; dances choreographed by Gillian Lynne; and a grand masque-like conclusion in which Hymen appeared on a cloud with a rainbow arched above him. To support all this a 'side-stage orchestra of a dozen' was 'kept busy throughout the evening' by Stephen Oliver's score.⁶⁵ The effect of ornate unreality was supported by John Napier's fantastic pictorial scenery – complete with flying effects – and costumes whose sources were variously identified by reviewers as *The Three Musketeers*, the court of Charles II and the paintings of Watteau. The 'alert and scholarly Nunn' was revealed once again in character-centred detail closely integrated with the narrative, such as the arrival in the Forest of Arden of other exiles from the tyrannical Duke's court – notably Le Beau and Charles the wrestler, the latter engaging in a good-humoured bout with Orlando. But to those who looked for a sense of direction in the company's artistic policy, *As You Like It* was a puzzling throwback to scenic pictorialism and the proscenium stage and a venture into the unwelcome territory of pseudo-opera.

In *Shakespeare Survey* Roger Warren suggested that the production was another sign that Nunn's productions of the comedies had become 'increasingly bizarre'. Characters 'had to switch off their characterisations for uneasy and quite unnecessary attempts to sing bits of text', and the backcloths, front drop and painted trees 'seemed even more affected, irrelevant, and old-fashioned than the mock Elizabethan stage of 1976'.[66] The wintry nature of the production's first three acts was sustained beyond the interval, which followed the first 'wooing' scene (3.2), staged as a 'skating' episode. Spring arrived somewhat belatedly, in 5.3, with a show of greenery prompted by the seasonal references in 'It was a lover and his lass.' Warren observed that this 'company celebration of the coming of spring to a snowy Arden, a big ritual celebration just *before* the point where Shakespeare wrote one, meant that Hymen's entry in fact misfired'. Nunn's productions would continue to be as unsatisfying as the concluding pseudo-operatic Hymen scene 'while he substitutes ear- and eye-tickling externals for an exploration of the text and its meanings'. 'It is really very odd,' Warren concluded, 'that a director who illuminated [the 1976] *Macbeth* with an imaginative probing of the text can be content with such a dimly superficial view of a masterpiece in another kind.'[67] There were few cuts in a relatively full text, and the running time settled down – after the removal of the prologue – to a consistent 3 hours 15 minutes, including the interval: at the first Stratford dress rehearsal it had been 3 hours 17 minutes *excluding* the 20-minute interval.[68]

One consequence of the quasi-operatic framework, redolent of the Restoration theatre's 'improvements' of Shakespeare, was that many reviewers paid more attention to it than to the results of the 'imaginative probing of the text' that had in fact taken place. In this respect, the crucial consensus was that the individual performances were all satisfying and, in the case of Rosalind and Orlando, fresh and innovative. In the last inch-and-a-half of the seven column inches he devoted to the production, John Peter in the *Sunday Times* finally turned to the performances, praising Peter McEnery's 'lean, tense' Orlando, 'a gauche country boy barely past his adolescence and clearly a trifle unstable', who was first seen practising wrestling. Kate Nelligan was 'a nervous thoroughbred: a girl who doesn't quite feel at home with emotions and observes her own with uneasy joy'.[69] Irving Wardle was especially eloquent on the subject: 'an athletic high-pressure performance, courageously breaking the bounds of Shakespearean decorum'.[70] Noel Witts, in *Plays and Players*, commented on Peter McEnery's 'ravaged Orlando in a West Country accent ... far from the mooning lover', and seeming at times to be 'desperately trying to break out of the conventions that surround him', while Kate Nelligan's 'exuberant Rosalind – all darting hands and flying ringlets – [had] precisely the kind of humanity that these conventions try and control'.[71]

As You Like It became yet another production to achieve refinement through transfer to the Aldwych, with simplifications in its staging and cast changes. Although an adapted version of the scenery remained, the prologue had gone, repeated verses in 'It was a lover and his lass' and sung responses in the marriage ceremony in the Oliver Martext scene had been shortened. (Some of these changes may have been effected during the Stratford run.)[72] 'Purged of the excesses that clogged it last year at Stratford,' wrote B.A. Young, it was now 'as charming and as funny an *As You* as anyone could wish.'[73] Charlotte Cornwell and James Laurenson took over as Rosalind and Orlando, and some reviewers regretted the departure of Nelligan and McEnery. Peter Hepple, in the *Stage*, thought Cornwell played Rosalind 'with more of a hearty instinct than an appreciation of the verse'.[74] Young noted that Laurenson's Orlando seemed to be 'treating his love-making as a game rather than the serious courtship Rosalind is after'. Although the reception was warmer than for the initial Stratford run, there were still reservations about the scenic and musical elaboration. Eric Shorter complained that there was 'plenty going on', but it was a pity 'that the various contributing arts seem to have smothered the play's urgency of narrative', and in the *Spectator* Peter Jenkins suggested Nunn's 'invention [ran] somewhat riot' in the final scene, with Alan David as Touchstone 'try[ing] to lead the audience in an "all together now", as a male Hymen [was] lowered in a cardboard cloud and as the hey-ding-a-dings threaten[ed] to outnumber the reprises of *A Chorus Line*'.[75] (The backstage musical, with its finale's reprise and repeated choruses of 'One – singular sensation', had arrived from New York in 1976.)

Between 1977 and 1981 Nunn oversaw the London transfer of *As You Like It* and, with John Caird, co-directed *The Life and Adventures of Nicholas Nickleby*, an epic work of the kind (according to the assistant director Leon Rubin) he had wanted to commit the RSC to for some time. The Dickens project not only fulfilled Nunn's ambition to exploit and showcase the resources of the company and its capacity for ensemble work in a large-scale show, it was also a brave response to yet another financial crisis. A deficit thought likely to reach £400,000 by the end of the financial year, and an increase of only 7 per cent in Arts Council grant for the coming year, threatened the RSC's ability to sustain its London season once the Stratford plays from 1979 had completed their run at the Aldwych.[76] With John Napier as designer, Stephen Oliver as composer and David Edgar as scriptwriter, Nunn and Caird embarked on a production that would correspond in some respects to the cycles of history plays and the 1972 'Romans' season as a form of 'event theatre'. When the two parts played on one day, the audience's sense of participation in a marathon provided the kind of communal theatrical experience Nunn had often hoped for, enhanced by the playing of multiple roles by the actors, the energetic use of the platforms and walkways of Napier's constructivist set, and such inspired pieces of improvisation as the creation of a stagecoach from items of luggage. The playfulness of the show balanced the unabashed sentimentality of Dickens' novel as well as sharing its comic and melodramatic theatricality. The latter was emphasized in the treatment of the Crummles troupe of players and their performance of a version of *Romeo and Juliet* with a comically happy ending. Critical response to the marathon press day was mixed, and despite the enthusiastic reception by audiences during the first weeks, word of mouth was slow to be reflected in bookings. Then, in the 8 July issue of *The Times*, Bernard Levin praised the show extravagantly, rebuked its critics ('some of the criticism ... makes one despair not just of criticism but of the human race') and precipitated a rush to the box office. The rest of the six-week run quickly sold out.[77]

Nicholas Nickleby was revived at the Aldwych in April to June 1981. It subsequently transferred to the Old Vic for a seven-week run, during which it was filmed for Channel 4 television, and played on Broadway for 16 weeks. A largely recast revival in 1985 played for a brief season at Stratford, followed by a tour in the UK and Continental Europe. The Stratford box office suffered from the loss of eighteen performances in the 1981–2 season, possibly amounting to some £81,000, but the loss incurred by making space in the schedule for exploiting the production was compensated by the estimated net contribution to the company's finances of £100,000.[78] More significant than the financial dimension of *Nicholas Nickleby* were the excitement generated not only in audiences but also in the company and the creative team, and the sense of ensemble and risk-taking. This is conveyed vividly in Leon Rubin's account of the process. Nunn told the company at the outset that 'Brechtian improvisation' as distinct from Stanislavskian, would be adopted. As Rubin notes, he believed that 'in all his work he should begin with character and then move into situation and incident. Then an audience is involved and moved'. At the same time he carried out 'his usual microscopically detailed examination of each thought, word and deed', even when this resulted in delays in the rehearsal schedule.[79]

Shakespeare meets Shaw and Chekhov in 1981–2: *All's Well That Ends Well*

In contrast to the 'operatic' *As You Like It* and the epic *Nicholas Nickleby*, Nunn's production of *Three Sisters* for the 'small-scale tour' of twenty-six regional venues between July and October 1978 had been a venture into the kind of intimate theatre that suited The Other Place. Its emotional intensity and naturalistic domestic detail not only foreshadowed the 1989 *Othello*, but also seemed to inform *All's Well That Ends Well*, which Nunn had described in advance as 'Shakespeare's most Chekhovian play'.[80] The production, which opened in Stratford on 17 November, was another landmark in Nunn's career and the company's work, combining his ability to embrace the opportunities offered by the larger stage with an impressive degree of nuanced and sensitive performance from the actors. Gareth Lloyd Evans wrote in the *Stratford-upon-Avon Herald* that 'Trevor Nunn was at his best: the hallmarks of his production being a flowing intelligence, visual imaginativeness and a care for the speaking of the text.'[81]

'They say miracles are past,' says Lafew, 'and we have our philosophical persons to make modern and familiar, things supernatural and causeless' (2.3.1–3). As well as Chekhov, the playwright cited most frequently by reviewers, Nunn's *All's Well That Ends Well* evoked an age when Shavian philosophical persons were doing just that, locating in humankind itself the Life Force that changes the world and secures what they want for its inhabitants. In contrast to the teeming world created in *Nicholas Nickleby*, this was an elegant and tightly focused production, centred in the sense of calm and mature reflection of Peggy Ashcroft's Countess. The elegiac quality of her scenes was balanced by the Shavian energy of Harriet Walter as Helena and the humanity with which even Parolles, the lying chancer, was treated.

The adaptation of the text was conservative: 160 lines were cut from the total of approximately 3,000, with only two places where the order of the text was changed.[82] The epilogue 'spoken by the King' was omitted. The deleted lines were for the most part brief elaborations of a thought already expressed or passages where an obscure or anachronistic reference would be a distraction. Because 3.2, when Helena resolves to depart from Rossillion, was played as if at night, her soliloquy (followed by the interval) concluded with 'End night, come day! / For with the dawn, poor thief, I'll steal away', instead of 'Come night, end, day! / For with the dark, poor thief, I'll steal away' (128–9).

The more radical revisions, with the transposition of blocks of dialogue, occurred in the second half of the performed script. At the end of 3.5, after Helena, Diana, the Widow and Mariana watched the parade of the troops, the women's thanks to Helena for her promise to 'bestow some precepts of this virgin [Mariana] / Worthy the note' (99–100) were followed by the first seven lines of 3.7, with Helena assuring her hostess that she is the lady wronged by Bertram – though she has not hitherto revealed this – concluding with the Widow's response that she 'would not put [her] reputation now / In any staining act'. Helena's 'Nor would I wish you' (8) ended the scene, which gave way to the initiation of the plot on the part of the two Dumaine brothers (the text's First and Second Lords) to unmask Parolles. After 3.7, in which Helena secures the complicity of her new friends in her plan to take Diana's place with Bertram, the first two scenes of Act Four were almost intact, with the capture of Parolles and Bertram's arrangement of his tryst with Diana. In the long scene of Parolles' interrogation, 4.3, speeches at 241–55 and 276–82 were moved to follow 192 ('What is his [Captain Dumaine's] reputation with the Duke?'), bringing together the passages in which the Dumaine brothers are slandered, and allowing the revelation of Parolles' opinion of Bertram to stand alone as the climax of the episode.

In John Gunter's elegant set, white columns supported a roof that could be transformed to that of a conservatory, a gym, a railway station, a field hospital or a palace. This was the end of the 'long' nineteenth century, and although he characterized the setting as 'a kind of *fin-de-siècle* mishmash, a glossy Edwardiana, more hindsight than Forsyte', John Elsom in the *Listener* welcomed the 'clarification' Nunn had brought to the play through this choice: like many other reviewers, he noted the implicit evocation of Shaw's *Man and Superman*, 'where the device of the anti-sentimentalists was to have the woman chasing the man'.[83] The spirit and enterprise of Helena, Parolles' optimism that 'simply the thing I am / Shall make me live' (4.3.322–3), and the success of the old doctor's 'receipt' in curing the king became part of this world. Stephen Moore's Parolles was an amiable realist, a coward still, but with shades of Bluntschli in *Arms and the Man*. Helena was reminiscent of Ann Whitfield, who 'inspires confidence as a person who will do nothing she does not mean to do', but she did not, as Shaw's heroine does, inspire the fear that 'she will probably do everything she means to do without taking more account of other people than may be necessary and what she calls right'.[84] In the *Financial Times* Michael Coveney described the opening scenes as 'a Chekhovian wash of disappointed love, silhouetted walzters, ticking clocks and comfortable armchairs'.[85] Irving Wardle, reviewing the Barbican transfer, associated Chekhov with the 'off-stage nocturnes and autumn leaves drifting down on a country estate', and suggested that the scene between the Countess and Lavatch (the opening of 3.2) evoked *The Cherry Orchard*, 'as if Ranevskaya had decided to stay behind with Firs'.[86] In his 1981 Stratford review *The Seagull* had provided a comparison for Harriet Walter's 'love-sick' Helena, 'black-dressed like Marsha [*sic*] with keys at her waist, sitting dejectedly by the Countess as Bertram hovers at the door eager for his getaway'. Nicholas Shrimpton, in *Shakespeare Survey*, seems to have been the only reviewer to associate the setting not with Chekhov but with 'the vivid sense of life in a late nineteenth-century French country-house', where 'a distant bell and a twitter of birdsong sketched in the landscape of Provence'. He declared that this production's 'tutelary novelist' was Marcel Proust.[87]

Nunn established the men-only (or *Boys' Own Paper*) world of the young men rushing off enthusiastically to war, and preserved the etiquette of class distinctions, as in Bertram's disdain for Helena's social standing, and Parolles' status as the kind of personality who might expect to blackballed from a club and was only in the officers' mess on sufferance. In the *Daily Mail,* Jack Tinker wrote that 'an entire epoch [was] fleshed out and the layers of its society peeled back to reveal a social conscience one scarcely suspected Shakespeare possessed'.[88] Michael Billington, noting the Chekhovian 'wicker furniture' and the clocks at Rossillion, suggested that the play then moved to 'a Novello court' – with young officers dressed as if in one of Ivor Novello's romantic Ruritanian musical comedies. This gave way in the wartime scenes to 'a world of brass bands, smoky estaminets, and peachy nurses who might have stepped out of *Oh What a Lovely War*'.[89] A station sign descended from the flies to indicate 'Firenze' and after a brisk battle suggested by offstage pyrotechnics, the slightly damaged 'conservatory' set represented a field hospital.

In the opening moments two shadowy figures had appeared, dancing a tentative waltz in silhouette, before screens with grey shutters slid across between the pillars of the set and the furniture of the countess's drawing room was brought in. As the lights faded before the interval, Helena stood, one arm raised against the door-jamb, gazing into the world outside the chateau, and at the final curtain she and Bertram moved, hesitantly and not quite holding hands, towards a new life – one hoped. In the first scene Bertram left a world of love: giggling maidservants fussed round, suggesting that he had been the observed of all observers in Rossillion, while the Countess was its central figure, linking youth and age in her affections. The fine balance of her opening words – 'In delivering my son from me I bury a second husband' – was maintained by Ashcroft, wistful but not overly melancholic. Stanley Wells observed that 'Even so it was with me when I was young' (1.3.123) was 'not (as Edith Evans made it) a meditation but a statement', an indication of the way Ashcroft 'shift[ed] the balance of her role away from poetic generality to personal expression'.[90] Despite her appearance in only six scenes, Ashcroft's Countess was a keynote in the 'Chekhovian' temper of the production. Michael Billington's review of the 1982 Barbican performance captured the effect: 'as the seasons pass on her rural estate, she views the life around her with a gentle wit ("This was your motive for Paris, was it?" she asks of Helena, raising an eyebrow at the overpowering urge to cure the king's fistula) and total respect for other people's dignity'.[91]

It was clear throughout that this was a warmly accommodating home, in which it was affection rather than mischance that was remembered and where the clown had his place as well as the gentleman Lafew. (Lavatch's habit of flirting with all available women was tolerated as an amiable human flaw.) The bond between countess and the shrewd, unhappy clown, bent nearly double with what seemed to be crippling arthritis, was simply conveyed in the pleasure she took in sharing jokes with him, the care with which she straightened his muffler when he set off for Paris, and the pat on the head she gave him before he shuffled off. The courtesy of her conversations with Lafew illuminated the sense of a kindly woman at ease with her contemporaries and able to make the young – Helena, if not Bertram – at ease in her presence. Even the steward Rinaldo, with his report on Helena's overheard intentions, was considerate and dutiful rather than nosey and was treated accordingly by his mistress. Nunn extended this warmth to the army and the diplomatic corps, making the Dumaine brothers earnest and compassionate spectators of Bertram's reprehensible career. Their discussion in 4.3 of his dealings with Diana and Helena was the culmination of the kind of observation that had run throughout the whole play. This gave fresh authority to the first brother's reflection that 'As we are ourselves, what things are we!' (18–19), reinforcing its connection with Parolles' acceptance of the 'thing' he is and with the play's central problem: what sort of thing is Bertram?

Mike Gwilym, in Stratford, played him as an aggressive, often graceless youth. 'An overgrown adolescent,' Shrimpton suggested in *Shakespeare Survey*, 'desperate to escape from home and mother, and to live in a world of men.'[92] He was constantly offered affection but his confused adolescent sense of the need to assert his own worth in the wider world drove him away. (At the Barbican, Philip Franks made him less assertive and more sympathetic but still a callow and unperceptive youth.) Gwylim's Bertram was often simply gauche, lacking the manners to disguise his anxiety to get away from Rossillion and not even thinking to put down his suitcase to shake hands with the king. His brutal rebuttal of Helena after the 'elimination dance' in which she chose him from among the other young lords produced a barely controlled breakdown of her nervously maintained composure, a reaction quite foreign to Shaw's brilliantly rational women. For Billington this prompted thoughts of another Scandinavian dramatist: 'At first, there is a teasing playfulness about her selection of Bertram as a husband ... But Nunn turns this to naked anguish when Bertram spits out "I cannot love her" [2.3.145] with Strindbergian intensity [Figure 5].' Shrimpton, one of the few reviewers to sympathize with Bertram, deduced that 'a sense of being dragged home to mother lay behind his dismay', and found this consistent with what he interpreted as an 'entirely reasonable account of how a young man in Bertram's position' might see the situation: 'Helena did not seem wrong to want Bertram. But she did seem wrong to want him so soon.'[93] Arguably, Gwilym did little to encourage such sympathy. His Bertram was crudely spiteful when he openly declared 'here comes my clog' as Helena entered to say goodbye to him (2.5.53). His embarrassment was disturbing and inescapable, from the callous parting from his wife to his 'boggling shrewdly' in the final scene.

For all his preening himself as a would-be lady's man in his most Parolles-like moment, Bertram was altogether out of his depth with Cheryl Campbell's worldy-wise Diana. (An accomplished chanteuse at the behind-the-lines estaminet, her claims to a spotless reputation were perhaps endangered by her saucy delivery of 'Je m'en fous', a song of Campbell's

FIGURE 5 All's Well That Ends Well *(Royal Shakespeare Theatre, 1981)*, 2.3: *the King of France (John Franklin-Robbins) gives Helena (Harriet Walter) to Bertram (Mike Gwilym). Photo by Reg Wilson © RSC.*

own devising.) He offered her a chair, but she sat in another one; he poured champagne, but she didn't drink; and when his opening gambit, 'They told me that your name was Fontibel', was met with 'Not so, my lord, Diana', he was completely nonplussed. He tried to deny her the all-important ring as 'an honour 'longing to [his] house' (4.2.42), but could not find anything to say when she flung his words back at him. Nevertheless, the supposed one-night-stand with Diana seemed like a triumph to him. Nunn gave it a counterpart in the hitherto unexplored love-life of Parolles: after flirting with Mariana as the little army with its brass band left the stage in 3.5, an episode in pantomime at the café showed them seeming to make up, and when the troops departed 'finally leaving her in tears trying to drown her sorrows'.[94] The ebullience of Bertram after his fling with Diana was short-lived when the unmasking of Parolles betrayed his own shallowness. Then, just when he might have been expected to have profited by his experience, he started lying to the king. All this might have been true of any performance of the role, but Gwilym's earlier brashness had made Helena's acceptance of him almost incredible. Nothing could redeem the snobbery of his rejection of Diana. Nevertheless his silence when confronted with Helena and the whole truth seemed to come from astonishment as much as from fixed habit of callousness, and the 'if' was wondering rather than sceptical or flatly conditional in 'If she, my liege, can make me know this clearly / I'll love her dearly, ever, ever dearly' (5.3.309–10). Responses to this moment reflected the essential ambiguity that no special pleading on Bertram's behalf can remove. Irving Wardle thought Gwilym's recoiling from Helena 'like a loathsome food, uncontrollably vomiting up his refusal in the king's face' in the scene where she chose him from among the other lords may have been 'a powerful moment, but it also [made] nonsense of the final reunion'. James Fenton, in the *Sunday Times*, came to the unusually charitable conclusion that '(a) he is indeed sincere when he says that he loved Helena all along; that (b) what motivates him is not mere snobbery but a profound loss of face. If there had been a way for their love to be realized, *he* should have found it.'[95]

The qualified nature of the interpretation's Shavianism was most evident in Helena's decisiveness and determination in her pursuit of Bertram. Although she did not set out for Saint Jacques de Compostella with the express purpose of encountering Bertram, and retained her references to the pilgrimage, her practicality was reflected in venturing to the war zone not specifically as a pilgrim but as a nurse from the Voluntary Aid Detachment (VAD) in the 1914–18 war. In any case, Helena seized the opportunity offered by her (admittedly strange) detour from Provence to Florence on the way to Spain. So far, so Shavian: in Act Three of *Man and Superman* Octavius offers to tell John Tanner that Ann Whitfield loves him, but she replies: 'Oh, no: he'd run away again ... there's no such thing as a willing man when you really go for him .... I doubt if we ever know why we do things. The only really simple thing is to go straight for what you want and grab it.'[96] Harriet Walter's Helena may have resembled Shaw's heroine in pursuing her man, but she did not have Ann's opportunities for engaging with him in argument – and Bertram did not have the wit and verbal dexterity of Tanner: this was *Man* without the *Superman*, and 'Life Force' was all on the woman's side. 'In a society where so much has been given to men like Bertram,' John Elsom asked, 'isn't Helena entitled to use her wits to redress the balance?' The important difference between Shaw's heroine and Shakespeare's, as interpreted by Nunn and Walter, lay in the intensity of feeling that complemented the 'wits' of her strategies.

Walter's ability to project both passion and reason made Helena's reappearance in the final scene, like her curing of the king, a mystery of human resourcefulness rather than divine intervention. From her first-act discussion of virginity, with Parolles speaking directly and unwittingly to her own concerns while thinking he was simply enjoying bawdy talk with a respectable girl, to the stratagems she devised once arrived in Florence, she was innocent without being ignorant of sexuality and the world. She did not suggest cunning, but was not mawkishly devoted to her unworthy husband. In the *TLS,* Stanley Wells, noting the connection between the Shavian 'New Woman' and the dramatist's favourite contemporary, cited Shaw's comparison of the play with *A Doll's House*, and his identification of Helena as 'an early Ibsenite heroine'.[97] Her devotion to Bertram was conveyed by such subtle touches as her caressing of his wooden cigarette box with 'my idolatrous fancy / must sanctify his relics' (1.1.95–6), but it was clear that the fancy was rooted in powerful physical longing. Michael Billington recognized her as 'not a ruthless Shavian go-getter but a love stricken medico's daughter, seemingly always on the verge of tears and bursting with undentable passion'. James Fenton identified her progress as being from 'a state of high distress ... towards one of mysterious fulfillment', remarking that the realization that she had forgotten her father's death (1.1.76–81) came across 'with the full force of panic and dismay'. One consequence of this engagement with Helena's suppressed desire was to make her warmer and less calculating than might have been the case in a more thoroughly 'Shavian' character: for all her talk about the Life Force, Ann Whitfield – possibly like her creator – is more talk than passion. Robert Cushman observed that in this reading 'Helena's imperative [became] not to get a man, but to get his love'.[98]

Nunn's most notable achievement was to place the action in a believable near-contemporary world, while retaining an element of wonder, appropriate to the 'old tale' of the curing of the king and the discarded wife who returns. In his review of the Stratford performance Billington identified the strategy as one of 'putting real, suffering people into an unreal situation'. The brief opening tableau and the moment before the interval when Helena gazed towards the distant world as if searching for her 'bright particular star', were echoed in her entrance in the final scene, resolving Diana's riddle (5.3.296–8), framed upstage in the same position, bathed for a few moments in a roseate light, radiant in herself and evoking the figures of Hermione or Thaisa. It was hardly surprising, even in this age of scepticism, that the king should ask 'Is there no exorcist / Beguiles the truer office of mine eyes? / Is't real that I see?' but Helena's answer, 'No, my good lord, / 'Tis but the shadow of a wife you see, / The name and not the thing', pulled the play back into reality from its seeming divergence into romance when (as J.L. Styan notes), although speaking to the king she did not take her eyes off her husband (5.3.298–302).[99]

These touches, subtly suggesting kinship with the 'late romances', further qualified the production's quasi-Shavian acknowledgement of the kinds of explanation required by 'philosophical persons'. Enough mystery was left, residing in Helena's unfathomable need to woo and pursue her unworthy 'bright particular star'; Bertram's lack of honesty and only a faintly dawning good sense; and the tentative nature of the ending. As the lights faded the pair were framed in the central doorway of the set, not quite holding hands, their fingers barely touching. Walter explained that this was a compromise between the three divergent views of the actors and the director: she saw them as a couple of realists making the best of it, Gwilym thought the ending should be 'bitter for Bertram', and Nunn preferred an optimistic ending with Helena as Bertram's 'redeemer'. Walter thought that she 'couldn't make redemption out of the messiness'.[100] The temper of the play was reflected in this difference of opinion in the rehearsal room, and its resolution in this tentative image was entirely appropriate. It was entirely appropriate that there should be a hint of the conditional in the emphasis given by John Franklin-Robbins as the king when he announced that 'all yet *seems* well' (5.3.327).

1981: Into the Barbican

After playing in New York, *All's Well That Ends Well* had to wait for its London transfer until the spring of 1981, when it followed the two parts of *Henry IV* into the newly opened Barbican Theatre. The two histories were an appropriate choice for the opening of the new theatre, having been the first plays staged in the new Shakespeare Memorial Theatre in 1932. Although the productions had a degree of panache and energy appropriate to the occasion, reviews reflect a sense that they were more dutiful than accomplished: James Fenton in the *Sunday Times* felt that they were 'full of remarkable things but … nothing like Mr. Nunn's best work'.[101] Unsurprisingly, given that once again Caird joined Nunn as co-director and Napier designed, critics traced the influence of *Nicholas Nickleby*. Irving Wardle described the set as 'a medieval counterpart of his all-embracing *Nickleby* design: a massive and intricate group of timber constructions, with cat-walks, rusting pulleys, roped hatches, which are tricked [*sic*] off laterally to form an ever-changing module of streets, tavern and palace interior, Shallow's orchard, and the ominous forest where York's party are betrayed'.[102] Stephen Wall in the *TLS* identified signs of 'Trevor Nunn's remarkable talent for thickly populated, energetically sustained stage life' with the result that 'during scene changes we tend to get sudden bursts of music and actors crossing the stage at speed, as if they had an urgent appointment in the wings opposite'.[103] As for the broader interpretive approach, Michael Billington felt that the directors regarded the plays as 'an extension of *Nicholas Nickleby* by other means'. The plays were treated 'as if they were a long novel called Fathers and Sons', with a 'Dickensian obsession with detail' rather than the pattern of the plays in an 'emblematic Morality tradition'. Nunn was 'very good on psychology', but lost 'something of the physical momentum and medieval clarity of these extraordinary works'.[104]

There was evidence of an innovative approach to the psychological complexity of other leading characters: Joss Ackland was an unusually conflicted Falstaff, described by Nicholas Shrimpton in *Shakespeare Survey* as 'Not, in fact, particularly funny ... A manic depressive, by turns insufferable and subdued'; and Wardle observed that Patrick Stewart's King Henry played 'from behind a saintly mask, consciously cultivating a mildly benevolent manner that is repeatedly torn aside by eruptions of rage (as when he counsels Hal to adopt "humility", shrieking the word at the top of his voice)'. Gerard Murphy's Hal was 'a hippy Prince, with long blonde hair and a petulant manner, who had dropped out without much liking for the alternative society'.[105] 'For all its force,' wrote Wall, 'his Hal does not suggest an interesting and complex interior life.' In the *Sunday Telegraph* Francis King dismissed him as 'perversely awkward and plebeian'.[106] Psychological innovations of this kind, interesting as they might be, seem to have sapped the vitality of the plays. Paradoxically, the two parts of *Henry IV* – especially the less eventful second part – emerged as less coherent and well-made than the carefully crafted treatment of the 'epic' qualities of the Dickensian adaptation. The productions also suffered by comparison with the dynamic theatricality of Terry Hands's stagings of the *Henry IV* plays and *Henry V* in 1975–6 and the three parts of *Henry VI* together with *Henry V* in 1977–8. When *All's Well*

That Ends Well entered the London repertoire it seemed like a reminder of where the director's real strengths lay, at least so far as Shakespearean production was concerned.

Nunn took leave of absence twice during this period to direct two musicals for commercial managements: *Cats* (1981) and *Starlight Express* (1984). For the RSC he collaborated again with Caird on *Les Misérables*, a co-production with the impresario Cameron Mackintosh. The musical opened at the Barbican in September 1985 for an eight-week run and transferred to the Palace Theatre in December. The enduring international success of these productions has provided another element in the narrative of his career constructed by critics, in which the 'classical' director, nourished by the subsidized sector, yields to the financial and artistic siren song of the commercial theatre. As for *Les Miz* (as it soon came to be known), its staging and the skillful filleting of a long novel suggested comparison with *Nicholas Nickleby*. In his 1978 review, Michael Billington had admired the 'breathtaking panache' of Nunn and Caird's direction of this 'high-class melodrama' and the 'impeccable' designs by Napier, but in 2007, in his overview of postwar theatre, *State of the Nation*, he complains that 'what was so depressing' about it was 'the way it reduced Hugo's epic structure and social detail to a few well-chosen banalities'. The production 'may have offered the RSC a vital financial lifeline', but it 'also represented a degradation of standards and a vulgarization of taste that seemed neatly to encapsulate the philistine spirit of the Eighties'.[107]

The Comedy of Errors and *As You Like It* had already provided some evidence for these arguments, but arguably those productions, like his discovery of the potential of intimate theatre at The Other Place, had also 'unlocked' another important element of Nunn's creativity as a director. In contrast to the work of this 'epic', expansive and sometimes 'showbiz' Nunn, the next chapter examines the 'chamber' productions of *Macbeth* (1976), *Othello* (1989), and his 1991 *Measure for Measure* at the 'new' Other Place as further developments of his penchant for tightly focused, psychologically expressive detail.

3

'Chamber' Shakespeare at The Other Place

During his tenure as artistic director, Nunn directed *Macbeth* (1976), *The Alchemist* (1977) and *Three Sisters* (1979) at The Other Place, the last being a production created for the company's small-scale tour. He returned to direct *Othello* in 1989 – the final production at the theatre – and in 1991 his *Measure for Measure* and an adaptation of *The Blue Angel* opened the new Other Place, built on an adjacent site. Two of these productions, *Macbeth* and *Othello*, were remarkable in redefining approaches to the plays themselves as well as marking developments in his own work, excursions into a practicable form of the 'chamber theatre' he had been trying to achieve in the intractable spaces of the Royal Shakespeare Theatre and the Aldwych.

The Other Place owed its existence as an addition to the company's range of performance spaces – and the consequent developments in its repertoire – to the initiative and energy of Buzz Goodbody. John Barton had recruited the twenty-year-old Sussex University graduate as his assistant after seeing her production of Dostoevsky's *Notes From the Underground* in the 1967 National Union of Students/*Sunday Times* Student Drama Festival. In 1968 she worked with Terry Hands on *The Merry Wives of Windsor*, providing research on daily life and the class background that supported improvisations she led in rehearsal and was reflected in the programme notes. She became involved in the small-scale touring productions of Theatregoround, and in 1969 joined Nunn as assistant director for *The Winter's Tale*. After Theatregoround was disbanded in 1971, her productions included Trevor Griffiths' *Occupations* at the Place in London. In 1972 she joined Nunn and Euan Smith for the Roman plays, assuming increased responsibility when Nunn was taken ill. Her most notable specific contribution was the social realism of the treatment of the Plebeians in *Coriolanus*, but she also worked on 'solo calls' with actors. Tim Piggott-Smith, whose roles included Pompey in *Antony and Cleopatra*, recalled her as 'very supportive to Trevor, always toeing the party line, which is important' and 'someone who spent all her time thinking about other people'.[1] The performances of her Theatregoround *King John* production on the main Stratford stage in 1971 had made her only the third woman to direct a play there.[2]

In 1973 she was given oversight, with Jean Moore as administrator, of performances in the 'tin shed' that had been used in the early 1960s as a studio space by Michel Saint-Denis. Now designated as The Other Place, in a wry reference to Hamlet's suggestion (4.3.33) that Claudius might seek the body of Polonius 'i' th' other place' – that is, in Hell – it offered the opportunity to create an intimate theatre of the kind favoured by alternative theatre groups. In that sense it would be 'other'. It would also answer to Goodbody's vision, expressed in a remarkable policy document, for a theatre that fostered a community of audience and performers, as well as accommodating new plays, devised work and new approaches to familiar classics. Her first season included versions of *King Lear* and *The Tempest* adapted to the needs of school audiences, as well as four new works plus *Uncle Vanya* and David Rudkin's *Afore Night Come*. Her acclaimed production of *Hamlet* opened the second season in April 1975 but, as Colin Chambers writes, it was 'overshadowed' by the shock of her suicide four days later. She was 'a pioneering figure who opened the company up to new ways of thinking and provided the impetus for the rejuvenation of the RSC in the mid-1970s'.[3] Peter Thomson, reviewing the 1975 season, observed that 'the achievements of The Other Place over the last two years offer a vital criticism of attitudes that still govern performances in the main house'.[4]

Nunn described the impact of her example on his own work in an interview with Richard Eyre published in 2011: she had 'changed [his] mind completely about Shakespeare in small theatre spaces when in 1975 she did her formative, groundbreaking production of *Hamlet*'. Using an adjective applied only with caution in the theatre, he declared that for him 'there was something definitive about that'. Over and above the quality of the interpretation, he was impressed by the technical and aesthetic consequences of the theatre's intimacy:

> With her *Hamlet* there was a conversational tone; there was the certainty that thought was producing the text, because we were so closely involved we could hear every breath and sort of see into the eyes of each and every character. Therefore we could see the origin of thought, and that in itself banished textual music as a propriety completely and overnight. ... She left an extraordinary legacy, and the production that I did of *Macbeth*, which was the following year, was created with the purpose of carrying on that work.[5]

Although, judging by this interview, the broader social dimensions of the enterprise may not have been uppermost in his mind, this was effectively the kind of 'in one room' formula he had so far been pursuing with only qualified success. During the first season the seating had been flexible, in the sense of not being fixed to the floor, lending productions an element of improvisation of the kind associated with small-space fringe performance.

For the 1976 season John Napier designed a new arrangement, with fixed seating for the audience on three sides of the almost square acting area and a permanent balcony on all four sides. There was no flying space or trap, and lighting was still provided with equipment no longer needed at the main house. Facilities for audience and cast were minimal: there was no foyer, and any refreshments were provided on an ad hoc basis by an ice-cream van or hot-dog stand.[6] Budgets were also minimal: Ian McKellen recalled that *Macbeth* was budgeted for £250, with some of the costumes bought from secondhand shops. (His uniform jacket, with buttons all the way down, was from Birmingham's Fire Department, and he and John Woodvine – as Banquo – wore their leather coats over their shoulders because they were too small to be fastened at the front.)[7] Nunn's productions in this venue differed greatly in their use of its intimacy, and although *The Alchemist*, with Ian McKellen as Face and John Woodvine as Subtle, was well received, its subsequent transfer to the Aldwych rather than the Warehouse was felt by some to have given it a greater scope for its expansive, fast-paced comedy. Michael Billington suggested that in its first incarnation in May 1977 it 'looked cramped and lacked any sense of escalating panic among its trio of cony-catchers'. Now it had 'taken wing almost literally'.[8] This was a rare example of a production from The Other Place benefitting from the move a larger stage: the brief revival of *Macbeth* at the RST in 1977 was considered a mistake, and Nunn's other 'chamber' productions depended for their impact on the venue's sense of confinement and tight focus.

Although the television versions of both *Macbeth* and the 1989 *Othello* were restaged in a studio, archive evidence shows that both reproduce almost completely the detail of the theatre performances. The contrast with *The Comedy of Errors*, videotaped by ATV in the 1976 season, is instructive. The television version of the comedy conveys most elements of the stage performance faithfully, but brings cameras into the actors' space to allow closer proximity with the action and includes points of view from onstage positions and business directed towards the camera that would not have been possible in the theatre. Audience members are shown arriving and leaving (in the rain), and cutaways to the responses of an audience are included along with the off-screen laughter and applause. One purpose of the broadcast seems to be advertising: to show the viewing public that a visit to the RSC would (or could) be fun. Nevertheless, the result is artificial, and less convincing than the techniques commonly used to establish audience presence in television comedy.

For the tragedies it was not important or perhaps desirable to include or simulate the responses of a live audience. The intensity, immediacy and at times disturbing proximity of the performances in The Other Place corresponded closely to the effect of privately viewed television drama. The videos of *Macbeth* and *Othello* use this potential differently, responding to the differences between the productions and, indeed, the plays. The video version of *Macbeth*, directed for television by Philip Casson, creates an even deeper darkness around the action than was possible in the theatre, and although close-ups and speeches direct to camera intensify one aspect of the production, the metatheatrical effect conveyed by the theatre's visible props table and thunder sheet and the close proximity (and visibility) of the audience is absent. The available documentation for *Macbeth* also includes a remarkable record compiled by Sue Dommett, a graduate student at the University of Birmingham's Shakespeare Institute. Based on twenty-one viewings of the production in Stratford and London as well as the available archive material, this annotated script records textual changes (including those of the 1974 and 1975 productions), staging effects, movement and – in many cases – gesture and emphasis.[9] The extensive archival material and, above all, the existence of the television versions have facilitated detailed retrospective commentaries, notably those on *Macbeth* by Bernice W. Kliman and *Othello* by Lois Potter and Virginia Mason Vaughan.[10]

Macbeth, 1976–8: Intimacy, ritual and the powers of darkness

Like his previous stagings, Nunn's 1976 production began by establishing the opposing powers of light in the white-clad

Duncan's saint-like demeanour, and of darkness in the weird sisters' 'black mass'. The words 'ritual' and 'rite' recur in reviews. In *The Times* Ned Chaillet described 'a battle of the sacred against the profane' in which 'the two strands of primal ritual and modernity' were 'combined in Macbeth's collapse', and Michael Billington in the *Guardian* suggested that Nunn had now 'hit the right balance between verbal clarity and depraved religiosity'.[11] When the audience entered they saw a bare stage with a black ring defining an empty circle in the centre and black-painted orange boxes around its perimeter. Kliman suggests that the circle was 'suitable for a communal rite, for purging Scotland of the evil that infects it, evil in the person of Macbeth and, to a lesser extent in this production, Lady Macbeth'.[12] The actors entered and sat on the boxes, facing centre. Organ music accompanied the lowering of the house lights, and – as the other characters watched – the witches moved into the centre of the circle and spread a cloth on the floor to begin their rites. Throughout the play the tone of their softly spoken exchanges was confidential, as though this was a regular occasion, effectively a planning meeting. They were distinct personalities with a business-like relationship. Later, at the opening of 1.3, the oldest, who seemed to be in authority (Marie Kean), asked the second, younger sister (Judith Harte) where she had been as if reproving a latecomer. The reply, 'Killing swine', was spoken as if to say 'Doing something useful, what else?' The youngest (Susan Dury), with her staring eyes and spasmodic movements, was the medium through whom information would be conveyed from the spirits they served. In the opening sequence their incantation, 'Fair is foul, and foul is fair', was juxtaposed with the murmured prayers of Duncan, kneeling within the circle on the audience's right-hand side, deep in self-accusing prayer and tapping at his breast with repeated murmurs of 'mea culpa'.

The opening shots of the video convey the staging, with an initial top-shot looking down onto the circle, a view as if from the audience looking across it, and then a travelling shot moving slowly from one face to another. In televisual or filmic terms this produces the kind of discomfort associated (for example) with the use of penetratingly intimate close-ups in the films of Ingmar Bergmann. There was nothing picturesque or 'historical' about the characters' appearance, except for Duncan (Griffith Jones) with his white beard and flowing hair. Costumes were eclectic and vaguely modern, with the exception of the cope and crown that represented kingship and the breastplate Macbeth donned in the final act. Lady Macduff and Lady Macbeth wore similar turbans and floor-length dresses, the former white, the latter black and more tailored. In the video, the muted colour palette and the darkness that always seems ready to encroach upon the actors go some way towards compensating for the absence of a crucial element of the audience's experience at The Other Place, where they were effectively a congregation as well as onlookers for whatever took place only a few feet in front of them. The presence of the cast members seated on the boxes suggested that some kind of re-enactment was taking place within the circle, a rite more directly shared than had been possible in either of the previous stagings. Although the RSC had left behind the experiments of the 1963–4 'Theatre of Cruelty' season, this was an experience close to the kind of physical engagement and the psycho-physical impact sought by Artaud and his followers. Intense concentration, tightly focused on the part of actors and audience, confined in a room for the duration of an uninterrupted performance, generated a tension so completely shared that the off-stage noises in the scene of Duncan's murder were as alarming to the spectators as to the characters within the action. Ominous storm effects came from the visible thunder sheet, and at some points 'sound effects', such as the birdsong heard when Duncan arrived in Dunsinane, were provided by watching actors. In his *Observer* review Robert Cushman mentions the uncanny effect of 'the scratching of the murderers at Lady Macduff's door' in 4.2.[13] (In the video, this is replaced with an indistinct off-screen thud.)

'There was a kind of even-handed stillness', Nunn recalled. The audience believed that they were 'in some way party' to the murder 'because they could hear the breathing of the other people asleep in the household in the middle of the night'. Having disposed of the 'detritus' of realism that had 'kind of barnacled the play over most of the century', he was able pursue 'an examination of the mental state of two people who were approaching an acknowledged act of evil, and then an investigation of the consequences of that act of evil upon their mental state, and upon their marriage'.[14] J.W Lambert, hailing this as 'the most fulfilling production of this dark and difficult work' he had ever seen, identified the creation of feeling for the Macbeths as one of its most remarkable achievements: 'The first half of the piece ... has the scheming couple, looking towards the world they see as their oyster, and then, never damaging our empathy with this dreadful pair, shows us that outside world, no oyster but a giant octopus, closing in on them.'[15] An overwhelming sense of apprehension permeated every action long before Lady Macbeth's 'Nought's had, all's spent / Where our desire is got without content' (3.2.5–6). This was a world in which, from Duncan's arrival at Dunsinane onwards, 'content' was to be glimpsed only fleetingly.

The emotional relationships and psychological states of the principal characters had an extraordinary impact, an urgency conveyed by what Richard David identified as a frequent 'jaggedness of movement and gesture, like a tremor that, though violent as measured on the seismograph, is yet strictly confined within the narrowest limits of time and space'.[16] Within the circle, the actors' intense 'energy, intelligence and concentration' were such that, as Robert Cushman suggested, 'an adequate critique would need as many lines as the play'. Dommett counted cuts of 235 complete lines and 120 part lines, approximately 10 per cent of the text. The performance lasted 135 minutes, without an interval.[17] All the Hecate material was omitted, but the description of the English king (4.3.147–59) was included, given especial relevance by the religious emphasis in the treatment of Duncan and the forces of evil. The Siwards, father and son, did not appear, and the scenes leading up to the catastrophe were trimmed to make them more concise. Apart from the murder of Macduff's family and the 'England' scene (4.3), the focus was relentlessly on the relationship between the Macbeths. The dual emphasis on naturalistic acting and symbolism, familiar in Nunn's previous productions of this and other plays, seemed in retrospect to have marshalled him the way he was going towards this text. In this respect, the naturalism with which the witches were characterized as they dealt with the symbolic props of their rites was especially significant.

The temperamental difference between Macbeth and Banquo was established in their first encounter with the witches: Banquo urbane and calm, Macbeth already registering a more nervous, eager state of mind as he scrutinized the sisters, holding his dagger towards each of them in turn. He turned away as Banquo questioned them, and his subsequent reaction (1.3.129–44) to the news of his elevation to the title of Thane of Cawdor, fulfilling the first of the witches' predictions, anticipated – as the text suggests – the vocal and physical embodiment of the shaking of his 'single state of man' as he worked his way through the maze that led from 'present fears' and 'horrible imaginings' to the realization that the thought in which 'murder yet is but fantastical' might now take on a real form. In *Shakespeare Quarterly*, Gareth Lloyd Evans noted that in the aside reacting to the nomination of Malcolm as Prince of Cumberland (1.4.48–53) 'his face took on an extraordinary blending of eye-flashing greed and youthful anticipation'.[18] In this and the subsequent soliloquies, patient reasoning was gradually overwhelmed by strong emotion and the 'vaulting ambition' he seemed reluctant to admit but could not help feeling. Benedict Nightingale found him 'a still, secretive Macbeth, watching himself helplessly as his darker longings overwhelm him'.[19] In McKellen's vocal and physical performance an air of self-possession with occasional flashes of humour was repeatedly undermined by each new and vividly embodied idea. The actor's virtuoso exploration of every new thought was reflected in vocal delivery that at times could be over-elaborate. It now seemed appropriate, for, as Cushman observed, this Macbeth could 'retreat within himself in a second; he [was], as they all say, "rapt," a few feet away from us and impenetrable'. The striking contrast between this febrile, anxiety-ridden usurper and Judi Dench's calm, decisive Lady Macbeth made her eventual psychological collapse all the more shocking. The play became the story of the couple's moral and psychological disintegration. McKellen remembered suggesting that, because they were rehearsing soon after the Watergate revelations precipitated the fall of the US President Richard M. Nixon: 'of course they're the Nixons, aren't they?' Nunn replied that at the beginning of the play they were the Kennedys, 'the golden couple everybody wants to be with, whose house everybody wants to visit, including the King'.[20]

Dench's first entrance moved the tragedy into a new intensity. Her face and hands were thrown into relief by her black dress and the tightly drawn turban hiding her hair. (Apart from silver studs as earrings, there was no other adornment until the brief coronation procession that preceded the play's third act, when she assumed a gold coronet and a thin necklace.) Engrossed in the letter, she quoted the phrase 'Hail, King, that shalt be' from memory, questioningly, and then scrutinized the letter as if to confirm the significance of words she had already studied carefully, repeating some of them in a murmur and finally clutching the paper to her as she repeated the memorized final sentences. She sat to contemplate Macbeth's being 'too full o'th' milk of human kindness', then spoke 'Thou wouldst be great' as though he were already before her, until she rose with 'Hie thee hither', which was effectively the first of her invocations. Seyton entered to report Duncan's imminent arrival, and once he had left, the nature of the opportunity seemed to strike her: 'The raven, himself is hoarse' (1.5.38). After a few moments' pause she turned slowly and lowered herself to the floor, holding her hand above it with 'Come you spirits'. A momentary pause before the word 'cruelty' was followed by an involuntary cry of fear and she turned to face the darkness behind her before continuing. The horror of each successive idea seemed to strike her in a gradual crescendo of whispered entreaty, so that the offer of her woman's milk and the thought of the 'murdering ministers' registered with increasingly awestruck urgency until with 'Hold, hold!' she stood with outstretched arms in unwitting readiness to embrace 'Great Glamis' as he entered, emerging from the darkness behind her as though himself summoned by her conjuration. Their exchanges were erotically charged as they embraced tightly, hands and mouths caressing each other and breathing with the intensity of physical passion. Reviewing the 1997 transfer of the production to the Warehouse in London, Irving Wardle described this as revealing 'the inner life of the production ... a long embrace in which the first hints of the plot are smothered in endearments and hypnotic reassurance'.[21]

The moment-by-moment workings of their acts of imagination were marked in physical and vocal emphasis throughout. In 1.7 Macbeth's 'If it were done, when 'tis done' (1–28) began with a degree of intellectual detachment, but when the significance of the killing of Duncan became more vivid – 'He's here in double trust' – his voice caught momentarily on the word 'subject'. The virtues of Duncan, pleading 'like angels, trumpet-tongued' against the 'deep damnation of his taking off' led to the extraordinary image of 'Pity, like a naked, new born babe' as Macbeth moved from a degree of detachment into the kind of 'horrible imagining' that would recur from now on. Reflection that his only motive was 'vaulting ambition' seemed to suggest he might decide not to commit the crime, but then his train of thought was interrupted by Lady Macbeth's arrival.

As the planning and execution of the plot progressed during this sequence, the couple's physical intimacy was qualified by the urgency with which Lady Macbeth asserted the practicalities of the crime in the face of her husband's spiritual and emotional agonies. His explanation that he had 'won golden opinions of all sorts of people' – the last phrase spoken with a wry smile – left her unmoved and coldly indignant. As he went to embrace her, she pulled away, with 'From this time / Such I account thy love' (1.7.38–9). Movement towards and away from physical endearment marked stages in their relationship from now on. When he emerged, daggers in hand, from the exit leading to Duncan's chamber, she was close to him, urging resistance to the thoughts of being unable to say 'Amen' with the determined admonishment that 'these deeds must not be thought / After these ways' (2.2.34–5). At his description of the voice that seemed to call 'Macbeth shall sleep no more' (44), she pulled back from him, covering her ears as if refusing to listen, and resisted his talk of an imagined or ghostly 'voice' by making 'Who was it that thus cried?' a practical enquiry. Advising him to wash the blood from his hands – 'Go, get some water' – with comforting solicitude, she pulled his coat around his shoulders, but in doing so she noticed that he still had the daggers, which clanked together in his bloody hands. She shifted back into indignation that he had been distracted from the necessities of the business in hand. She was dismayed when, after the discovery of Duncan's body, Macbeth, his hands once again bloody, admitted killing the king's grooms.

The play's third act began with a coronation ceremony, not included in the video, after which Macbeth was isolated in the centre 'in a pool of bright light' clad in the golden cope and wearing the crown.[22] He and Lady Macbeth, now in a coronet and necklace, then processed round the perimeter of the circle. Banquo stood observing from outside the circle, close to the audience, and his reflection, 'Thou hast it now' (3.1.1–10), was shared as if in reaction to the spectacle. For a moment he seemed to savour the possibility of his own issue being kings, but his face hardened with 'But, hush; no more' (10). Macbeth and Lady Macbeth re-entered together, both smiling genially, and Macbeth enquired about the plans of their 'chief guest'. Macbeth then came up to him to tell him the news about 'our bloody cousins'. As he was about to leave the stage, Banquo suspected the likely implications of Macbeth's asking 'Goes Fleance with you?' (35) he turned, came back and knelt to kiss Macbeth's hand fervently, bowing to Lady Macbeth as he left. She acknowledged this more qualified homage with a curt nod of the head. When Macbeth sent away Ross and the others with 'Let every man be master of his time / Till seven at night' (40–1) she smiled as she moved confidently towards him, as if expecting that he wished to confer privately with her, but he dismissed her with a curt 'Well then, God be with you' (44, for 'While then') and turned away, killing her smile. As she exited she turned sharply on hearing Macbeth's sudden call of 'Sirrah!' and then encountered Seyton, who had entered in response to it and paused for a moment looking her full in the face. This was the first sign of exclusion from her husband's plans and the rise of Seyton as his confidant: she had been banished from the circle that represented power and he had been invited into it.

At the beginning of 3.2 it was Seyton who told her with almost insolent matter-of-factness that Banquo has gone from the court, and her soliloquy – 'Nought's had, all's spent' (5–8) – was followed by Macbeth's rejection of her as she greeted him with 'How now, my lord' and approached him, smiling and clearly expecting an embrace. Once again the smile faded rapidly from her lips at his cold response, and she moved away. She turned back towards him, asking 'Why do you keep alone?' (8) in a pleading, bereft tone. As Macbeth's disturbance of mind became more and more evident, her reaction was one of dismay and sympathy, culminating, as he continued to dwell on the necessity to 'lave our honours in those flattering streams', with 'You must leave this' (36). This was a cry of anguish, hand to brow, rather than a stern rebuke. She was crying as he turned towards her with 'O full of scorpions is my mind – dear wife', the last words spoken as an endearment and an implicit appeal. They embraced at last, and the plan to deal with Banquo and Fleance was broached as he nuzzled her face and ear, pulling back and touching her face with his fingers on 'be innocent of the knowledge, dearest chuck', and passing his palm across her eyes with 'Scarf up the tender eye of pitiful Day' (48). (Dommett notes that he looked at his hand as though 'looking for blood'.)[23]

These moments of intimacy recalled the others that coincided with the planning of a crime. The banquet (3.4) ended with another of the same kind, by which time their relationship had advanced a stage further and she had discovered she was unable to control Macbeth's deranged state of mind or excuse it convincingly. The scene would also confirm her suspicions of the increasing ascendancy of Seyton.

At the beginning of the scene, the boxes were drawn into the circle and placed close together to form an intimate group. Seyton handed a silver chalice to Macbeth, who took it round from guest to guest. Seyton had been the 'third' murderer and it was he who reported Banquo's death, and as the two talked Lady Macbeth watched from the seat where Macbeth had placed her on the other side of the circle. The ghost did not appear to the audience or the thanes: from his first sight of it, evidently seated next to Ross, Macbeth's reactions were extreme. The invisible spectre seemed to be moving around the room, and he lurched towards it, his voice agonized and his features contorted, so that Lady Macbeth's 'Why do you make such faces?' (66) was entirely appropriate. When she sat on the 'stool' where the ghost had appeared, he launched into an even more frenzied paroxysm –'Pry'thee, see there! / Behold! Look! Lo! How say you?' (65–6). Regaining his composure briefly, he raised the chalice in a toast to 'our dear friend Banquo, whom we miss' (88): at this point, Lady Macbeth clearly realized what Seyton had reported. After a few moments' silence, looking fixedly in front of her, she started a slow handclap to initiate a new drinking ritual. The guests responded, clapping and shouting rhythmically to encourage Macbeth to drain the loving cup, but as he did so he saw the ghost again. From now on anxiety about what might be revealed by his 'admir'd disorder' added to her dismay. She held him back as he yelled 'Avaunt! and quit my sight!' almost screaming herself as she tried to assure the peers that this was merely 'a thing of custom' (95), but with 'Hence, horrible shadow!' he broke from her and lunged at the apparition with his dagger. As the fit subsided he gasped between each phrase of 'Why – so – being gone – I am a man again', then commanded the ghost 'Pray you, sit still', as she looked on, open-mouthed. When Macbeth wondered that the company could 'behold such sights' and 'keep the natural ruby in [their] cheeks', Lady Macbeth placed her hand over her husband's mouth with 'I pray you speak not' to silence him, rather than in answer to Ross's 'What sights, my lord?' (114–15). Ross kissed Macbeth's hand to take his leave, but when Lennox tried to do the same she shrieked 'Stand not upon the order of your going / But go at once', and after managing to utter 'A kind good night to all!' her head bent back in a silent cry of anguish before she subsided into Macbeth's lap. He grew more composed and apparently detached as he considered what must be done with Macduff. The scene now ended with another of the couple's embraces, this time even more agonized than the last. She collapsed to the floor but he raised her, supporting her head as he assured her 'We are yet but young – in deed' and helped her from the stage.

At the beginning of 4.1, the weird sisters arranged themselves in the centre of the stage around a small 'cauldron' and placed four candlesticks around it, as if in a parody of an altar. As they added the ingredients of their brew they repeated 'Double double toil and trouble' to a tune resembling the *Dies irae*. In a homely touch, the 'baboon's blood' was poured into the mixture from a small saucepan. The young witch suddenly perceived that 'something wicked this way comes', and Macbeth entered upstage. In response to his demands for information they seized Macbeth, pulled him to the floor and stripped him to the waist, marking him with black crosses on face, chest and back and making him drink the brew from what seemed to be a communion cup. He was shown puppets representing the first three apparitions, their lines voiced by the sisters in turn. When he persisted in wanting to know more, they blindfolded him, holding candles before his face. With cries of agony as they passed the candles close to his face, he 'saw' the show of eight kings and Banquo. The witches withdrew, vanishing by leaving the circle and stepping into the darkness beyond it. When Seyton and Lennox entered to make their report that Macduff had fled to England, they found him still half-naked and clutching the talismanic figures. He even addressed 'The castle of Macduff I will surprise' (149) to one of the dolls, as though they were already taking place of the thanes who would desert him.

In the final movement of the play, after the murder of the white-clad Lady Macduff and her son – her throat was slit by the now ubiquitously evil Seyton – the scene in England (4.3) began with lucid and passionate urgency in the perplexing testing of Macduff (Bob Peck) by Malcolm (Roger Rees). In one of the production's less convincing touches of symbolism, the whiteness of Malcolm's roll-neck cable-knit pullover (some reviewers thought that together with his wellington boots it made him look like a trawlerman) seemed to be intended as a sign that he was on the side of good, but the eloquence of his recital of his supposed sins was not easily discounted. Was the legitimacy of his claim to the throne really the guarantee of his being the morally appropriate person for it? Malcolm was able to speak with authority, but in the final scenes he was not involved in any fighting: that would be the task of Macduff.

Throughout the play, McKellen's Macbeth had seemed fascinated by his hands and what they could or might do: Dommett notes that with 'This supernatural soliciting / Cannot be ill; cannot be good' (1.3.132–3) he '[held] his ungloved hand out, palm upwards, as if asking the audience to adjudicate the matter', and that in the next scene on 'the eye wink at the hand' (1.4.52) he looked 'with detachment at the hand that will murder Duncan', immediately connecting it with the 'black and deep desires' that must be hid.[24] In their passionate and increasingly fraught embraces, the video's close-ups show that Macbeth's hands are always active and prominent – around Lady Macbeth's face, shielding her eyes, stroking and supporting her. Billington wrote that he 'accomplishe[d] the murder in a state of headlong hypnosis but holding his incarnadined hands thereafter, he gaze[d] at them like a child walking from a bad dream'. As well as an inevitable emphasis on bloody hands in the 'dagger' speech in 2.1 and in the scene of the murders in 2.2 there is the kissing of the king's hands, which recurs as an act of fealty, and Macbeth's hands desperately clutch the talismans given him by the witches. Cushman observes that with 'What hands are here? Ha! They pluck out mine eyes' (2.2.60) McKellen 'look[ed] as if he might well blind himself with his jabbing fingers'. The hands were 'the key' to his performance: 'at first they are alert and sensitive; when he meets the witches they tense and stiffen, bunched fists inside black military gloves. At the end they are lifeless; they have gone, with his conscience and his sensibilities into decay, and he knows it.' Lady Macbeth's obsessive 'washing' of her hands in the sleepwalking scene (5.1) was thus both an arresting culmination of the play's visual and verbal imagery, as well as the logical consequence of her commitment to evil and suppression of any humane sympathy. It would be difficult to better Kliman's description of 'the number of changes Dench [could] ring on the predominant emotion of soul-wrenching despair':

> Without even the simple jewellery that marked her investiture as queen, she remembers everything horrible, nothing hopeful. Eyes glistening with tears, she tries to obliterate a stain on her hand, biting and mouthing it, then stares searchingly at the hand she holds to the candle, the better to see the irremovable stains. Her voice rises to an incredulous shriek as she cries, 'Here's the smell of the blood still.'[25]

In his *Shakespeare Quarterly* review, Gareth Lloyd Evans interpreted the subtext as 'a long regret that seemed to encompass not only the memory of the deeds to which she had been accessory, but also a love which had disappeared'.[26]

In the final scenes Macbeth had piled up the crates at the centre of the circle, with the cope of kingship to one side on a stand, a reminder of the illusory glory for which he had sacrificed his soul. He held the stage without interruption from 5.3 onwards, the abbreviated scenes of preparation by his enemies being spoken from outside the circle. J.W. Lambert found 'a terrible grandeur' in the moment when he sat 'among the ruins of his life' while 'the voices of his destroyers, firm and practical, sound[ed] from their shadows in the outer darkness'. His reaction to Seyton's report of the queen's death was blank and frighteningly detached: Cushman noted that in 'tomorrow, and tomorrow, and tomorrow' (5.5.18) the words were 'separated by a silent chasm, beyond which wait sickening vistas of despair'.

There was no exultation after the death of Macbeth and the confirmation of Malcolm as king. Macduff stared at his bloody hands as though they reminded him of a similar action on Macbeth's part after the murder of Duncan – and Malcolm did not declare that his 'thanes and kinsmen' would be earls. Dommett records an element of the final moments not replicated in the video:

> Malcolm turns and exits [at the back] ... Angus slowly follows him. Lennox moves the cope stand out of the circle. He exits ... Ross and Macduff look at each other. Ross takes the crown and puts it on the stage right table. Macduff stands slowly staring at the blood. He goes to the table and puts the daggers down. Ross and Macduff leave together.[27]

The props were thus returned to their place at the edge of the circle, as though marking their readiness for a repetition of the tragedy. (Like the onstage thunder sheet, in the video version the props table is not visible.) The daggers, now bloody, with which Macbeth had been killed offstage – no head was produced – now had their place alongside the crown. In this stripped-down version, the few hand-properties had the same kind of emblematic significance as those in Barton's 1973 *Richard II*. The others were the chalice that served as loving cup at the banquet, the paraphernalia of the witches' rites, and the dolls Macbeth had been given by the witches on his second encounter in 4.1. He had clung to these until in his final despair he hacked at one of them with his sword: now they lay on the floor where he had dropped them. The material objects associated with the tragedy, and endowed during it with spiritual significance, were thus left ready for the next time they would be needed. The cope and crown had been worn twice: when Duncan had been invested with them at 1.4.35 ('Sons, kinsmen, thanes') as he nominated Malcolm as his successor, and again in Macbeth's coronation.

The television version's loss of a sense of the theatrical as well as symbolic status of these props is unfortunate, as is the omission of any sense of characters watching the action from the perimeter of the circle: consequently we do not see the witches remaining on stage during 1.6 and 1.7 to witness the initial stages of the seduction of Macbeth and Lady Macbeth. Moreover, the production's two most remarkable metatheatrical effects are present but are not fully realized. In 2.3, when Ian McDiarmid, whose Ross was a precisely spoken and dapper civil servant, entered as the Porter he clicked his fingers and the lights suddenly illuminated the audience as well as the stage. He was bare-chested, his hair was tousled under his soft cap, and he thrust his hands deep into his pockets, as if threatening to lower his trousers below the level of decency. In a Scottish accent – itself a rarity in the production and here broadly demotic – he picked out members of the audience as examples for his harangue. Dommett describes business not present in the video: deciding to 'devil-porter it no longer' he went to the stage-right table, 'pick[ed] up a board with a length of chain attached to it' and 'rattle[d] them noisily'. After throwing the board so that it clashed against the double doors at the right he clicked his fingers, returning the lights to the previous dark state.[28] The televisual equivalents for this are the manner in which the Porter, brightly lit, speaks direct to camera, and the actor's undisguised doubling of the roles, but it remains an element of the staging that depended on the presence of the theatre audience.

The other notable moment in which illusion was broken – or rather, intensified – in the theatre by a striking effect was Macbeth's action in 5.5 when on 'I 'gin to be aweary of the sun' he shielded his eyes from the beam of a lamp hanging above him and sent it swinging, its light flashing across his face as yelled his defiance with 'Blow, wind! Come, wrack! / At least we'll die with harness on our back' (50–1). In the video the effect is still present, but the lamp that he has reached up to is not visible, so that it appears to be an unseen feature of the room he is in rather than part of the theatre's equipment. Dommett's account and the promptbook show it as part of a carefully plotted series of actions, which include Macbeth himself pushing four boxes under the hanging light at the centre, piling up the boxes and placing a fifth on top: 'He climbs on the boxes, grasping the hanging light with both hands. He shines it on the gallery and then the doll's face held next to his own' and 'squints into the light' with 'I 'gin to be aweary of the sun' (5.5.48), and then after 'And wish the estate o'th' world were now undone' he 'drops the doll pushing the light with both hands. It swings backwards and forwards across the circle just clearing his head', and on 'Ring the alarum bell' he 'flings his arms wide'.[29] The spectacle of Macbeth piling up the boxes became a desperate piece of make-believe, the interplay with the doll was a sardonic reminder that this was a representative of 'the Fiend / That lies like truth' (5.5.42–3), and the shining of the light towards the gallery made his final lines a defiance of the outside world, represented by the spectators as much as by his opponents outside the circle.

The 1976 *Macbeth* was a successful amalgamation of detailed naturalistic acting with stylized and expressionistic staging and metatheatrical effects. The casting, especially of Dench and McKellen, gave Nunn a company who could mine the text in the way he had always valued. The exploration of the possibilities of engagement with an audience in an uncomfortably confined space fulfilled in one way the ambition for intimacy that had informed much of his main-stage work. Simpler and more forceful expression was found for ideas that on the larger stages had been represented more elaborately. Macbeth was now beleaguered in what Chaillet described as the 'cold world in the empty circle', and his stronghold had been scaled down to the heap of boxes that seemed to show him as the temporary caretaker of an attic rather than the possessor of a castle whose walls would 'laugh to scorn' any siege. Dennis Kennedy suggests that, like Goodbody's *King Lear* and *Hamlet*, this was an interpretation 'deeply rooted in family matters', but there is an important difference: here the family was embedded in a world of symbolism, in which the psychodrama of the central couple, the battle for their souls, was played out with minimal domestic detail, and nothing handled by the actors was devoid of symbolic significance.[30] This 'Magnificent *Macbeth*' (Lambert's *Sunday Times* headline) and 'Triumphant Tragedy' (Cushman's in the *Observer*) was Nunn's most effective venture into the kind of theatre represented by Barton's treatment of *Richard II*, but with a greater intensity of psychological exploration. At The Other Place and later at the Warehouse it had qualities subsequently associated with immersive theatre.

Othello, 1989: Selective naturalism and the audience as *voyeurs*

The intimacy of The Other Place was used to different effect in August 1989 when Nunn returned to Stratford to direct *Othello* in the final production staged at the theatre, which had closed officially in January. This was sometimes referred to informally as a 'leaving gift' for the director, and its cast did not appear in any of the season's plays at the other Stratford theatres. It played for thirty-four performances at Stratford, followed by forty-six in London at the Young Vic, and was subsequently videotaped for television in a version that corresponded even more fully than that of *Macbeth* to the theatre performances.[31] This was another production with a very full text, running for four hours including a ten-minute interval. Among the few cuts were Iago's enigmatic reference to Cassio as 'a fellow almost damned in a fair wife' (1.1.20) and the indication that Iago has 'looked upon the world for four times seven years' (1.3.312–13). Lines from the end of Cassio's exchange with the 'clown' at the beginning of 3.1 were used for the cashiered lieutenant's enquiry to a soldier as to whether Emilia was 'stirring' yet. The setting was an indeterminate period in the late nineteenth century, with military costumes that evoked the American Civil War, although this identification was perhaps more vivid for American than for British audiences: in any case its relevance to the racial dimension of the play was debatable. The set by Bob Crowley left the acting space free, with doors in a wall under the upstage balcony, which was fitted with slatted shutters to form an 'above' area used by Brabantio in the first scene. After the move to Cyprus, the removal of carpeting laid for the council scene revealed a sand-strewn expanse of floor that served for both interior and exterior locations during the rest of the play. Furniture was placed as the action required – including camp beds and a washstand for the barrack-room in 2.3, and a simple iron bedstead, a dressing table, open trunks and a *prie-dieu* for the bedroom.

The naturalism of Ibsen and Chekhov was a point of reference in some of the commentary on *Othello*, but there was a notable contrast between the ways the two playwrights had figured in Nunn's career since the 1970s. For *Hedda Gabler*, produced on tour and at the Aldwych in 1975 with Glenda Jackson in the title role, John Napier had provided a 'wondrously extravagant set' that, with its 'figured-glass French windows, oriental rugs, palm fronds and all' suggested to one reviewer 'the reception lounge of some magnificent *fin-de-siècle* hotel near Cannes', and an indication that the Tesmans were living beyond their means.[32] Nunn's directorial engagement with Chekhov three years later could not have been more different. This was his contribution to a new venture, a tour of *Three Sisters* and *Twelfth Night* to small-scale, non-theatrical venues under the overall direction of Ian McKellen, whose experience with the Actors' Company made him an appropriate leader of a small but high-powered ensemble. Constrained – or rather, liberated – by the logistical requirements of the tour, *Three Sisters* had been conceived as a minimalist production, with few properties and the simplest possible set by Napier. It used 'no more than the necessary furniture against an eloquent backdrop, the ikons of Holy Russia visible, but fading', and the review in the *Glasgow Herald* noted that the action was 'unimpeded, the scenes merg[ing] into one another like the lapse of time itself'. A 'beautiful little extra' was the appearance before the last act of 'an ordinary scene-shifter, who walk[ed] about the open stage scattering autumn leaves'.[33] Nunn recalled that after a 'period of panic' occasioned by the text's demands for 'rooms, doors and elements of furniture' he 'started to think of *Three Sisters* as a poetic play, as a play of heightened language and poetic ideas. In a sense, I started to think of it in Shakespearean terms', because 'the seventeenth-century bare stage and back wall provided actors with the capability of entering and leaving an uncluttered environment, the specificity and detail of which could be created through language'.[34] There was no dining table for the lunch party in Act 2, with the actors 'making' a table 'using only chairs, forks and napkins', and in one of the production's most haunting moments the noise made by the humming top presented to Irina was provided by the actors:

> In rehearsal, I developed the possibility by asking each character to make their wish – in the spirit of the question 'What would your birthday wish be?' Then I asked each of them to concentrate on that wish, and to transform it into a single and sustained sound.

When the sounds were put together the result was an 'unplaceable, indefinable haunting sound', as though 'the characters were hearing their inner thoughts about their future – their imaginations captured at a moment in time'.[35] This was part of an overall strategy in which 'textual and improvisational disciplines more or less kept pace with each other' during 'more than two weeks' in which meticulous analysis of the text was followed in the evenings by 'situational and individual improvisation work'.[36]

In *Othello* the moments of stillness and contrasting emotional intensity in the rhythms of the play and the exploration of behavioural alongside textual detail – long a feature of Nunn's work – were suggestive of Chekhov. Ibsen was evoked in the accumulation of physical detail, the endowment of domestic objects with significance, and the fraught sexual relationships of the central characters. In his *Observer* review Michael Ratcliffe added to the list of playwrights evoked, identifying Ian McKellen's Iago as a 'hellhound' from Strindberg, presumably referring to Edgar, the captain of an artillery battery in a desperately destructive relationship with his wife in *The Dance of Death* (1905).[37]

In *Macbeth* the audience had been witnesses to a rite, and effectively made to assume involvement of the kind associated with a religious congregation. Now they were situated as voyeurs on the edge of an uncomfortably intimate domestic drama. 'If there has been a more powerful, more eloquent, more emotionally shattering production of this great play, then I must have missed it', wrote Jack Tinker in the *Daily Mail*. With its 'deeply claustrophobic ... barrack-room and bedchamber atmosphere' the production 'discover[ed] a momentous domestic intimacy in the work which at times turn[ed] us into embarrassed eavesdroppers'.[38] The programme essay by Norman Sanders (editor of the 1984 New Cambridge edition of the play) reflected the production's aims, citing the shift towards indoor theatres in the 1600s as a factor in 'this most claustrophobic of the tragedies', since 'every aspect of the play seems designed to produce intense concentration'.[39] In *Shakespeare Survey* Stanley Wells commented on the 'rare intimacy of communication and directness of emotional impact' and Robert Smallwood observed in *Shakespeare Quarterly* that the tiny theatre was 'an excellent space in which to explore the intensity of the private family relationships'.[40] For John Peter, the 'family tragedy of blind faith and short-sighted judgment' was 'all the more shocking as the characters are almost within touching distance'.[41]

It was unsurprising, then, that connections would be made between 'intimacy' in the sense of both the theatrical experience and the treatment of sexual and emotional intimacy in the play. Virginia Mason Vaughan takes this further, suggesting that in this *Othello* 'the search for meaning in human relationships, the struggle to find trust and intimacy in a world of appearances, the fragility of human bonds' is an emphasis 'symptomatic of the 1990s, when each day's newspaper features the story of another battered woman murdered by her husband or boyfriend, and talk-show hosts probe people's most intimate secrets on nationwide television'.[42] Even if there was no specific intention to refer to this, it was inevitably an important element of the production's impact on audiences, sharing the focus with issues of race and class. Because Bianca was played by a black actress, Marsha Hunt, her treatment by Cassio and his amusement at the notion he might marry her had racist overtones that were consequently present in Emilia's virtuous disdain for her ('Fie upon thee, strumpet!') when the wounded Cassio is discovered in the penultimate scene (5.1.121). Hunt commented that there was 'a sense of three women in the play rather than two', and that in all three relationships 'the power of jealousy is destructive and in all of them, the men are eating the women up and spitting them out. It's very modern. It's feminist.'[43]

The class element was particularly striking in Ian McKellen's Iago, and the ensign's resentment at his failure to achieve promotion to lieutenant. As he and Othello settled down to deal with the day's paperwork in 3.3, he seemed the model of efficiency (Figure 6). He had what Michael Coveney in the *Financial Times* described as a 'suburban rapacity for promotion' that was 'almost a comic symptom'.[44] He was a born non-commissioned officer, literally buttoned up in his immaculately pressed uniform tunic, doing up its high collar and straightening his cap as he moved on to the next stage of his strategies. In the play's first scenes Roderigo (Michael Grandage) in his lightweight suit and panama was more a man-about-town than a soldier, and Cassio (Sean Baker) appeared in 3.1 after his demotion in similar civilian attire: he seemed like a debonair but tentative wooer when he came to

FIGURE 6 Othello *(The Other Place, 1989), 3.3:* Othello *(Willard White) and* Iago *(Ian McKellen) (Joe Cocks Studio Collection © Shakespeare Birthplace Trust).*

ask Desdemona's intercession and presented her with a box of sweets. His courtliness and suavity and the ease of his intimacy with Desdemona (Imogen Stubbs) marked him out from the other soldiers on his arrival in Cyprus, as did his tactless insistence in the drinking scene that 'the lieutenant is to be saved before the ancient' (2.3.105–6).

Class distinctions – the status of the 'senators' – had been evoked in the play's second scene. The council meeting was that of war cabinet, seated round a table covered with green baize under a hanging light and furnished with brandy and cigars. (At the end of the scene as he described Othello as being of 'a free and open nature / That thinks men honest that but seem to be so' [298–9], Iago pocketed a handful of these, subsequently handing them round to his fellow soldiers on arrival in Cyprus.) In this club-like setting Willard White's Othello, described by Wells as 'an imposing figure of great natural nobility with a darkly resonant speaking voice of unforced power and authority', moved with confident ease and dignity while Iago stood dutifully to attention to one side.[45] Desdemona entered tentatively, moving forward to respond to Brabantio's 'Come hither, gentle mistress' (1.2.179). After replying to his demand that she declare to whom she owed allegiance she retreated to a seat in the background until she made her case for accompanying her husband to Cyprus, and before her father's exit she moved round the table towards him in an attempt to secure a sign of affection. Adam Mars-Jones in the *Independent* noted that Clive Swift 'show[ed] plainly that Act One of Othello's tragedy is Act Five of Brabantio's'.[46] Nunn's direction of the scene thus encompassed Desdemona's spirited invasion of a world normally closed to her, the family drama of her being disowned by her father, and the contrast between Othello's easy acceptance as a member of the meeting and Iago's respectfully formal demeanour.

In Cyprus the action clearly took place in a garrison where the time of day was marked by off-stage sounds of bugle calls, and even of a hymn played on a harmonium at the beginning of 3.3. (The exchange between Desdemona and Othello at 3.3.56–61 implies that the scene takes place on a Sunday.) Cicadas were heard in the background and the distant voice of a muezzin suggested to Anne Barton that this was 'a place ... with larger racial tensions of its own'. At appropriate junctures strict military drill was observed, and the drinking scene and brawl in 2.3 took place in a barrack-room. (When Desdemona came into it she was clearly fascinated by this hitherto unfamiliar aspect of the military life.) This was the world in which Iago could thrive, 'a trained NCO to whom detail is all' and whose 'attention to detail [was] matched by the almost technical precision of the way he works on Othello'.[47] 'Every detail is correct', wrote Michael Billington, 'down to the little baccy-tin for half-smoked cheroots and the obsessive way he tidies his barrack-room blankets'.[48] In preparation for the celebrations in 2.3 Iago prepared the drink that would intoxicate Cassio, pouring wine into an enamel basin, adding spirits to it from a flask and then, after dipping his finger in the mixture to taste its potency, adding more. He was equally adept in caring for the wounded Montano and administering a pick-me-up to the distraught and already massively hung-over Cassio – he carefully cleaned the bowl after the lieutenant had vomited in it – and convincingly punctilious in his reluctance to incriminate the lieutenant under Othello's questioning. His methodical manipulation of his victims could be passed off as diligent and loyal, though this took some effort with the querulous Roderigo. Iago's soliloquies were delivered with ruthless rapidity in his clipped and incisive Lancashire accent, itself a marker of class. Stanley Wells observed that 'McKellen's insolent scorn extended even to the audience in his baleful, challenging gaze'.[49] This made the venom of 'I hate the Moor' in his explanation to Roderigo (1.3.366–7) and the momentary anguish of return to his suspicion that the 'lustful Moor' had cuckolded him, now repeated in the privacy of a soliloquy (2.1.292–5) all the more shocking as revelations of suppressed passion. Another dimension of this was clear at the end of 3.3 when Iago knelt alongside Othello and joined hands with him to pledge allegiance in the murder of Cassio, and the determination to kill Desdemona. The final line of the scene, Iago's 'I am your own for ever' (482), was like the confirmation of a marriage vow.

The marriage at the centre of the play was characterized by the calm but intense responses of her husband to Desdemona's impetuous expressions of affection. Harry Eyres's observation that 'Passion connects them with electro-magnetic force; in crowded rooms they only have eyes for each other' suggests the effect of the staging's intimacy – the theatre was, after all, a crowded room – and the sense that their love was an implicit challenge to the world about them.[50] Billington thought that her 'squeal of excitement ... as if it's her first trip abroad', at the news that they were to embark immediately for Cyprus, 'already separate[d] her from the Moor far more than the colour of her skin'. Anne Barton, in her *TLS* review, described her as 'fragile, lovely, manipulatively aware of her charm, and very young'. In the senate scene she was 'self-possessed' in a 'known world' but went 'adrift' immediately in Cyprus.[51]

She threw herself into Othello's arms when he arrived there and Stubbs made clear Desdemona's readiness to enjoy herself in this new and exciting environment. She describes the work done in rehearsal on 'the happiness and giddiness and laughing together' that characterized the 'huge secret love' she shared with Othello.[52] Desdemona joined in with Iago's extempore joking in the same scene, even when he manipulated her physically into playing along with his act, but her mood was suddenly dashed by apprehension for Othello's safety. Her acceptance of comfort from Cassio was watched by Emilia (Zoë Wanamaker), seated at the other side of the side of the stage, and Iago turned towards the audience with 'He takes her by the palm' (2.1.167). Nunn's staging thus created a microcosm of the play's intertwined relationships, with Iago and Emilia as witnesses of a moment that would prove instrumental in Iago's destruction of Othello's trust in his wife.

For all her wariness, at first Emilia seemed affectionate towards Iago and unsure about her young mistress, perhaps embarrassed to witness her displays of conjugal affection. She whistled thoughtfully during the long pause after Cassio's comment on her husband that 'you many relish him more in the soldier than in the scholar' (165–6). The equivocal nature of Iago's marriage to Emilia, and her growing suspicion of him, were marked subtly throughout the play. The brutality of his rejection of her after seeming to initiate an embrace once he had Desdemona's handkerchief in his grasp (3.3.319) seemed to be a turning point.

At the beginning of 3.2 Emilia and Desdemona were preparing a jug of lemonade. Desdemona gave Othello a glass – evidently it lacked sugar, causing him to wince and put it down – before sitting on his knee to raise the question of Cassio's demotion. The cajoling mood continued when she returned to summon Othello to dinner, and she failed to notice any double significance in his claim to feel pain 'upon [his] forehead' (288): Desdemona's insouciance in this and her solicitude for his health underlined the gravity of the scene that had just passed between him and Iago. At the end of the scene she returned to the stage, and for a moment it seemed that she might pick up the dropped handkerchief, but she had come for the watch she had placed on the desk. The handkerchief that had remained on the floor as the production's first part ended was retrieved by Emilia at the opening of the second: it was an ironic suggestion of what might have been the plot's development such as a Victorian novelist might have devised.

During the 'temptation' dialogue, Othello had swept the papers from the table at which he and his ensign had been working, and Iago had collected them carefully and placed them in their proper place in a portfolio, with another gesture of control disguised as dutiful care. But perhaps more disturbing was the thought that these were aspects of the same mentality: Othello's relationship with Desdemona needed to be dealt with as a disruption of orderly life, and Iago's behaviour was such as would soon be familiar by the clinical term 'obsessive-compulsive'. (At one performance I attended, McKellen, no more than two feet away from my seat, dropped his box of matches: it was Iago who calmly picked them up one by one.) In 4.2, when Iago held Desdemona in his arms to comfort her after Othello's insults, he had achieved a degree of intimacy with her that recalled ironically Cassio's behaviour in 2.1, but this was a temporary fulfilment.

The most moving moment of warmth between Desdemona and a character other than Othello came in her scene with Emilia at the end of 4.3, when the discussion of the ways of men was given a familiar, homely touch by their sharing the box of sweets Cassio had given her in 3.2: it had been locked in the drawer of her dressing table, which Othello had tried to open in 4.2, but had failed to find the key. Now it was seen that the key was kept in the casket Roderigo in his turn had rifled through looking for the jewels he thought he had given her through Iago. A stage property, linking five characters, was thus revealed as innocent, although had Othello found it he would undoubtedly have seen it as further proof of Desdemona's unfaithfulness. Far from being a gimmick, this was a notable example of Nunn's skill in using an object that was significant rather than symbolic. It was typical of the production's movements from metaphor to object that as he struggled with the lock Othello should declare that Emilia was 'a subtle whore, / A closet lock and key of villainous secrets' (4.2.21–2). This was a more sophisticated device than – for example – the outsize nursery toys in *The Winter's Tale*, but as potent as the humming top in *Three Sisters*. After Desdemona's entrance the scene alternated between violence and tenderness: Othello sat on a chair for the reflection 'Had it pleas'd heaven / To try me with affliction' (48 etc.) and she knelt beside him, trying to soothe his alarming dejection, but he forced her to look at herself in a hand mirror on 'turn thy complexion there' (63) and in a premonition of the final scene he turned her from an embrace to grasp her by the throat on 'O thou black weed, why art so lovely fair?' (68–9: quarto reading).

Othello made Desdemona stand on a table, taunting her with the name of 'whore' and then dragged her to a *prie-dieu*: in the video the camera takes Desdemona's point of view when he circles her as she stands on the table, recalling ironically a similar moment after his arrival in Cyprus. The intensity of Othello's scrutiny, once loving, had become a form of violence in itself. The 'willow' scene (4.3), with its commonplace preparations for going to bed ('unpin me here' referred to her hair) and the dispassionate discussion of the ways of men, marked the firmness of Desdemona's bond with Emilia. At the end of it Desdemona knelt at the *prie-dieu*, this time for the prayer 'God me such usage send, / Not to pick bad from bad, but by bad mend' (103–4). Here, as elsewhere, every detail showed Desdemona's willingness to understand her husband's puzzling shifts of mood and to support him lovingly, to bring him back from the dark place to which he had gone. The end of the scene marked a development in the relationship between the two women. Lois Potter observes that 'Emilia has resisted Desdemona's attempts at intimacy until now; but, at the end of the scene, when Desdemona says "Good night", Emilia impulsively seizes and embraces her'. She points out that 'this brief moment of friendship ... explains why, contrary to all the indications she had given earlier, Emilia cannot let the death of Desdemona remain unexamined'.[53] It was also a sign of the subtlety with which Wanamaker marked Emilia's growing understanding of the husband whose 'fantasy' (3.3.303) must have prompted him to ask repeatedly for the handkerchief.

Throughout the play, beginning with his taunting calls to Brabantio in the first scene, Iago had dwelt on crude and vivid images of love-making and intimacy. Nunn's direction of the murder of Desdemona seemed to fulfil for the audience the ensign's response to Othello's demand for proof of her adultery with Cassio: 'Would you, the supervisor, grossly gape on, / Behold her topp'd?' (3.3.398–9). At first Othello's tenderness towards the still-sleeping Desdemona, his care not to wake her as he kissed, established a quality in their love that was presently to be destroyed. With 'will you come to bed, my lord?' (5.2.24), she stretched out her hand across what was clearly his side of the bed, in a gesture that suggested the contented sleep they had shared until now. The pacing of the scene changed swiftly as Othello assured her that the threat of immediate death was real. Confronted with the allegation regarding the handkerchief her alarm grew into indignation as she yelled, 'He found it then, / I never gave it him' (5.2.66–7). After a desperate struggle, in which she crashed against the locked door of the bedroom, Othello flung Desdemona onto the bed and then lay on top of her to smother and then strangle her, completing the action with what seemed like post-coital gasps and rolling over to lie beside her on the bed. Nunn and the actors thus achieved a performance of the scene that intimated the marital happiness granted to the couple's 'sheets' – Iago's ironically down-to-earth wish at 2.3.26 – before moving to the sexual violence of the murder. Brought to 'look on the tragic loading of this bed' (5.2.361), Iago stared at it with apparent fascination but betraying no glimmer of either triumph or remorse, 'his face still hungry for their secret', as Mars-Jones observed. Smallwood describes 'a stare of cold, detached, emotionless curiosity, the last thing we [saw] as the lights went down'.[54]

Iago's gaze – obsessive but unrewarded – was doubly discomforting because not only was there no sign of satisfaction for him but also no special secret in the couple's love. He would never comprehend the marriage he had destroyed, or for that matter his own. The mundane details of the production's world, the humdrum military and domestic routine (dinner time, a banal barrack-room, hints of an offstage church parade, documents to be signed) had diminished any romantic exoticism in the couple's love affair. Desdemona loved her husband wholeheartedly but simply, and the lack of 'local colour' in this colonial garrison made a normal domestic life eminently possible. Wells noted that 'the depth of her love was most apparent after her fate was sealed, as she listened entranced to Othello's tale of the handkerchief [3.4.57–77] and for a moment one sensed a return to an earlier stage of their relationship, when she would listen with similar fascination to his traveller's tales'.[55] As if in acceptance of his standing outside the Venetian world, Othello appeared as an exotic figure in the final scene, clad in a white and black robe and wielding a scimitar for the first time, the warrior of the tales by which he had wooed Desdemona. In White's delivery of the most eloquent of the character's speeches there had been none of the self-dramatizing manner attributed to Othello by Leavis in his 1937 essay on the play. Anne Barton suggested that the directors' interpretation was 'far closer to that of John Bayley in *The Characters of Love* (1960)'.[56] Now Othello seemed to be accepting a role that had been imposed on him, a reversion not to a more 'primitive' character but rather an acceptance of the appropriate role for a wronged husband. The otherness conveyed by his colour was secondary to a deeper cultural divide, an obligation to perform a violent action required and sanctioned by standards of a society foreign to that he had adopted.

How did the production deal with the question of race? It was, after all, only the second time a black actor had appeared in the title role at Stratford – the first being Paul Robeson in 1959. Virginia Mason Vaughan points to a paradox of the production's treatment of racial tensions: although 'global conflict' was not 'highlighted' racial issues were 'emphasized' without being 'stressed explicitly', largely through Nunn's casting of White, who had appeared as Porgy in his recent Glyndbourne production of *Porgy and Bess*: 'The theme remains understated ... throughout the production, as if it were implicit in the situation but not dominant.'[57] My own initial reaction to his performance at The Other Place was that Othello moved and spoke impressively in a mode different from that of those around him on stage, with an 'otherness' that was attributable, it seemed, to the actor's operatic rather than his ethnic identity. He was, Robert Smallwood suggested, 'an alien among the Venetians, the black opera singer among the white Shakespeareans'.[58] His stature and the timbre of his voice were unusual in the context of the RSC. The contrast between his measured, sensitive and sonorous speaking of the verse and the virtuosity of McKellen's articulation of Iago's lines – which at times bordered on fussiness attributable to the actor rather than the character – suggested a contrast that seemed to be a factor in the ensign's enmity. It was an additional element in the tangle of mostly obscure motivations in a far from motiveless character, and the colour of Othello's skin seemed a contributory matter, to be dredged up and given voice with racist vehemence as occasion suggested. As Vaughan notes, Iago's compulsive physical caresses – even including at one point the comradely ruffling of Roderigo's hair as he passed by him – did not extend to his approaches to Othello: they did not make eye contact until the end of the temptation scene and he was 'only intimate with the other characters when Othello [was] offstage'.[59]

Othello was marked throughout by meticulous attention to textual detail, prepared for as usual by thorough tablework in which the cast read and discussed the text. 'Before any blocking,' Marsha Hunt recalled, 'we'd all taken part in deciding what Shakespeare had to say.'[60] As well as properties endowed with significance – such as the cigars purloined by Iago, the box of sweets and the unsweetened lemonade – Nunn added details that responded to a degree of realist logic not always observed in productions. One notable example was that of the two letters from Iago 'found in his [i.e. Roderigo's] pocket' (5.2.305) and a third – also found on 'the discontented Roderigo's body' (311–12), which was to have been sent to the ensign by his dupe. Roderigo consulted what one assumed was the first of these at the beginning of 5.1, when he reassured himself by reading aloud Iago's 'satisfying reason' that '"Tis but a man gone' (10) before pocketing it again. Details of this kind were magnified by the intimacy of the theatre and register effectively on video. Nevertheless, the overall effect of the period chosen was to provide a believable but not in some way 'accurate' depiction of a society in which the play might work effectively: there was no specific analogy between the Venetians in Cyprus and armies of occupation anywhere or at any time, either past or present, let alone any reference to the American Civil War era. *Measure for Measure*, Nunn's next 'chamber' production for the RSC, again as a freelance, would make more direct reference to the intellectual and social circumstances of the places and historical periods in which it was set.

Measure for Measure, 1991: Freud's Vienna and the psychiatrist's couch

Three years after *Othello* closed The Other Place, a new, permanent version of the theatre opened with productions of *The Blue Angel*, adapted from Josef von Sternberg's film, and *Measure for Measure* directed by Nunn, whom Michael Coveney now dubbed 'the RSC's wunderkind turned *éminence grise*'. The new theatre 'not only restored the precious intimacies of the former galleried arena, but also retained its special atmosphere', and exuded 'a palpable sense of workshop and powerhouse'.[61] The stage floor, at 9 by 13 metres, was larger, and the seating accommodated 240 on three sides (270 if all four sides were used), roughly 100 more seats than the old theatre. There was a trap, and the audience entrance now faced the back of the stage rather than the side.[62]

In March 1991 Nunn had directed *Timon of Athens* at the Young Vic, whose thrust stage and 450-seat auditorium had provided an acceptable 'middle way' for the transfer to London of the RSC's studio productions. *Timon* differed from most of his previous Shakespearean work in its bold treatment of what was in any case a problematic text and the transposition to a specifically contemporary world. 'Athens' stood for the London of financial gambling, corporate excess and contrasting poverty, and reviewers reached for analogies in Oliver Stone's film *Wall Street* (1987), and the plays *Serious Money* by Caryl Churchill (Royal Court, 1987) and *Singer* by Peter Flannery (produced by the RSC at the Swan Theatre in 1989). Paul Taylor, in the *Independent*, suggested the prodigality of Scott Fitzgerald's Jay Gatsby and the tasteless opulence of Hugh Hefner's Playboy Mansion as models for Timon's affluent lifestyle.[63] There were a few dissenting voices: in the *Tribune* Ian Dodd described the production as riding 'a cliché-ridden route from computerised office to squash-club locker-room' and in the *TLS* Peter Holland complained that the 'world overflowing with material objects' had become 'less a representation of a fiercely materialist culture than a self-regarding tribute to Nunn's directorial imagination'.[64] Nevertheless, on balance judgements were in favour of what Carl Miller in *City Limits* described as a 'careful reworking' that fitted 'the Young Vic's tradition of intelligent, accessible interpretation'.[65] Intriguingly, Irving Wardle in the *Independent on Sunday* thought that Nunn had delivered 'the kind of show that Michael Bogdanov was directing at this address 15 years ago', as though the challenging social activism of the ESC had caught up with the erstwhile director of the RSC.[66] The final movement of the play, after Timon (David Suchet) exiled himself from the city (or 'The City') found him in an urban wasteland where he and Barry Foster's Apemantus, a 'laid back and insidious philosopher-tramp',[67] inhabited a landscape that for some evoked that of *Waiting for Godot*, albeit one cluttered beyond Beckett's dreams with the detritus of a self-destructive consumerist society. John Peter regretted that Nunn had removed the sense of 'something mythical' in 'Timon's determination to bury himself by the seashore'. Having him shoot himself in the back of the van he had adopted as a hovel 'reduce[d] him to the level of a sad crackpot'.[68]

On this thrust stage and in a theatre seating a hundred more than the new Other Place, Nunn seemed to have addressed a new constituency with a production more directly contemporary in its engagement with social issues than had been customary in the RSC's combination of textual orthodoxy and 'relevance'. This contrasted with the creation of a world for *Measure for Measure* that resonated with that of the 1990s without asserting direct identity with the audience's own circumstances.

Maria Bjornson's basic set, shared by *Measure for Measure* and *The Blue Angel*, had been designed for touring to venues that called for more than the austerity of the old Other Place, and was consequently more elaborate than would have been possible there. A cobbled street, incorporating tram tracks, crossed the stage from back to front at an angle, bounded by steps and backed by metal staircases. Gates and bars moved across as required for the prison scenes. Tall bookcases identified the office location and a pavement café could be established as necessary with tables and chairs. Although a large clock face seemed to register the 'real' time of the action, it was speeded up or slowed down as required. (It moved rapidly through thirty minutes while Isabella explained the Duke's plot to Mariana.) This was a fragmented image of *fin-de-siècle* Vienna, the significance of which was made explicit in the progamme with a photograph of Freud and quotations from his works, together with an extract from Anna Freud's introduction to 'Repression' in *The Essentials of Psychoanalysis*. The title page cited Freud's definition of repression as 'a preliminary stage of condemnation, something between flight and condemnation'. In case there was any doubt, on stage at the opening in the ducal office was the classic psychiatrist's couch, copied from Freud's preserved original. The production opened and closed with couples waltzing to Johann Strauss the Second's 'Emperor Waltz', marking the location of the play and evoking a romantic and imperial vision that its action would question. The pairing with *The Blue Angel* suggested that the two plays shared a common environment of a world where repressed desires broke surface and decorum was threatened or simply ignored.

The script was cut sparingly, with minor alterations in 1.2 (lines 78–85, for Pompey and Mistress Overdone were moved to open the scene), 3.1.28–32 (the Duke's exhortation to Claudio lost a few of its medical details) and five of Abhorson's lines in 4.2.[69] The most important alteration was the division into three sections of the Duke's soliloquy, 'He that the sword of Heaven will bear', which concludes the text's third act. The first (517–23) was placed at the beginning to form a prologue spoken by the Duke (Philip Madoc) as he examined press cuttings and a photograph:

> He who the sword of Heaven will bear
> Should be as holy as severe,
> Pattern in himself to know
> Grace to stand, and virtue go,
> More nor less to others paying
> Than by self-offences weighing.

Robert Smallwood noted the 'thoughtful, quizzical reading' of this 'as it were from his own notebook anthology of verse'.[70] The second, beginning 'Shame to him whose cruel striking / Kills for faults of his own liking', came at the end of the play's third act and immediately before the interval, summing up the Duke's reflections on the way his deputy had responded to the test of his integrity. The third, with its justification of using 'craft against vice' (533–8), was spoken after 4.1.57 while Isabella took Mariana aside to explain the 'bed-trick' device to her. One consequence of this arrangement was to reinforce the impression of the Duke as a strategist, overseeing and commenting on his plan to the audience at each stage. The newspaper cuttings, shown to Isabella to explain the story of Mariana and Angelo in 3.1, were appropriate to the production's choice of time and place, but the discovery of the Duke reflecting on Angelo's past misdemeanours as the play opened suggested a level of deviousness – or even salacious curiosity – in motives that would turn out to be at the very least mixed when in 1.3 he admitted to the Friar that he had abstained from taking measures against the city's vices to avoid accusations of 'tyranny' and was using Angelo 'in th'ambush of [his] name' while conducting an experiment to see 'If power change purpose, what our seemers be' (1.3.54). Nunn thus reminded the audience at significant points of the character's combination of self-examination and case-study research. Peter Holland noted that 'what in Shakespeare is troublingly discontinuous' – if the Duke knew about the Mariana affair, one asked how that affected his treatment of Angelo – was now made 'completely apparent', and the other reasons for his actions were now subordinate to the 'heavy emphasis' on 'Lord Angelo is precise' (1.3.50).[71]

Having placed the Duke initially as an analyst on his own couch, Nunn did the same with Angelo (David Haig), bearded like Freud and, in Michael Billington's words, 'a humourless bureaucrat whose vanity is indicated by a brocaded waistcoat' in whom the production showed 'the ego battling unavailingly with the id'.[72] After his first encounter with Isabella, during which she repeatedly touched him as she pleaded for her brother's life, he clutched his crotch as if transfixed by the realization that long-suppressed desires had asserted themselves. Before she arrived for their second interview, in which he came close to raping her, he 'lolled' on the couch 'biting the flesh of his own arm as if it were hers and breaking into cackles of surprise at this unlikely behaviour'.[73] Under pressure, Claire Skinner's Isabella showed signs of 'some buried trauma that makes this warm and likeable young woman react with shrill hysteria at the mention or (worse still) threat of sex'.[74] She responded with what more than one reviewer called a 'tantrum' to Claudio's suggestion in that she might reconsider her rejection of Angelo's proposition, pummelling him with her fists: 'O, you beast! / O faithless coward, O dishonest wretch!' (3.1.138–9). The uneasiness of reviewers in describing Skinner's performance reflects an underlying challenge to gender assumptions that was perhaps inevitable in a production that implicitly invoked Freudian attitudes to the magic word 'hysteria'. Informed by the Duke that Angelo had gone back on his word to pardon her brother, she reacted with screams and tears and pounded a table with her fists. Identifying the play's character as 'an obvious forerunner of the woman who refuses to be told how to dispose her body' in 'an odd meeting of religious morality and feminism', Martin Hoyle, in the *Independent on Sunday*, characterized Skinner's Isabella as 'adorably vulnerable, with schoolgirl bob and black lace-up shoes' and a 'piping little-girl voice' that 'assume[d] a monotonous rant that evoke[d] the priggish head prefect and old-fashioned puritanism'.[75] Billington thought the Duke's final offer to Isabella, 'although gratefully received', made him look 'dangerously like Humbert Humbert', the child-loving protagonist of Vladimir Nabokov's novel *Lolita*.

In the final scene the Duke remained the 'scientific' observer, 'making little notes' on Isabella's statements, wrote Robert Smallwood, 'as at a consultation' and making the offer to her 'his last psychological experiment'. After a long pause, in which she seemed to realize she could not think of anything to say, her hand reached slowly towards his. Smallwood expresses vividly the misgivings elicited by this moment:

> They made a most curious couple, this slender, youthful little girl, so quiet and still, so tired now after all the turbulent suffering and danger she had passed, and the middle-aged, tubby, grizzled physician, her only remaining friend, to whom she timidly stretched out her hand. Were they really about to go to bed together, one felt a little vulgar for wondering, or does she see in this moment the possibility of that trusting paternal relationship that her past must somehow have denied or distorted?

Smallwood reflects that 'If, of course, one's imagination placed *her* thoughts in this latter area and *his* in the former, then this was a very bitter moment indeed'.[76]

The combined effect of the specific associations of *fin-de-siècle* Vienna and Nunn's by now familiar tendency to leave no action without its correlative object, presented *Measure for Measure* as a problem play in the Shavian sense of a play about a societal problem. John Gross suggested that an element of perplexity had been introduced by the naturalistic rather than 'allegorical' conception of the Duke.[77] Both Billington and Holland expressed reservations about a process that, while anchoring the play in a 'fixed, concrete world' and 'illuminating individual psychology',[78] deprived it of any mystery. Holland, whose reservations regarding Nunn's *Timon* have already been cited, identified the approach with reference to that production, as well as to the 1989 *Othello*:

> What had seemed experimental in *Othello* was now becoming a recognizably fixed style: emphatically naturalistic acting as if the plays were Ibsenite social dramas, consequently a phenomenal density of detail, a certain literalism with the text and above all a belief in the plays' explicability.[79]

Martin Hoyle's *Independent on Sunday* review was symptomatic in its assessment of the consequences of Nunn's approach: 'this engrossing production leaves one wondering why the work was ever included among Shakespeare's problem plays'.

Minor effective details of social behaviour, as well as contributing to the construction of an intelligible world for a play's action, also produced vivid cameos which reviewers enjoyed describing. Abhorson was 'a top-hatted Masonic hangman equipped with tape-measure and diabolical case of instruments';[80] the 'dandies of café society' were 'Puccini's Bohemians grown up';[81] and the low-life characters provided 'the full reek of unregenerate humanity'.[82] Robert Smallwood observed 'a slopping out parade of bucket-carrying prisoners, interrupted by a trivial but sordid outbreak of violence between two women prisoners', newspapers printed in historically appropriate German *Fraktur* type in the café scene, and the 'prison skivvy' serving an enamel mug of tea to the Provost 'who in a little gesture of compassion edge[d] it across to Claudio'. Some of these incidental touches were visual explanatory footnotes of the kind exemplified by the identification of the paper found on Roderigo's body in *Othello*. Smallwood identifies one in Lucio's ringing the receptionist's bell when he arrived at the gaol in 4.3: 'So that's what he's doing here: he's come to visit Claudio, though Shakespeare never got round to telling us.' But having noted the 'coherent, exciting, but deliberately narrow path through the play's vastness' steered by Nunn's 'incisive and efficient' decisions, Smallwood reflects that 'within its chosen limits, the production made total sense; it would be ungrateful to ask for more'.[83]

The 'more', though, might consist of the kind of 'fairy tale' element that Nunn had supplied in *All's Well that Ends Well*, a sense of the inexplicable that might defy rational analysis, either psycho- or ordinary. Isabella's acceptance of the Duke's offer of marriage sidestepped one of the play's most debated issues, and the play had been delivered into the hands of those 'philosophical persons', remarked on by Lafew, who 'make modern and familiar things supernatural and causeless' (*All's Well*, 2.3.1–3). Comparisons were inevitably made with Jonathan Miller's 1974 production at the National Theatre, effectively revived in his 1975 'Bed Tricks' season at the Greenwich Theatre, but Miller's Vienna had been as much Kafkaesque as Freudian, the multiple doors of its set designed to evoke 'that clerkly 1920s world'.[84] In the words of Penelope Wilton, who played Isabella in 1975, this approach was appropriate to a play 'about sexual frustration and repression'.[85] Her Isabella reacted with the same violence as Skinner's to the advances of Angelo and Claudio's suggestion of compliance, but the tenor of the productions differed. Nevertheless Miller, though never shy of applying medical or psychological perceptions to his productions, had not placed Freud at its centre. In Miller's, the evocation of Kafka's work introduced an element of the inexplicable, the kind of distortion of reality that Freudian psychology seeks to explain.

Of Nunn's three 'chamber' productions for the RSC, *Measure for Measure* was the least innovative in its approach to the play, partly because in the new and slightly larger theatre it lacked the at times alarming intimacy of *Macbeth* and *Othello*. Maria Bjornson's set seemed elaborate enough to suggest aspirations for development into a full main-house staging, and although the actors' performances were compelling at no point was the audience as uncomfortably near the couch as they had been to the magic circle in *Macbeth* or the bed in *Othello*. This was also close to being a 'concept' production, in which the ideas of the great psychoanalyst were presented as the key to the play. There was less of the feeling created in the two tragedies that – in the words of the doctor to the Gentlewoman in *Macbeth* – the audience had 'known what [it] should not' (5.1.44). Nunn's next intimate theatre version of a play by Shakespeare, *The Merchant of Venice* at the National Theatre, would offer the combination of incisive interpretation and direct access to potentially disturbing ideas and emotions that had been achieved in his 'chamber' work in Stratford.

4

1997–2007: The National Theatre, and beyond

Between 1991 and 1997, when he succeeded Richard Eyre as Director of the National Theatre (hereafter, 'NT'), Nunn directed a well-received film of *Twelfth Night* but staged no new theatrical productions of Shakespeare. He had not directed *Twelfth Night* at the RSC, and he was able to take advantage of the opportunities for a more expansive depiction of the play's social milieu that the medium afforded. At the same time, the nineteenth-century setting, like that of his *All's Well*, accommodated the play's treatment of status and gender. Illyria was made enough of a warlike state for Antonio (Nicholas Farrell) to need to keep away from Orsino's court and, indeed, hide from the mounted officers who patrolled his beaches. In Olivia's household the position of Malvolio (Nigel Hawthorne) and his secret social ambitions were credible, while the self-indulgence of Olivia (Helena Bonham Carter) was complemented by an ambience of aesthetic luxury. A prologue, with accompanying blank-verse narration spoken by Feste (Ben Kingsley) showed how Viola (Imogen Stubbs) and her brother cross-dressed for a concert party on board ship, and this prepared the way for her adoption of a spare uniform of his as a disguise and – in the typically Nunn-style crossing of every 't' and dotting of every 'i' – how she acquired from a make-up box the moustache that completed her disguise.

A festive and engaging film, *Twelfth Night* suggests how strongly Nunn might have challenged nostalgia (or anxiety of influence) attendant on memories of John Barton's romantic RSC production of 1969.

The 'call' to the NT – it was effectively that, after an inconclusive search for a new Director to succeed Richard Eyre – came in 1996. Nicholas Hytner, Nunn's successor, describes this as 'a significant act of public service' by 'a mighty figure in the British theatre'. Nunn 'needed the National far less than it needed him'. This was not an auspicious time to take over, as during the 1990s subsidized theatres had been 'told to charge what the market would bear', resulting in a rise in ticket prices and the necessity of taking fewer risks, 'which led to the mainstream audience losing its appetite for risk'.[1] Two of Nunn's moves as artistic director recall aspects of his RSC tenure. The 1999 productions were part of an 'ensemble' season in which six plays were to be presented across all three theatres by a 40-strong acting company and, in 2001–2, as part of an ambitious 'Transformation' plan supported with £2.5 million of his own money, he implemented a reconfiguration of both the Olivier and the Lyttleton in an attempt to bring audience and performance closer together. The project also included the creation of an intimate (100-seat) venue, which eventually became the Loft, carved out of the foyer and exhibition space. In the event, the actors in the ensemble did not remain together after the completion of the six-play season. Scheduling rehearsals as well as performances across the theatres had been problematic, and, as in the case of the three-year contracts planned by Hall in the RSC's early years, actors were unwilling to forgo opportunities for other work. The major alterations to the two larger theatres did not survive after Nunn's tenure as Director.[2] Although a sophisticated sound system had been put in place to remedy the acoustical problems of the Olivier, Nunn decided to use body microphones, a development that aroused some controversy. Acceptable – indeed, necessary – in present-day musical theatre to allow for a balance between voices and orchestra, amplification of this kind for spoken drama was objected to on principle by many actors and critics, and brought its own technical difficulties.

1999–2003: Three plays at the National

Like his plans for an ensemble and for altering the performance spaces, the three Shakespeare productions Nunn directed during his tenure at the NT evoked the range of production styles and the kinds of challenge encountered during his RSC career. In 1999, *Troilus and Cressida* and *The Merchant of Venice* in the Olivier and the Cottesloe respectively represented his command of large-scale and 'chamber' staging, while in 2003 with *Love's Labour's Lost* in the Olivier he appeared to bring his experience with musicals to another Shakespearean comedy. Cross-cast with the musical *Anything Goes*, this was his final production as Director of the NT.

All were plays he had not directed in Stratford and in each the text was adjusted significantly: *Troilus and Cressida* began and ended with Cressida on stage; in the closing moments of *The Merchant of Venice* Jessica (Gabrielle Jourdan) moved away from the Christians who stared at her as she sank to her knees, clutching the legal document conveying Shylock's wealth to her, and sang the Hebrew song she had earlier shared with him: thunder 'rumbled ominously in the distance' and 'everyone froze as the lights went down'.[3] The opening scene of *Love's Labour's Lost* was preceded by the violent explosions and flashes of a battle as a soldier fell to the ground beneath a tree, and was visited by a black-clad figure who spoke one of the lines that appear without a speech-heading at the end of the text, 'The words of Mercury are harsh after the songs of Apollo.' In a spectacular transformation, the blasted tree regained its leaves and the stage became the park adjacent to a country house. What followed was thus a flashback to the pre-war summer, as though in the mind of the apparently dying

Berowne (Joseph Fiennes). At the end of the play, after the arrival of Mercade, now identifiable as the messenger of death from the opening scene, the abrupt turn towards seriousness was followed by a return to the battlefield, so that (as Charles Spencer observed) the comedy of love 'suddenly seem[ed] like a distant dream', illustrating 'the truth of Berowne's perception that it is impossible "to move wild laughter in the face of death"'.[4]

Nunn's textual strategies in *The Merchant of Venice* were treated with more respect by reviewers than his manipulations of the text in *Troilus and Cressida* and *Love's Labour's Lost*. Opinions on these diverged markedly. The ending of *Troilus and Cressida* was either a timely and effective reminder that Cressida silhouetted against the Trojan walls showed 'an individual victim' standing 'emblematically for her entire sex',[5] or a sign of the 'glow of romantic pathos' with which Nunn had 'bathed' the 'doomed love affair'.[6] As for the revised opening and ending of *Love's Labour's Lost*, David Nathan in the *Jewish Chronicle* hailed 'Nunn's triumph' in infusing the whole play with the effect of Mercade's news, while Nicholas de Jongh thought that the 'final, abrupt reversion to winter and war' was 'marvellous – all the force of a chronicle of death foretold'.[7] In the *Sunday Telegraph* John Gross identified it as 'one of those superficially bright ideas that simply creates a distraction' and insisted that for all its impressive stagecraft 'the whole concept' of the idyll recollected *in extremis* was 'sentimental in a way that Shakespeare isn't'.[8]

It is arguable that as a tightly-focused production played in traverse staging in a studio theatre and with a mesmeric individual performance by Henry Goodman as Shylock, *The Merchant of Venice* coincided with one aspect of the critical narrative on Nunn's career, while the Olivier plays fitted the alternative – or complementary – perception of him as an acutely intelligent director whose penchant for theatrical effect sometimes overwhelmed his gift for mining psychological and textual detail. The fact that *Love's Labour's Lost* played opposite *Anything Goes* attracted this interpretation, while its status as his departing production as Director prompted some reviewers to incorporate it in their ongoing biographies of Nunn as either a parting gift to the NT or a sign that it was time he moved on. In *Shakespeare Survey,* Michael Dobson, who complained that the 'lingering effect' was that of 'a production which patronized its audience and Shakespeare's play in about equal measure', wondered sardonically whether 'perhaps Nunn was being deliberately generous, departing on an uncharacteristically low note so that he might be an easier act for Nicholas Hytner to follow'.[9]

Dobson's use of 'uncharacteristically' is a reminder of the high standard achieved in *The Merchant*, which was acutely focused in terms of both individual psychology and the societal background of its period setting. Although this was 1930s Venice without any sign of the Mussolini's Blackshirts, anti-Semitism was explicit in the well-to-do circle of Bassanio (Alex Hanson), while the repressed homosexual Antonio (David Bamber) was a provincial outsider among the urban sophisticates. They were happy to patronize him and take advantage of his generosity, going so far as to pull out their empty pockets with insolent nonchalance when they left him with the bill at the café. (Shylock, however, was punctilious in paying his bill and leaving a tip.)

Shylock's sombre house was in contrast to the chic opulence of Portia's Belmont, placed at the opposite end of the traverse and dominated by a Klimt-like mural. The space in between, paved in black and white checkers, served for a piazza café or a louche nightclub. (The trial scene used the whole length of the stage.) Like the sepia photograph of her father on Desdemona's dressing table in the RSC *Othello*, a photograph of Shylock's dead wife Leah was a reminder of the family, in this case one overshadowed by bereavement. In his short scene with Jessica (2.5), Shylock's impatience with his daughter's housekeeping and anxiety about her association with Christians were inextricable from his deep affection for her. He slapped her face when she seemed too interested in Gobbo's message then embraced her. As Robert Smallwood observed, 'the lonely widower, desperate and demanding, over-protectively clinging to his treasured child's love, was vulnerably on view here', as they gazed the photograph of Leah and joined in a 'wistful Hebrew song'.[10] She completed his 'Fast bind' with 'fast find' (2.5.52): it was a shared proverb from a childhood intimacy soon to be lost forever. In this respect the melancholy song and distant thunder of Nunn's conclusion to the play seemed apt, a reminder of what might lie ahead for both Shylock and his estranged daughter. Preparing to leave his house, she kissed her mother's photograph.

In the nightclub, redolent of *Cabaret* with its dancing hostesses and *chanteuse*, Shylock was obliged to share a table with Antonio and Bassanio. Young Gobbo's jokes about his conscience and the 'fiend' (transposed from 2.2.1–28) became part of a standup routine he evidently performed here on his nights off, a change warranted arguably by their status as direct address in their original position but here deliberately insulting his master to his face. Shylock forced his way out and, in an extra-textual episode with a theatrical pedigree stretching back to Charles Kean and Henry Irving, ran the gauntlet of Christian revellers on his way home. Finding his door unanswered he fumbled with his keys, then pushed it open and entered. Shylock's anger at the deception by his daughter and the complicity of the obnoxious Christians in her escape appeared to confirm a longstanding sense of grievance. John Gross described him as 'shrewd, humorous, endlessly alert, hardened by a lifetime's blows but still sensitive underneath' and 'ultimately implacable'.[11] Even in the early scenes of banter with the Christians, and in the 'merry bond' that he regarded as both a generous offer and a joke, Charles Spencer found 'a depth of grievance beneath the smiling humour'.[12]

In the trial scene he was a formidable opponent for both Portia (Derbhle Crotty) and Antonio, but found himself unable to make an incision on the first attempt. This was another crisis for a man ruled as much by conscience and regard for the laws, both secular and religious, as by any other emotions. Only when, with characteristic preciseness, before his second attempt he tied a white cloth around his waist to protect his suit from the inevitable spurt of blood did Portia think of the statute that would save Antonio's life. Earlier, as she sat down opposite him to argue the ethical and religious case for mercy – a word she stumbled on – she seemed to have reached the limit of her newly acquired legal repertoire. It was at that point that, as Smallwood observed, her 'earnest intensity ... riveted his attention' as though '[N]ever before ... had a member of the Christian community spoken to him with this degree of immediacy and it was curiously welcome.' Nevertheless, 'a returning awareness of the Gratiano mob' in the court behind him 'rekindled his resolve, and he just managed to find the strength to say "My deeds upon my head"'.[13] In this reading, the omission of blood from the bond was not a trick that Portia had kept up her sleeve as if to see how far Shylock would go or to subject Antonio to a traumatic test. The interaction between her and the Jew, so strange and moving to both of them, was at the emotional centre of the scene. At the end of it, told that he must become a Christian, Shylock bundled his yarmulke and his prayer belt together in one of pans of the scales he had brought with him. His lonely walk away from the court – his friend Tubal had earlier left quietly in revulsion at his determination to exact the penalty – was a final demonstration of the isolation he had been driven into.

Portia had met her own test – or series of tests – with fortitude and a degree of resigned merriment, and Nunn built up a sense of her household by redistributing lines so that the suavely efficient Balthasar and the little group of female attendants shared in her moods and were believably involved in her plight. She and Nerissa discussed the suitors who had decided to take their leave while watching a home movie of them, and there was a degree mock-solemnity in ritual of the scenes with Aragon and Morocco, with a gold curtain drawn ceremoniously by two of the maids to reveal the stand holding the caskets. But Morocco (Chu Omambala) in a hybrid costume of flowing robes and pinstripes evidently charmed her, so that she was clearly moved by his dejection at failing in his quest: 'Let all of his complexion choose me so' (2.7.79), often omitted in modern performances as incongruously racist, was spoken as if to hide her true feelings from her entourage. She was unequivocal, though, in her anxiety that Bassanio should succeed, and their speeches after he had chosen, 'recited as rhetorical formalities', were followed by whoops of joy 'to show their true feelings'.[14] Here, as in the trial scene, Nunn's direction explored shifts of tone and emotional temperature meticulously while keeping the flow of the action compelling and credible.

In *Troilus and Cressida,* Nunn was addressing for the first time as sole director a play whose theatrical credentials as a bitter satire relevant to the times had been established by productions at the RSC, in particular that directed by Peter Hall with John Barton in 1960, as well as Barton's own productions in 1968 and 1976. The 1960 production had been an assertion of the new company's credentials as being radical and innovative both in repertoire and methods. The 1968 *Troilus* confirmed Barton's standing as a major directorial talent in his own right. It was also akin to the 1966 *Revenger's Tragedy* with its portrayal of decadence among the Greeks, notably in the preening, camp Achilles of Alan Howard, although Barton insisted that there was no intention to present him as a homosexual.[15] Three notable RSC productions since the 1970s – directed by Ron Daniels (1985), Sam Mendes (1990) and Michael Boyd (1998) – had shifted the play away from the earlier versions of an 'ancient' historical setting with varying degrees of success, but the cynicism of Thersites, especially as performed in 1990 by Simon Russell Beale, and disgust with the brutal futility of war had remained as persistent elements in its appeal.

In the Olivier, Rob Howell's design reminded some reviewers of the 'sandpit' in Leslie Hurry's set for the RSC's 1960 production, which Allan Brien had interpreted as 'the waste land at the outskirts of an empire, the playground of overgrown schoolboys – the symbol of barrenness and shiftiness'.[16] Robert Smallwood describes the Olivier set as 'a circular arena of a stage, a sort of bull-ring, its floor blood-red gravel; a curved wall behind, broken by six wide doors, with a cyclorama of sky above, serene blue or threatening red according to the lighting, represented the walls of Troy'. The Trojans, played (with the exception of Pandarus) by black actors, wore 'loose robes in gleaming white, reminiscent of North African tribesmen' and the Greeks, 'apart from the non-combatant Achilles and Patroclus, who were in loose caftans', had 'battered leather jackets'. It was clear that although 'we were not exactly in the Ancient World', these were 'very much swords-and-shields armies'.[17] What was not clear to some critics was the significance of the not-quite-diverse casting. In the *Financial Times*, Alastair Macaulay identified the whites as 'ruthless schemers'; and the black Trojans as 'honourable, open-hearted, noble'.[18] This interpretation seems hazardously close to a racist cliché, with a 'tribal' community opposed to one that is more strategy-minded. In *The Times* Benedict Nightingale asked whether it was not 'odd' that 'a theatre which has often and effectively asked us to blind our imaginations to its actors' colour should suddenly expect us to make a point of not noticing it'.[19] Michael Billington proposed a less contentious interpretation: the Trojans were 'weighed down by a doomed paternalism' and the Greeks by 'a warring individualism'.[20] When Cressida was 'welcomed' to the Grecian camp in 4.5 her reception was hardly chivalrous, a 'mauling' thought John Gross, when she ought to have been kissed in turn by the generals.[21] One might expect that responses to this scene, effectively the spectacle of a black woman sexually assaulted by a gang of white men, would elicit comment in terms of its sexual and racial politics, but there was little hint of this in the reviews. Smallwood, though, felt that the scene 'had something of a gang rape about it' and noted that after being passed roughly from one man to another she 'found the presence of mind to mock Menelaus and then, to his fury offer[ed] Ulysses her foot to kiss'. She 'then managed to keep her end up in a rhythmic clapping dance in which she was flung from one to another before making an exhausted exit on Diomed's arm'.[22] After being 'passed round like an exhausted doll', her capitulation was 'less lusty', wrote Michael Coveney, 'than defeated'.[23]

Nunn had stressed Cressida's situation as a female victim of society by the revisions to the text, at least in its final scene, but in retrospect it seems that a potentially disturbing effect of the casting had gone by the board. Nevertheless, the image of victimhood was powerful enough and perhaps all the better for being separated from racial politics. Smallwood describes Nunn's rearrangement of the text as it led up to the final image of the production:

> [T]he ending ... had Pandarus coming on accompanied by Cressida, her face smeared with lip-stick, to Peter de Jersey's Troilus, whose 'Hope of revenge' speech [5.11.11–31] had just been delivered with a chilling ferocity and bleakness. His 'Ignominy and shame / Pursue thy life' [5.11.33–4] was then spoken, savagely and witheringly, to both of them. Thersites then entered to return Cressida's glove and to sneer about 'wars and lechery', before Pandarus, whose obviously terminal coughing had started when Cressida left for the Greek camp, croaked and wheezed through his gloomy envoi.

Cressida was 'left alone, circling helplessly in the growing darkness as the distant sound of gunfire was heard'.[24] Bridget Escolme, in a detailed analysis of the production, finds that the ending deprived Cressida of agency, pointing out that during his final speech Pandarus crawled to Cressida, stood her up and took a pot of rouge from his bag to smear her lips before making to lead her off stage. He stopped to think, and she then returned to the centre of the stage: 'as the lights dim to black, she makes two slow circles on the spot'. This was 'the figure of myth and history, Cressida the whore'.[25] It is difficult to reconcile this image with Nicholas de Jongh's complaint that the director 'bathes Troilus and Cressida's doomed love affair in the glow of romantic pathos'. As with the glamour of the Trojan warriors' return to the city in the first act, racing down centre aisle through the audience as if coming from a sporting event, Nunn's intention seems rather to have been to play the early stages of the love affair so as to suggest a glimmer of light before allowing it to be snuffed out.

There were a few dissenting voices, notably those of de Jongh, who had 'never seen such an arid Nunn production' and Susannah Clapp in the *Observer*, who thought the occasion lacked 'a pervasive sense of waste' and asked 'Should Shakespeare's most pessimistic play be so luscious?'[26] In the *Daily Express* Robert Gore-Langton admired 'a fine production ... full of piercing ideas and good performances and boldly staged as a mature epic for the Olivier stage' before exclaiming 'But my God, it's boring', and complaining about a show that lasted 'four hours with no let-up'.[27] The consensus, though, was overwhelmingly favourable, with applause for the production's 'masterly sweep and precision of focus' and 'virtuosic blend of intimate detail and epic sweep'.[28] Robert Butler, in the *Independent on Sunday*, discerned the influence on Nunn's 'bravura staging' of the 'blockbuster' musicals, with their 'scale, fluidity and use of simple contrast'.[29] Billington emphasized what was by now firmly established as a Nunn hallmark, the 'psychological questing' and the capacity to 'recreate' a play 'by redefining character'. This was especially effective in Roger Allam's Ulysses, 'a flawed ironist who relishes his power'. This *Guardian* review amounts to a celebration of the 'two Nunns' in a production that made 'exciting use of the space' and united 'intimate detail and symbolic gesture'. The point recurs elsewhere in the critical reception, and Sheridan Morley in the *Spectator* suggested that work itself played 'directly to Nunn's considerable strengths as a director – a huge, epic, sprawling tapestry of the Trojan Wars, with a spotlight forever switching from one character to another and one subplot to the next'.[30] Expressions of impatience with the play itself were not uncommon, but *Troilus and Cressida* was greeted by most of the critics as a reassuring sign of Nunn's ability to lead the theatre from the front. In the *Mail on Sunday*, Georgina Brown hailed 'a promising debut by the new multi-racial company'.[31]

In the *Sunday Times,* John Peter asserted that the production, Nunn's first Shakespeare production at the theatre since his appointment eighteen months previously, had 'reconfirm[d] his place among the great Shakespeareans'.[32]

The range of responses to the frame placed around *Love's Labour's Lost* – from 'marvellous' to 'sentimental in a way Shakespeare wasn't' – reflected the reservations expressed about what Nunn and his cast had put into the frame. Nightingale, in *The Times*, had 'hoped from more fun from the subordinate classes' but reflected that this might be 'the price of Nunn's approach'.[33] John Peter's respect for a 'flawed but unforgettably moving' production, in which Nunn 'like all great directors ... had read the play as if it had been a brand-new text', was qualified by a tendency he had detected recently in Nunn, 'a fondness for bringing on apple-cheeked urchins and other colourful extras, whether the text call[ed] for them or not'.[34] Familiar critical tropes from the three decades' worth of reviews reappeared: Charles Spencer (*Daily Telegraph*) wrote again of Nunn's combination of 'wondrous stagecraft with novelistic attention to the revealing detail'; Jane Edwardes (*Time Out*) suggested that anyone seeing the play for the first time this 'richly detailed but also sometimes over-explanatory' staging 'might well judge the playwright to have been exposed both to Victorian novels and to Chekhov at his most lethargic and wistful'; Susannah Clapp (*Observer*) admired the 'exquisite' detail of such moments as that achieved with one of the production's many sound effects when 'young couples, intent on badinage, follow the flight of an unseen bee as if tracing the line of their wit', but felt that the 'visual lushness ... swaddle[d] the complications of the dialogue'.[35]

The 'complications of the dialogue' that exercised the minds of many of the reviewers were, as is usual with this play, of two kinds: the wordplay and pedantry of Nathaniel and Holofernes, and the sophistication of the lovers' dialogue. Michael Coveney thought that the sonnets composed by the king's companions were 'sung first in Elgarian pastiche, then like something jauntier out of *Me and my Girl*'.[36] Nevertheless,

Nunn elicited a subtler psychological quality from the wooing games, centred on Joseph Fiennes's Berowne, 'full of feeling and of the irony some intelligent people feel about their feelings' and 'a touch of that melancholy that does not know its cause, that people like to cling to'.[37] There was unfinished business to be done here that was not merely the subduing of an overexuberant wit, and Nicholas de Jongh detected an unamiable trait in the character, who had 'the smug self-absorbed manner of a caddish Edwardian homme fatale, too deeply in love with himself to fall for Kate Fleetwood's equally self-admiring Rosaline'.[38] It was a moot point whether this was served or undercut by the portentous opening scene or what some took as the forced jollity of 'The Owl and the Cuckoo', treated as a big musical number

As Nunn's final production as Director, *Love's Labour's Lost* prompted reflections on his term of office. It was his 'last labour of love', according to John Thaxter in *The Stage*, whose review of this 'enchanting production of Shakespeare's most poignant comedy' was headed 'Nunn finds his perfect match'.[39] Most commentators were appreciative of the retiring Director's achievements, although in the *Independent on Sunday* Kate Bassett described the production as 'one helluva lavish, sugary farewell' that was like 'drowning in a vat of condensed milk', but qualified her apparently 'ungrateful' review by noting Nunn's 'splendid' contribution of 'some of his own money' to the theatre.[40] More balanced views included John Gross's observation that this production was 'uneven, but at its best very good indeed – and the same could be said of Nunn's term of office in general'. His achievements had been underrated, but would 'stand out more clearly in retrospect'.[41] Sheridan Morley's *New Statesman* review can stand for similar balance sheets of the theatre under Nunn's direction. It would be remembered for 'its triumphs as well as its disappointments', which of course included productions of plays other than the three by Shakespeare: 'He achieved on the Olivier stage a permanent acting ensemble, only to see it fall away after a season, while his choice of musicals [had] been far more conservative than was originally promised.' Like his predecessors, Peter Hall and Richard Eyre, he had 'not often been able to tempt living playwrights to the forbiddingly vast open spaces of the Olivier, but his work at the Lyttleton and the Cottesloe, as both director and producer, [had] seldom been without courage'.[42]

2003–11: Beyond the National Theatre – a young Hamlet, a modern King Richard II and an ageing Lear

Once again the critics' construction of a *Bildungsroman* with Nunn as the hero – he would never be as much of an anti-hero as Peter Hall – had influenced the reception of his productions, this time informed by the various storms and stresses of the NT's internal politics and external relations. Only *The Merchant of Venice* was free from the critical attitude that insisted that a director (or Director) of Nunn's standing was not so much 'only as good as his last show' but rather 'only as good as one he had directed years ago'. This, though, was among the productions by which he was recognized as having a claim to have changed the way the play was thought about. Like *Troilus and Cressida* and *Love's Labour Lost*, several of the Shakespeare productions he has directed since leaving the NT have been of plays he had not undertaken at the RSC: *Richard II*, *The Tempest*, the early histories in the RSC's 1964 *Wars of the Roses* adaptation, *A Midsummer Night's Dream* and *Pericles*. He has also returned to texts with which he has a longstanding relationship: *Hamlet* (2004) and *King Lear* (2007). Rather than survey all Nunn's post-NT productions, this chapter focuses on two in which he revisited plays from earlier in his career, and a third representing the 'unexplored' territory. While *Hamlet* at the Old Vic was a radically new approach to a text he had directed only once, in 1970, his *Lear* for the RSC was his third encounter with the play as a professional director. In the case of *Richard II*, produced at the Old Vic in 2005 in the second season of Kevin Spacey's artistic directorship and with the American actor as the king, Nunn was taking on a play that, like *Troilus and Cressida*, had been directed in a memorable production at the RSC by John Barton. For *Hamlet* and *Richard II* Nunn turned again to the modern-dress contemporaneity he had experimented with in *Timon of Athens* at the Young Vic.

The tragedy revisited his understanding of the play, expressed in his 1970 RSC production, as a family drama, this time in explicitly contemporary terms. The casting of Ben Whishaw (age 23) as Hamlet and Samantha Whittaker (19) as Ophelia placed the generation gap at the centre of the play, with Gertrude who, in Imogen Stubbs's own description, was 'living in a fantasy, a fantasy of being young forever, ... pretending you can be sexy and a mother at once', and who 'cherished a celebrity-magazine idea of glamour around herself, trying to inhabit a world in which all was smiles, everyone loved her and everyone around her was another perfect accessory to her perfect life – whereas in reality she herself had been the accessory all along'.[43] Her feelings towards Hamlet were those of a woman who wanted him to still be a child. Stubbs describes the way she and Nunn constructed the character and her relationship with her world. In the first 'court' scene she clearly relished her role as a wife who had secured a trophy and was besotted with him. After she and Claudius had kissed on 'taken to wife' (1.2.13) she made 'a rather kittenishly abashed play' of wiping the lipstick from his face, and she made sure that as they exited she gave the press a perfect photo-opportunity by 'smiling back at them over her shoulder' and holding the pose long enough for the cameras.[44] She tried to treat Ophelia as 'a "let's-go-shopping-together" protégée' and showed her wedding ring to her when she said that she hoped the girl's 'beauties' might be the cause of Hamlet's wayward behaviour (3.1.38–44). As the play progressed she took more and more shocks to her self-confidence and gradually 'diminished': 'Trevor had a very cunning idea for suggesting that', so that in her first scene she wore four-inch heels, but 'over the course of the action the heels got progressively lower, so that [she] looked more and more dwarfed by Claudius (Tom Mannion), more and more dependent on him, and more and more little-girlish, until by the last scene [she] was in flat shoes'.[45] She also took to drink, fortifying herself during the play scene, sitting with a bottle in front of her before Ophelia's entrance in her 'mad scene' and 'having another stiff drink in the closet scene'. It was hardly surprising that she should drink down the poison in one go despite Claudius's warning – 'Gertrude, do not drink!' – during the fencing match.

In their first appearance as a royal family, his mother and stepfather held their first joint press-conference in their sharply tailored white suits, Hamlet, his woolly hat pulled down over his ears, slouched like 'a skinny gap-year layabout in angry black combat fatigues'.[46] He was 'intensely distressed, hardly able to speak his first soliloquy for sobbing', and Kate Bassett interpreted him as 'verging on a nervous breakdown, neurotically twisting his hands and shuffling like an old tramp, derelict before his time'. But there were 'glimpses of his younger undamaged self' when he flung his arms round his old college friends and, in the closet scene, 'momentarily curl[ed] up in his mother's lap'.[47] In Hall's 1965 production, David Warner, with whose performance some reviewers compared that of Whishaw, had been very credible at the age of twenty-four as a representative of youth rebelling not just to itself but to whatever was on offer. His articulacy and clarity of speech suggested that the intellectual climate of Wittenberg was having its effect. In Nunn's 1970 Stratford production, the anguished and, later, antic disposition of Alan Howard, aged 33 at the time, resulted from the effects of grief on an already mature man. When the 'skinny' Whishaw, as comically unlike to Hercules as any Hamlet, hugged himself or gnawed at his nails and spat out the pieces, his rejection of the world was more immediately recognized as that of an immature but alarmingly articulate 'stroppy teenager'. As the reviewers reach for terms to identify him, the modern immediacy of the performance becomes apparent. John Nathan in the *Jewish Chronicle* identified 'the archetypal, misunderstood, tragic teenager, without whom no dysfunctional family would be complete'.[48] Alastair Macaulay thought his appeal lay in sincerity: 'He speaks with his heart – his whole nervous system – in his mouth, and he moves as if not yet in control of his gangling limbs.'[49] The expression of almost inarticulate feeling seemed to be wrenched from him, so that at times his nose ran even as he spoke. 'To be or not to be', transposed to its earlier position in the first quarto to and made into a scene on its own, was spoken as he sat on a bench holding a bottle of water and a handful of pills, and the murder of Polonius was 'an act convincingly born out of teenage rage'[50]. Michael Dobson, conspicuously resistant to Whishaw's performance, thought that his delivery of 'To be or not to be' simply 'reduced the speech's philosophical content to a mere whining personal complaint about what a miserable time Hamlet was having and how unfair it all was'.[51]

Modern dress helped to 'clarify' character, wrote Michael Billington in the *Guardian*, so that Ophelia became 'a gauche gymslip schoolgirl with a fatally not-particularly interested Hamlet', but in his emphasis on the family Nunn had failed to address the political significance looked for by commentators since at least the 1960s – and Jan Kott's essay on it in *Shakespeare Our Contemporary*. There was little sense, Billington reflected, 'that Elsinore is a deeply corrupt tyranny poisoned by usurpation'.[52] New scenes had been added, including Hamlet 'silently observed in Ophelia's bedroom ... and Claudius later seen beating up Hamlet' in what had become 'an everyday story of murder, madness and retribution in a modern royal family'.[53] In another interpolation, Ophelia was discovered dancing alone in her bedroom to music reviewers identified as that of the New York rock band The Strokes, played full-blast. This was the most determined bid for engagement with youth culture that Nunn had made since the 1969 *Winter's Tale*, and in a moment of social reportage rare in theatre reviewing, in the *Daily Telegraph* Sarah Sands reported evidence that news of it had filtered through to its target audience. As she 'peered short-sightedly at the wine list', feeling that she might be 'the oldest person in the theatre', she noticed that 'an exuberant herd of teenagers in low-slung trousers and cropped T-shirts moved into the foyer'. In an age of anxiety about audience demographics her description of how they brought their 'generational idiosyncracies' into the theatre is worth quoting in full:

> They drank water from bottles rather than crackling cough sweet wrappers. They checked the time on distractingly luminous mobile phones. They rolled their tickets up into joints.

The allegation about the use of the tickets in a public place should perhaps be treated with scepticism, but the report of responses during the performance carries more conviction:

> They laughed at shouting or bloodshed, they nudged each other during recognizable A-level text passages. When Hamlet records his stepfather's behaviour in his notebook, my youthful neighbor whispered to his friend 'What's he doing? Why is he writing stuff down? Strange boy.'[54]

Sands's report has an element of bemused condescension, as she ponders whether 'written comprehension may be a neglected module', and she finds the production, with its 'curious lapses into populism', unsatisfying and 'strangely, unmovingly reductive'. Other reviewers, setting aside their more mature sensibilities, acknowledged that the Nunn and the Old Vic had offered a version of the play designed, as the weekly listings magazine *What's On* put it, 'to get the kids away from their computer screens and into stage Shakespeare'.[55]

Richard II began with the royal regalia displayed in a perspex case at the centre of the stage in a cross-shaped pattern of light. Richard entered wearing 'a purple jacket with gold trim, white knee breeches and white stockings'. White-gloved officals removed the crown, orb and sceptre from the case, and two women helped him into a coronation robe, holding up a mirror for him to adjust the crown on his head. Handel's 'Zadok the Priest' grew to a climax as Richard, followed by a crucifer, processed diagonally across the stage between rows of peers in their ceremonial robes. The scene quickly shifted to a parliament-like setting in which the robes were removed to reveal formal business suits and the barons opposed each other across the floor of the house. There were now video screens showing crowds waving Union Jacks, and footage from the 1953 coronation.[56] Later the screens would show scenes of civil conflict and motorcades as well as 'live' reporting of the goings-on in government.

Stage business denoting the production's here-and-nowness was inventive and comprehensive: John of Gaunt (Julian Glover) delivered his 'This England' speech as a televised party political broadcast, clips of which recurred in subsequent scenes; Richard was in a private club relaxing with friends when news of Gaunt's death was received via text-message, and he learned of the troubles in Ireland from a copy of the *Daily Telegraph* (the gardener's paper of choice was the *Sun*); the queen received news of the rebellion during a fashion photo-shoot; Bolingbroke (Ben Miles) led his rebellious army in body armour; and the Duchess of York arrived at court in a motorcycle helmet to plead for her son's life. According to taste, this was either 'a bombastic grey suits production that makes a fetish of its modernism', or one in which 'in Nunn-style, every crook and crevice in the action is filled with revealing detail and whispers'.[57]

Although tournaments, trial by combat and any meaningful invocation of medieval ideas of kingship were not on the production's agenda, the presentation of the symbols of the monarchy was as almost as insistent as it had been in John Barton's 1973 production, with a similar use of symmetrical business. 'Among the recurrent gestures', wrote Patricia Tatspaugh in *Shakespeare Quarterly*, 'were the care with which

Richard placed the crown on his head and his contemplation of the "hollow crown"' (3.2.160), so that the mirror was seen again in the abdication (4.1) and the image of the cross reappeared in the prison scene. At the conclusion of the play 'Richard's coffin was brought on, Henry and the court entered in long black coats, and Aumerle gave Henry the crown, which he placed on the black casket. Light closed on the crown.'[58] Michael Dobson reflected that although this *Richard II* 'looked as though it ought to be a play about contemporary politics', the cast, 'apart from the monarch, all resembled Tory grandees, and even the Conservative Party is no longer controlled or even fronted by Tory grandees'.[59] There were moments, however, when the use of the paraphernalia of modern public life chimed with an important thematic aspect of the play: Benedict Nightingale noticed that 'with characters sometimes changing tone and tune before the cameras' the media opportunities emphasized 'one of the play's points, that there is a big difference between public statement and private feeling'.[60]

At the centre of the production was Spacey's Richard, far removed from any of the feyness or clichéd self-indulgence often associated with the role, but insecure under a desperate performance of authority. Nunn's programme note included what Quentin Letts in the *Daily Mail* testily called 'sixth form clichés about how *Richard II* plugs in to today's "republican debate"'.[61] Few of the reviewers discerned any reflection on current representatives of the House of Windsor: a notable exception was Jane Edwardes in *Time Out London*, who found Spacey's king 'very much a Windsor, who loves the glory but not the responsibility of ruling'.[62] Unlike Nicholas Hytner's recent *Henry V* at the NT, this was a production in which the element of contemporary setting did not directly address the specifics of policy and governance in modern Britain. The focus was more generally on the exercise of power and the personal psychology of those who possessed or assumed it. Michael Billington described the Richard of the first acts as 'a man who combines the empurpled trappings of power with a self-delighting irony', but who reaches a degree of desolation in the final scenes: 'Used to the comfortable accoutrements of power, he seems sadly empty and desolate without them. And when he says "I have no name," you realize that this is a Richard who has no real identity when divorced from office.'[63] Benedict Nightingale observed that Spacey 'gives us the pain and sometimes the rage of that discovery', and Kate Bassett observed that in the opening sequence Richard was 'caught in a kind of royal time warp' as he stepped slowly to the front of the stage and gazed ahead while he was robed: 'Nunn's brilliant stroke [was] then to have this monarch turn his hands outwards, confidently expecting orb and scepter.'[64] Whether actor or director was the source of this brilliance is not in question here: Nunn's direction accommodated, or rather, fostered, attention to such moments of psychologically convincing personal behaviour. Symbolism and realism complemented each other. In the abdication scene Richard was 'teasingly and stubbornly unreadable', heading straight for the throne when he entered until a servant restrained him, he was 'deliberately rather than petulantly making a scene' and, as Dobson noted, 'Just when Bolingbroke finally thought that the worst of this irregular spectacle was over, Richard took the crown back, and to general dismay insisted on ascending the dais and crowning himself, to stunned silence, before at last renouncing the throne at "Now mark me how I will undo myself"' (4.1.193ff.).[65]

Nunn's 2007 production of *King Lear* opened at The Courtyard Theatre, the temporary Stratford home for the RSC between 2006 and 2010 during the demolition and rebuilding of the 1932 theatre. This was like a larger, less intimate version of the Swan. With its thrust stage, enfolded by galleries and raked stalls seating, it might have seemed like the kind of space that Nunn had been striving to achieve since the 1960s, although Ian McKellen, who played Lear, has suggested that 'Trevor didn't like it, and used our production to try and convince the authorities not to take it as a blueprint for the new permanent theatre'.[66] Paradoxically, Christopher Oram's set represented a 'traditional' theatrical auditorium, with gilded boxes and crimson hangings, that curved away at an angle behind the platform on which the main action took place, a 'great stage of fools' that the audience viewed, as it were, from backstage: arguably, the design came into its own in venues such as the Harvey in Brooklyn, a reconditioned former cinema built in 1904, where the preserved and artfully distressed proscenium-arch theatre mirrored the onstage image (Figure 7). The set disintegrated in the course of the play, with the destruction of the regal world that Lear's actions had reduced to civil war: pieces of the upstage ceiling fell in, the chandelier was shattered and the hangings were pulled down. In the scenes on the heath 'real' rain fell, and the hovel was lowered – somewhat awkwardly – from the flies.

Michael Dobson describes this as progressive 'desecration', appropriately enough as the play began with a mimed scene in which Lear entered in priestly robes and mitre, every inch an Orthodox patriarch, and blessed the kneeling courtiers with a grand, sacerdotal gesture that evidently came naturally to

FIGURE 7 King Lear *(Courtyard Theatre, 2007), 1.1: Cordelia (Romola Garai) speaks her mind. Photo by Manuel Harlan* © *RSC.*

him.[67] McKellen explains that this might be 'a daily event, in which he dressed as an archbishop, so to speak, to give his blessing'. He left the stage and the court relaxed, but the opening conversation between Gloucester, Kent and Edmund was interrupted by the sudden return of the king, which sent everyone back to their appointed places. Now in his crimson, gold-braided Tsarist military uniform with a small crown instead of a mitre, Lear seemed almost frail as he seated himself behind his large desk, obviously relishing in anticipation the chief item on the day's agenda. His speech was read from a set of filing cards, and a lectern had been set in place from which the daughters would make their declarations of love. But even in the normal run of business 'he [could] always call on this raised hand of blessing or banishment. Wonderful power'. Power of a less sanctified kind came into play when he punched Kent in the stomach with 'O vassal! Miscreant!' (1.1.160), which McKellen identifies as childish petulance: 'he clearly behaves inappropriately and takes advantage of the fact that he's king, and strikes people or shouts at them'.[68]

Cordelia (Romola Garai) was astonished and amused by the responses of her sisters to the test, taking the whole matter as some sort of game, and even laughing out loud until the moment when it became obvious that Lear's anger was earnest. Two cushions were placed downstage as if for a wedding or at least betrothal and her suitors were to kneel to receive the king's blessing, but instead Lear took them by the hand as they entered and asked Burgundy what dowry he would take 'in a soothing, unctuous voice, as if about to bless their union'. He then 'sneeringly' revealed his real attitude to Burgundy 'when, on the words "with our displeasure pieces / And nothing more [1.1.198–9]," ' he 'drop[ped] their hands, snatch[ed] up the crown where his anxious and awkward sons-in-law [had] placed it on the desk, and shout[ed] the word "nothing" through it, parroting the offending term back at Cordelia once again'.[69] Dobson's description conveys the manner in which a sense of being on display, enjoying his anger and his inventiveness in showing it, underlay Lear's ferocity. It was, in effect, a tantrum on a grand, kingdom-shattering scale. Charles Spencer found 'vulnerability behind the furious despotism', tracing this strain through his relationship with 'Sylvester McCoy's delightful, spoon-playing fool', to the scene of reconciliation with Cordelia, which had 'a gentleness that will move all but the hardest hearts'.[70] Lear's gestures struck John Peter as 'those of insecure old men who think they can command both obedience and pity'.[71] Michael Billington was struck by Lear's 'curiosity', that of 'a man who is always asking questions', so that 'by the end, you feel that this is a Lear who has somehow undergone a rigorous moral education'.[72] Benedict Nightingale in *The Times* identified 'a growing sense of the complexity of the humiliated, angry man who has always repressed the feelings that might tell him who he is'. When Lear said 'But I'll not weep', he 'promptly [did] so' – a moment that McKellen records as one of Nunn's suggestions: 'Trevor was very keen on that. He said: say you're not going to do it and then do it.'[73]

In the storm scene Lear stripped down to below the waist at 'Off, off you lendings!' (3.4.101–3), to the alarm of the Fool who solicitously pulled his master's trousers up once the image had made its effect. (The moment lent itself to much more-or-less inventive comment from the reviewers.) McCoy's Fool, too 'full of songs' for the taste of some reviewers, wore motley that resembled that of an old-time music-hall comedian, and carried a stick with a little model of his own head on the end of it: Lear had acquired this during the hovel scene and carried it when he reappeared in the field near Dover. (In 1976 Donald Sinden had appropriated the broken tambourine and motley coat-facings of Michael Williams's Fool.) This was a reminder of a companion who had been hanged at the end of the first part of the play and whose functions Lear had now effectively taken over in his conversation with Gloucester. (Consequently, in the final scene 'And my poor fool is hanged' [281] now referred unequivocally to him rather than to Cordelia.) Lear's catastrophic failure to achieve emotional maturity, revealed in the first acts of the play, had now been modified by the tenderness of his relationship with the Fool and his understanding of the plight of 'poor naked wretches', and his reconciliation with Cordelia in 4.6 was the culmination of the journey. Susannah Clapp thought that, in the final scene, Lear's 'Never, never, never, never, never' was delivered 'with a growing recognition that there is really no hope, no second life'.[74] Nevertheless, McKellen insists that Lear simply 'defines death in poetry, and feels it'. He has 'lived life to the full, comes to terms with events and develops understanding'. Jan Kott's 'idea of bleakness' is misguided: it 'suggests painting a colour on the play which disguises its essential subtleties and complications'.[75]

Once again, the director's love of explanatory details was remarked on. Some were more ingenious than illuminating. In the 'hovel' scene (which included the mock trial from the quarto text), to illustrate the line 'To have a thousand with red burning spits / Come hizzing in upon 'em' (3.6.15–16) Lear wielded a red-hot poker that had been used to heat the contents of the three goblets of wine. (Business that consequently required ingenious props: a glowing stove and a poker that would glow.) Others, such as Lear's play with his cue cards, were deftly expressive of character and 'told the story', or had the familiar effect of tying up loose ends that might well be left unknotted in a production less firmly grounded in naturalism. One such was Regan's addiction to alcohol, evident from the dialogue with Goneril that ends the first scene, fuelling her savagery in the blinding of Gloucester and culminating in the opportunity it gave her sister for the poisoning in the final act. This entailed the Doctor being brought on as a prisoner of war and obliged to leave his medicine chest behind on stage: Goneril sat on it, and surreptitiously purloined a small bottle with which she was then seen to spike Regan's celebratory champagne. This clarified by anticipation Goneril's 'If not, I'll ne'er trust medicine' in response to her sister's 'Sick, O, sick!' (5.3.96–7). Was this subtlety or literalism? Michael Dobson thought Nunn had achieved 'one of the most elaborately explained productions' of the play he had ever seen, 'not only in terms of psychological motivation but in terms of logistics'.[76]

Conclusion

Responses to Nunn's third *King Lear* ran the gamut from admiration to grudging acceptance, with many reviewers expressing their annoyance that because of a leg injury to Frances Barber it had been withheld from the press for nine weeks after its scheduled opening. It was variously described as 'a very ordinary production' in which Nunn steered the play 'away from kingship and epic folly into the lower depths of domestic drama' (Ned Norman, *Daily Express*); 'a high-calibre return for this director to the company he ran for almost two decades' (Kate Bassett, *Independent on Sunday*); 'one of the most lucid, powerful and moving productions of this great tragedy I have ever seen' (Charles Spencer, *Daily Telegraph*); and 'gaudily emphatic' (Nicholas de Jongh, *Evening Standard*).[1] In their reflections on Nunn's career and directorial predilections, some of the reviews seemed to be writing as though (to yield to the temptation of quotation) a particular wheel had come full circle. Dobson, noting that this was the final element of the RSC's 'Complete Works Festival' – indeed, its 'promised end' – wondered whether this typical 'Perfectly Composed Production' was concluding the year-long event with 'a gratifying reunion of the RSC of the 1970s rather than a vision of the company's future'.[2] In one sense an epoch in the RSC's history had been characterized by a production that exemplified once again a finely coordinated interpretive – indeed, thematic – approach and engagement with psychologically revealing detail mined from the text.

In 1968 Simon Trussler had prophesied that the strength of the newly-appointed Director of the RSC would 'probably lie less in the overt power he wields than in the potency of his work and the gradual exertion of his influence, for the personality which filter[ed] through his productions seem[ed] philosophical rather than flamboyant'.[3] During his time at the RSC, Nunn redefined approaches to a number of plays, with productions acclaimed by critics and colleagues alike. Peter Hall described his 1976 *Macbeth* as 'magnificent, refreshing, invigorating, utterly clear and original: also the only *Macbeth* I've seen which works', and Michael Blakemore in *Stage Blood* declares it 'ground-breaking', a production that 'changed the course of Shakespeare in performance towards pared-down productions in intimate spaces'. Peter Holland identified the 1981 *All's Well That Ends Well* as 'one of the finest Shakespeare productions of the century', and similar accolades have been awarded to Nunn's *Othello* and 1969 *Winter's Tale*. Martin White, in a collection of essays on 'Director's Theatre', acclaims him as 'incomparable in his ability to present a complex weave of stories on stage and to reveal the bigger picture while (by?) focusing on the smallest detail'.[4]

Nunn's best work at the RSC and elsewhere has achieved a balance between the two strains, contributing to the development of approaches to the plays that facilitated innovation and asserted the seriousness that co-exists with playfulness in theatre, with a degree of the commitment to ethical significance he learned (literally) at the feet of Leavis. In the rehearsal room, Nunn has fulfilled the essential duties of a director as defined by Peter Hall: 'to suggest and provoke and be a mirror for the actor and finally an editor'.[5] Actors have welcomed his responsiveness to their own work and the invariable presence of ideas, as distinct from 'high concept' direction and design, and the experience of a production growing out of their own expertise and emotional engagement as well those of the director. In the context of this book – and of this series – he may appear as an *auteur*, a lone creative artist, but he has also been a notable collaborator with designers, composers and directors – in particular with the director John Caird, with whom several of his larger projects have been conceived and carried through. Although reservations about Nunn's approach to directing Shakespeare have been expressed in many of the reviews that have been cited, paradoxically, the complaints as well as the encomiums speak both to his personal standing as an artist and, more generally, to debates – sometimes heated – in the British theatre of the last sixty years, and to its contentious vitality.

Appendix: Shakespeare productions directed or co-directed by Trevor Nunn

In addition to the Shakespeare productions listed below, Nunn's prolific career has included many productions of work by other authors. A summary of these appears at the end of the list.

Abbreviations

RST	Royal Shakespeare Theatre, Statford-upon-Avon
TOP	The Other Place, Stratford-upon Avon
Aldwych	Aldwych Theatre, London
Warehouse	Warehouse, London
TFANA	Theatre for a New Audience, New York
Tfr.	transfer

Year	Title	Venue or company
1967	*The Taming of the Shrew*	RST
1968	*King Lear*	RST
	Much Ado About Nothing	RST
1969	*Winter's Tale*	RST
	Henry VIII	RST

1970	*Winter's Tale*	Aldwych (Tfr.)
	Henry VIII	Aldwych (Tfr.)
	Hamlet	RST
1972	*Coriolanus*	RST
	Julius Caesar	RST
	Antony and Cleopatra	RST
	Titus Andronicus	RST
1973	*Coriolanus*	Aldwych (Tfr.)
	Julius Caesar	Aldwych (Tfr.)
	Antony and Cleopatra	Aldwych (Tfr.)
	Titus Andronicus	Aldwych (Tfr.)
1974	*Macbeth*	RST
	Antony and Cleopatra	TV version
1975	*Macbeth*	Aldwych (Tfr.)
1976	*Romeo and Juliet*	RST
	Macbeth	TOP
	The Comedy of Errors	RST
	King Lear	RST
1977	*Macbeth*	RST, then Warehouse
	Romeo and Juliet	Aldwych (Tfr.)
	Comedy of Errors	Aldwych (Tfr.)
	King Lear	Aldwych (Tfr.)
	As You Like It	RST
1978	*As You Like It*	Aldwych (Tfr.)
	Macbeth	TV version
	Comedy of Errors	TV version
1979	*As You Like It*	Aldwych (Tfr.)
	Merry Wives of Windsor	RST
1981	*All's Well that Ends Well*	RST

1982	*Henry IV, Parts 1 and 2*	Barbican, London
	All's Well that Ends Well	Barbican, London (Tfr.)
1989	*Othello*	TOP
	Othello	Young Vic, London (Tfr.)
1990	*Othello*	TV version
1991	*Timon of Athens*	Young Vic, London
	Measure for Measure	TOP (new theatre)
1996	*Twelfth Night*	Film
1999	*Troilus and Cressida*	NT, Olivier Theatre
	Merchant of Venice	NT, Cottesloe Theatre
2003	*Love's Labours Lost*	NT, Olivier Theatre
2004	*Hamlet*	Old Vic, London
2005	*Richard II*	Old Vic, London
2007	*King Lear*	Courtyard, Stratford
	King Lear	New London (Tfr.)
2011	*The Tempest*	Haymarket, London
2015	*The Wars of the Roses*	Rose Theatre, Kingston
2016	*Pericles*	TFANA, New York
	Midsummer Night's Dream	New Wolsey, Ipswich

Nunn's major non-Shakespearean productions for RSC have included *The Revenger's Tragedy* (Middleton, attributed to Cyril Tourneur: 1966), Vanbrugh's *The Relapse* (1968), Ibsen's Hedda Gabler (1974), Jonson's *The Alchemist* (1977), Chekhov's *Three Sisters* (1979), Kaufman and Hart's *Once in a Lifetime* (1979), O'Casey's *Juno and Paycock* (1980), Heywood's *The Fair Maid of the West* (1986), Chekhov's *The Seagull* (as a freelance: 2007) and Jonson's *Volpone* (2015), as well as *Nicholas Nickleby* (Aldwych, 1978), an adaptation of *Peter Pan* (Barbican, 1982) and *Les Misérables* (1985). For commercial managements, in addition to *Cats* (1981), he directed *Starlight Express* (1984), *Chess* (1986), *Aspects of Love* (1989), *The Baker's Wife* (1989) and *Sunset Boulevard* (1993).

Before becoming Artistic Director he had directed Stoppard's *Arcadia* (1993) for the NT. During his tenure, in addition to his three Shakespeare productions, he directed McGuiness's *Mutabilite* (1997), Pinter's *Betrayal* (1998), Gorky's *Summerfolk* (1999), Edgar's *Albert Speer* (2000), Chekhov's *The Cherry Orchard* (2000), Vanbrugh's *The Relapse* (2001), Stoppard's trilogy *The Coast of Utopia* (2002) and Williams's *A Streetcar Named Desire* (2002). There were four musicals for the NT: Rodgers and Hammerstein's *Oklahoma!* (1998), Lerner and Loewe's *My Fair Lady* (2001), Rodgers and Hammerstein's *South Pacific* (2001) and Cole Porter's *Anything Goes* (2002).

His non-Shakespearean work since 2003 has included plays by Ayckbourn, Rattigan and Stoppard as well as more musicals: *The Woman in White* (2004), *Acorn Antiques: The Musical!* (2005), the 'musical' version of *Porgy and Bess* (2006), *Gone with the Wind* (2008), *A Little Night Music* (2009) and *Aspects of Love* (2010).

NOTES

Introduction

1 Andrew Dickson, 'A Life in the Theatre: Trevor Nunn', *Guardian*, 18 November 2011.
2 Donald Bain, 'Midlands Miracle', *The Stage*, 11 April 1963.
3 Robert Cushman, *Observer*, 15 May 1977.
4 R. A. Foakes, ed., *The Revenger's Tragedy* (Manchester: Manchester University Press, 1996), 1.1.1–2. (In this edition, Foakes revises his 1966 Revels Plays edition and adopts the new attribution of the play to Thomas Middleton and Cyril Tourneur.)
5 Ibid., 1.1.14–16.
6 *Music by Guy Woolfenden for the Royal Shakespeare Company*. Abbey Records LPB 657 (Cambridge: Abbey Records, 1969).
7 Mark Amory, 'Emperor Trev', *Sunday Times Colour Magazine*, 19 September 1978, 32–6 (34).
8 *The Stage*, 13 October 1966.
9 Ronald Bryden, *Observer*, 30 November 1969.
10 For an account of the rewriting, together with transcripts of the added lines, see Stanley Wells, '*The Revenger's Tragedy* Revived', in *The Elizabethan Theatre VI*, ed. G. R. Hibbard (Toronto: MacMillan and the University of Waterloo, 1975), 105–33.
11 Stanley Wells, 'Shakespeare Production in England in 1989', *Shakespeare Survey* 43 (Cambridge: Cambridge University Press 1990): 183–204 (192).
12 Colin Chambers, *Inside the Royal Shakespeare Company: Creativity and the Institution* (London: Routledge, 2004), 70.
13 The subtitle of Hall's published diaries, edited by John Goodwin, reflects this aspect of his time at the NT: *Peter Hall's Diaries: The Story of a Dramatic Battle* (London: Hamish Hamilton, 1983).

14 Sally Beauman, *The Royal Shakespeare Company: A History of Ten Decades* (Oxford: Oxford University Press, 1982), 294.

15 Financial details in Beauman, *The Royal Shakespeare Company*, 293. Chambers, *Inside the Royal Shakespeare Company*, 59, identifies the situation as near bankruptcy, as does Nunn himself in his 'Afterword' to David Addenbrooke's *The Royal Shakespeare Company: The Peter Hall Years* (London: William Kimber, 1974), 181.

16 Programme for *Hamlet*, directed by Peter Hall, Royal Shakespeare Theatre 1966 (unnumbered pages). The same manifesto was printed in the *Revenger's Tragedy* programme, and versions of it appeared, with variations, for several seasons.

17 Addenbrooke, *The Royal Shakespeare Company*, 182.

18 Daniel Rosenthal, *The National Theatre Story* (London: Oberon Books, 2013), 662.

19 Peter Brook, 'Oh For Empty Seats!' (from *Encore*, January 1959), in *Encore Reader: A Chronicle of the New Drama*, ed. Charles Marowitz, Tom Milne and Owen Hale (London: Methuen, 1965), 69–74 (71).

20 David Selbourne, *The Making of* A Midsummer Night's Dream: *An Eye-witness Account of Peter Brook's Production from First Rehearsal to First Night* (London: Methuen, 1982), 231.

21 Peter Ansorge, 'Review of *A Midsummer Night's Dream* at the Aldwych', *Plays and Players*, Vol. 18, no. 11 (August 1971): 47.

22 John Heilpern, 'Directing Plays? It's Like Juggling', *Observer*, 4 February 1968.

23 Chambers, *Inside the Royal Shakespeare Company*, 48.

24 Clare Colvin, 'Hands to the Fore', *Drama: The Quarterly Theatre Review*, no. 164 (1987): 9–11 (10).

25 On the effect of a *Sunday Times* 'Insight' team report in 1986 attacking both Nunn and Hall for profiting excessively from transfers of RSC and NT productions, see Rosenthal, *The National Theatre Story*, 402–3 and Stephen Fay, *Power Play: The Life and Times of Peter Hall* (London: Hodder and Stoughton, 1995), 310–16.

26 William Gaskill, *A Sense of Direction* (London: Faber and Faber, 1988), 55.

27 Claire Cochrane, *Twentieth-Century British Theatre: Industry, Art and Empire* (Cambridge: Cambridge University Press, 2011), 173.
28 Catherine Itzin, *Stages in the Revolution: Political Theatre in Britain Since 1968* (London: Methuen, 1980), 7.
29 Mathew Morrison provides a succinct discussion in his 'note on terminology', in *The Soho Theatre, 1968–1981* (London: Society for Theatre Research, 2017), xv–xvi.
30 Roland Rees, *Fringe First: Pioneers of the Fringe on Record* (London: Oberon Books, 1992), 19.
31 Ibid., 9.
32 Charles Marowitz, *Burning Bridges: A Souvenir of the Swinging Sixties and Beyond* (London: Hodder and Stoughton, 1991), 236 (letter to Tynan).
33 Beauman, *The Royal Shakespeare Company*, 312.
34 Colin Chambers, *Other Spaces: New Theatre and the RSC* (London: Eyre Methuen and Theatre Quarterly Publications, 1980), 71.
35 Ibid., 19.
36 Graham Saunders, ed., *British Theatre Companies 1980–1994* (London: Bloomsbury Methuen Drama, 2015), 67.
37 Coveney, *The Citz. 21 Years of the Glasgow Citizens Company* (London: Nick Hern Books, 1990), 118.
38 Michael Bogadnov and Michael Pennington, *The English Shakespeare Company: The Story of 'The Wars of the Roses', 1986–1989* (London: Nick Hern Books, 1990), 19.
39 Michael Bogdanov, 'End Piece', *ESC News, Final Issue* (March 1999).
40 Irving Wardle, *The Times*, 19 October 1968.
41 Harriet Walter, *Other People's Shoes: Thoughts on Acting*, 2nd edn (London: Nick Hern Books, 2003), 95.
42 Addenbrooke, *The Royal Shakespeare Company*, 182.
43 Quoted by Rosenthal, *The National Theatre Story*, 596.
44 'All for Nunn' ('Atticus' column), *Sunday Times*, 20 August 1967.
45 'Young Man Looks at "The Shrew"', *The Times*, 1 April 1967.
46 John Goodwin, ed., *Peter Hall Diaries: The Story of a Dramatic Battle* (London: Hamish Hamilton, 1983), 347.

47 'Young Man Looks at "The Shrew"'.
48 Michael Bateman, 'Atticus', *Sunday Times*, 26 March 1971. Similar references to sitting at Leavis's feet, appear in 'Profile by Joan Bakewell: Trevor Nunn', *Illustrated London News*, 1 September 1977, 44–5 and Mark Amory's 1978 *Sunday Times* article, 'Emperor Trev' (see note 4 above). Nunn told Bakewell that it was necessary to sit literally at Leavis's feet because 'he didn't have any chairs and we sat on the rush matting'.
49 Trevor Nunn, 'Looking Back, Looking Forward', in *Summerfolk: Essays Celebrating Shakespeare and the Stratford Theatres*, ed. Stanley Wells (Ebrington: Long Barn Books, 1997), 131.
50 Ronald Hayman, *Leavis* (London: Heinemann, 1976), 20.
51 Ibid., x–xi.
52 Bakewell, 'Trevor Nunn', 44.
53 David Ellis, *Memoirs of a Leavisite: The Decline and Fall of Cambridge English* (Liverpool: Liverpool University Press, 2013), 12.
54 Peter Hall, 'interview' in *Talking Theatre: Interviews with Theatre People*, ed. Richard Eyre (London: Nick Hern Books, 2011), 43.
55 Michael Coveney, 'Talk Theatre', *Observer*, 28 June 1992.
56 Michael Cordner, 'George Rylands and University Shakespeare', in *Shakespeare on the University Stage*, ed. Andrew James Hartley (Cambridge: Cambridge University Press, 2015), 43–59 (58).
57 Simon Trussler, *'The Greatest Whore of Them All.* Peter Hall at Stratford, 1960–1968', *The Drama Review: TDR*, Vol. 13, no. 2 (Winter 1968): 169–74 (171).
58 Addenbrooke, *The Royal Shakespeare Company*, 227.
59 'Young Man Looks at "The Shrew"', *The Times*, 1 April 1967.
60 Jim Hiley, 'A Company with Direction: Jim Hiley on the Exuberance and Achievement of the RSC today', *Plays and Players*, Vol. 25, no. 1 (October, 1979): 14–21 (17, 18).
61 Chambers, *Inside the Royal Shakespeare Company*, 92.
62 Micheline Steinberg, *Flashback: A Pictorial History 1879–1979: One Hundred Years of Stratford-upon-Avon and the Royal Shakespeare Company* (Stratford-upon-Avon: RSC Publications, 1985), 121.

63 Frank Rich, *New York Times*, 4 April 1988.
64 Andrew Dickson, 'A Life in the Theatre: Trevor Nunn', *Guardian*, 18 November 2018.
65 Chambers, *Inside the Royal Shakespeare Company*, 76.
66 Rosenthal, *The National Theatre Story*, 170–1 (on the planned 1970–1 *Guys and Dolls*) and 549–55 (on 'The House of hit Musicals').
67 Rosenthal, *The National Theatre Story*, 681.
68 Alexis Soloski,'Trevor Nunn, British Shakespeare Master, Tries Something New: Directing Americans', *New York Times*, 22 February 2016.
69 Cicely Berry, *Text in Action* (London: Virgin Publishing, 2001), 36.
70 Andrew Lloyd Webber, *Unmasked: A Memoir* (London: Harper Collins, 2018), 400.
71 Julian Curry, ed., *Shakespeare on Stage: Thirteen Leading Actors on Thirteen Key Roles* (London: Nick Hern Books, 2010), x.
72 Ralph Berry, *On Directing Shakespeare: Interviews with Contemporary Directors* (London: Croom Helm, 1977), 57.

Chapter 1

1 Marian J Pringle, *The Theatres of Stratford-upon-Avon, 1875–1992* (Stratford-upon-Avon: Stratford-upon-Avon Society, 1994), 53–4.
2 Interview in *Flourish* (Spring 1968), n.p.
3 Beauman (*The Royal Shakespeare Company*, 301) suggests that Morley's design, as adapted in the 1969 season, had 'a palpable influence' on Brook's *Dream* the following season.
4 Sheila Bannock, 'The Angry Young Man from Verona', *Stratford-upon-Avon Herald*, 22 April 1967; John Peter, 'Fusion of Comedies', *The Times*, 4 August 1967.
5 Irving Wardle, '*Shrew* Set in Its Full Poetic Context', *The Times*, 6 April 1967.
6 Harold Hobson, 'Triumphs Unforseen', *Sunday Times*, 9 April 1967.

7 Rosemary Say, 'Angry Old Man', *Sunday Telegraph*, 14 April 1968.

8 *King Lear* 1968 programme, n.p.

9 J.C. Trewin, 'King Lear', *Birmingham Post*, 11 April 1968.

10 Herbert Kretzmer, 'Courage Pays Off in Nunn's Great *Lear*', *Daily Express*, 11 April 1968.

11 Harold Hobson, 'Eric Porter's Tumultuous Lear', *Sunday Times*, 14 April 1968.

12 Kretzmer, 'Courage Pays Off in Nunn's Great *Lear*'.

13 Sheila Bannock, 'Spectacle and Imagination are Fused in *King Lear*', *Stratford-upon-Avon Herald*, 19 April 1968.

14 Robert Speaight, 'Shakespeare in Britain', *Shakespeare Quarterly*, Vol. 19, no. 4 (Autumn 1968), 367–75 (368).

15 Philip French, 'Exemplary Lear', *New Statesman*, 19 April, 1968.

16 Speaight, 'Shakespeare in Britain', 369.

17 Irving Wardle, 'Lear of Solid Merit but Less than Sublime', *The Times*, 11 April 1968.

18 *King Lear* 1968 programme, n.p.

19 Ronald Bryden, 'Stratford Revolution', *Observer*, 20 October 1968.

20 Irving Wardle, 'Happy Strokes of Invention', *The Times*, 15 October 1968; Sheila Bannock, '*Much Ado* in a Set Like a Huge Vault', *Stratford-upon-Avon Herald*, 18 October 1968; Harold Hobson, review of *Much Ado*, *Sunday Times*, 20 October 1968.

21 Frank Marcus, 'Everything Turns Up Sunshine', *Sunday Telegraph*, 20 October 1968.

22 Gareth Lloyd Evans, '*Much Ado About Nothing*', *Guardian*, 15 October 1968.

23 Milton Shulman, 'What Nasty Little People Shakespeare Could Dream Up!', *Evening Standard*, 15 October 1968; Irving Wardle, *The Times*, 15 October 1968.

24 Irving Wardle, 'The Stratford Style', *The Times*, 19 October 1968.

25 Bryden, 'Stratford Revolution'.

26 Peter Roberts, 'Avon to Aldwych', *Plays and Players*, Vol. 16, no. 4 (January 1969) 32–4; 71 (34).

27 *Flourish*, Summer 1968.

28 Gareth Lloyd Evans, 'Interpretation or Experience? Shakespeare at Stratford', *Shakespeare Survey*, Vol. 23 (1970) 131–5 (132–3).
29 Harold Hobson, 'Where's the Greatness?' and Trevor Nunn, 'Plays Come Before Stars', *Flourish*, Vol. 2, no. 2 (Spring 1969), n.p.
30 *The Winter's Tale* programme, 1970 (London transfer), n.p.
31 Lytton Strachey, 'Shakespeare's Final Period', *Independent Review*, Vol. 3 (August 1904), 414–15.
32 Benedict Nightingale, 'Leontes Syndrome?', *New Statesman*, 23 May 1969.
33 The lines of this prologue are not included in the promptbook of the production, but are referred to in a cue sheet among the 'Production Records' file: RSC/SM/2/1970/Wint.
34 Herbert Kretzmer, *Daily Express*, 16 May 1969.
35 Philip Hope-Wallace, *Guardian*, 3 July 1970.
36 Patricia Tatspaugh, *Shakespeare at Stratford: The Winter's Tale* (London: Arden Shakespeare/Thomson Learning, 2002), 38–9.
37 Robert Speaight, 'Shakespeare in Britain', *Shakespeare Quarterly*, Vol. 20, no. 4 (Autumn 1969), 435–41 (437).
38 Tatspaugh, *Shakespeare at Stratford*, 69.
39 Six numbers from the production were recorded for an EP (Extended Play) record on the Grosvenor Records label (1970).
40 John Barber, 'Imaginative *Winter's Tale*', *Daily Telegraph*, 17 May 1969.
41 The source of the paragraph by Hall is not given, only its date, 1968.
42 Speaight, 'Shakespeare in Britain', 437.
43 Roy Porter, *Madness. A Brief History* (Oxford: Oxford University Press, 2002), 210–11.
44 Peter Ansorge, 'Director in Interview. Trevor Nunn Talks to Peter Ansorge', *Plays and Players*, Vol. 17, no. 12 (September 1970), 16–17, 21 (21).
45 Ronald Bryden, 'Time, that Conspirator', *Observer*, 18 May 1969.
46 J.W. Lambert, 'The past endures', *Sunday Times*, 18 May 1969.
47 Roger Warren, *Staging Shakespeare's Late Plays* (Oxford: Oxford University Press, 1990), 13.

48 Philip Hope-Wallace, 'Henry VIII', *Guardian*, 11 October 1969.
49 Ronald Bryden, review of 'Henry VIII', *Observer*, 12 October 1969.
50 Benedict Nightingale, 'Forget History', *New Statesman*, 17 October 1969.
51 John Barber, '*Henry VIII* as sombre study of *realpolitik*', *Daily Telegraph*, 18 December 1970.
52 Michael Billington, '*Henry VIII*', *The Times*, 18 December 1970.
53 Barbara Hodgdon, *The End Crowns All. Closure and Contradiction in Shakespeare's History* (Princeton: Princeton University Press, 1991), 233.
54 Ansorge, 'Director in Interview', 17.
55 Peter Thomson, 'A Necessary Theatre: The Royal Shakespeare Season 1970 Reviewed', *Shakespeare Survey*, Vol. 24 (Cambridge: Cambridge University Press, 1971), 117–26 (122).
56 Harold Hobson, 'Hamlet transformed', *Sunday Times*, 7 June 1970.
57 Ronald Bryden, 'Nunn's *Hamlet*: a Report from the Kitchen', *Observer*, 7 June 1970. The specific applicability of Laing's ideas to *Hamlet*, and perhaps to this performance, is evident from the account given by Charles Rycroft in the *Oxford National Dictionary of Biography*, quoting from *The Politics of Experience* (1967): 'when one person comes to be regarded as schizophrenic, it seems to us that *without exception* the experience and behaviour that gets labelled schizophrenic is *a special strategy that a person invents in order to live in an unlivable situation*'. Charles Rycroft, 'Laing, Ronald David (1927–1989)', rev. *Oxford Dictionary of National Biography*, Oxford University Press, 2004; online edn, May 2009 [http://www.oxforddnb.com/view/article/40071, accessed 28 March 2017]: Italics in original.
58 Peter Ansorge, 'A Pride of Hamlets', *Plays and Players*, Vol. 18, no. 5 (February 1971), 16–19 (18).
59 John Barber, 'Alan Howard's frail Hamlet lacks irony', *Daily Telegraph*, 6 June 1970.
60 Peter Roberts, 'Stratford-on-Avon: *Hamlet*', *Plays and Players*, Vol. 17, no. 10 (July 1970), 38–42 (39–40).
61 Thomson, 'A Necessary Theatre', 122.
62 Roberts, 'Stratford-on-Avon: *Hamlet*', 40.

63 Quoted in Jarka Burian, *The Scenography of Josef Svoboda* (Middletown, CN: Wesleyan University Press, 1971), 27.
64 Bill Nunn, 'Variable Geometry at Stratford', *Tabs*, Vol. 30, no. 2 (June 1972), 72–6 (71).
65 Details of auditorium alterations in Pringle, *The Theatres of Stratford-upon-Avon*, 54.
66 Beauman, *The Royal Shakespeare Company*, 315.
67 Figures in Beauman, *The Royal Shakespeare Company*, 314.
68 *Coriolanus* 1972 programme (n.p.); James Sargant, 'Barbican: A One-Room Relationship', *RSC Yearbook*, 1978 (n.p.). In the event, the first Barbican season did not take place until the spring of 1982.
69 Margaret Tierney, 'Direction and Design. Trevor Nunn and Christopher Morley talk to Margaret Tierney', *Plays and Players*, Vol. 19, no. 12 (September 1972), 23–7 (27).
70 Irving Wardle, 'This marvellous box of tricks', *The Times*, 13 April 1972.
71 Robert Speaight, 'Shakespeare in Britain – the Stratford Season', *Shakespeare Quarterly*, Vol. 23, no. 4 (Autumn 1972), 383–7 (383).
72 See Peter Thomson's detailed account in 'No Rome of Safety: the Royal Shakespeare Season 1972, Reviewed', *Shakespeare Survey* 26 (Cambridge: Cambridge University Press, 1973), 139–50. Details of the monument are confirmed by reference to photographs and the prompt copies.
73 Harold Hobson, 'Stage Struck', *Sunday Times*, 16 April 1972.
74 Wardle, 'This marvellous box of tricks'.
75 Frank Marcus, 'A Roman orgy', *Sunday Telegraph*, 16 April 1972.
76 Frank Cox, 'Stratford: *Coriolanus*', *Plays and Players* Vol. 19, no. 9 (June 1972) 36–9 (38).
77 J.C. Trewin, '*Coriolanus*', *Birmingham Post*, 16 April 1972; Speaight, 'Shakespeare in Britain – the Stratford Season', 383.
78 Thomson, 'No Rome of Safety', 143–4.
79 Irving Wardle, '*Julius Caesar*', *The Times*, 4 May 1972.
80 John Mortimer, 'Sing Ho and Hey with Matey', *Observer*, 7 May 1972 (includes review of *Julius Caesar*).

81 John Barber, 'Stratford has heroic Brutus in John Wood', *Daily Telegraph*, 4 May 1972.

82 Thomson, 'No Rome of Safety', 146.

83 Peter Ansorge, 'Julius Caesar', *Plays and Players*, Vol. 19, no. 10 (July 1972), 56–9 (57).

84 Speaight, 'Shakespeare in Britain – the Stratford Season', 385.

85 Thomson, 'No Rome of Safety', 146.

86 Michael Billington, 'Cleopatra', *Guardian*, 17 August 1972.

87 Charles Lewsen, 'Love as a Public Performance', *The Times*, 17 August 1972.

88 Speaight, 'Shakespeare in Britain – the Stratford Season', 386.

89 Benedict Nightingale, 'Decline and Growth', *New Statesman*, 25 August 1972.

90 Margaret Tierney, '*Antony and Cleopatra*', *Plays and Players*, Vol. 20, no. 1 (October 1972), 42–3 (42).

91 J.W. Lambert, 'Theatre', *Sunday Times*, 20 August 1972.

92 John Barber, 'Janet Suzman wrong sort of Cleopatra', *Daily Telegraph*, 17 August 1972.

93 RSC/SM/1/1972/ANT 1–3 (books 2 and 3 are labelled as stage manager's copies, 1 as 'prompt copy').

94 Thomson, 'No Rome of Safety', 147.

95 Billington, 'Cleopatra'.

96 Lambert, 'Theatre'.

97 Speaight, 'Shakespeare in Britain – the Stratford Season', 386.

98 Irving Wardle, '*Titus Andronicus*', *The Times*, 14 October 1972.

99 Thomson, 'No Rome of Safety', 148.

100 Harold Hobson, 'Savage Universe', *Sunday Times*, 15 October 1972.

101 Benedict Nightingale, 'Dance in an Abattoir', *New Statesman*, 20 October 1972.

102 Thomson, 'No Rome of Safety', 149.

103 Ibid.

104 Michael Billington, *Guardian*, 14 October 1972.

105 Jan Kott's *Shakespeare Our Contemporary*, published in 1964, has an appendix in which *Titus Andronicus* is discussed in the light of Brook's production, as well as chapters on *Coriolanus* and *Antony and Cleopatra*, but was represented only by a brief quotation in the *Antony and Cleopatra* programme.
106 *Titus Andronicus* programme, 1972, n.p.
107 Robert Ormsby, *Shakespeare in Performance: Coriolanus* (Manchester: Manchester University Press, 2014); Carol Chillington Rutter, *Enter the Body: Women and Representation on Shakespeare's Stage* (London: Routledge, 2001). On the social and industrial unrest, see Andrew Marr, *A History of Modern Britain* (London: Pan Books, 2008), 337.
108 Rutter, *Enter the Body*, 77.
109 Ormsby, *Shakespeare in Performance*, 73–85.
110 Peter Holland, ed., *Coriolanus* (London: Bloomsbury/Arden Shakespeare, 2013), 121.
111 Ormsby, *Shakespeare in Performance*, 86.
112 Thomson, 'No Rome of Safety', 141.
113 Trevor Nunn and David Jones, 'Writing on Sand', in Sheridan Morley, ed., *Theatre 73* (London: Hutchinson, 1973), 54–67 (56). David Jones was the RSC's company director at the Aldwych Theatre.
114 Nunn and Jones, 'Writing on Sand', 57.
115 Ibid., 60.
116 J.C. Trewin, 'The Roman tragedies', *Birmingham Post*, 23 October 1973.
117 Alan Brien, 'The Romans. Alan Brien Sees the RSC Cycle', *Plays and Players*, Vol. 21, no. 3 (December 1973), 32–7 (33).
118 Trewin, 'The Roman tragedies'.
119 Benedict Nightingale, 'The RSC's SPQR', *New Statesman*, 2 November 1973.
120 John Barber, 'Heroic Coriolanus of Nicol Williamson', *Daily Telegraph*, 24 October 1973.
121 Brien, 'The Romans', 33.
122 John Barber, 'Tactless Comic Touch in Saga of Murder', *Daily Telegraph*, 26 October 1973.

123 Brien, 'The Romans', 36.
124 Irving Wardle, 'The Romans', *The Times*, 25 October 1973.
125 Thomson, 'No Rome of Safety', 141.
126 Chambers, *Inside the Royal Shakespeare Company*, 64.

Chapter 2

1 On Barton's 1973–4 *Richard II*, see James Stredder, 'John Barton's Production of *Richard II* at Stratford-upon-Avon', *Shakespeare Jahrbuch* (West) (1976), 23–42; Stanley Wells, *Royal Shakespeare: Four Major Productions at Stratford-upon-Avon* (Manchester: Manchester University Press, 1977); Margaret Shewring, *Shakespeare in Performance: Richard II* (Manchester: Manchester University Press, 1996), 120–37; and Michael L. Greenwald, *Directions by Indirections. John Barton of the Royal Shakespeare Company* (Newark, DE: University of Delaware Press, 1985), 115–27.

2 *Shakespeare and the Idea of the Play* by Ann Barton (as Anne Righter) was published by Chatto and Windus in 1962, and was reprinted by Penguin Books in 1967 in the Penguin Shakespeare Library. She and John Barton were married in 1969.

3 Michael Billington, *Guardian*, 11 April 1973.

4 The added lines are transcribed from the promptbook in Shewring, *Shakespeare in Performance,* 133–4.

5 On Barton's *King John* (Stratford 1974, London 1975), see Greenwald, *Directions by Indirections*, 128–35; Geraldine Cousin, *Shakespeare in Performance: King John* (Manchester: Manchester University Press, 1994), 64–83 and R.L. Smallwood, 'Shakespeare Unbalanced: The Royal Shakespeare Company's *King John*, 1974–75', *Shakespeare Jahrbuch* (West) (1976), 70–99.

6 Smallwood, 'Shakespeare Unbalanced', 89.

7 John Russell Brown, *Free Shakespeare* (London: Heinemann, 1974), 25.

8 Ibid., 40.

9 Michael Coveney, '*Macbeth*', *Plays and Players*, Vol. 22, no. 3 (December 1974), 18–19 (18).

10 Robert Cushman, 'A famous thane', *Observer* (2 November 1974).
11 Coveney, '*Macbeth*'.
12 Programme, *Macbeth* (Aldwych, 1975), n.p.
13 Michael Billington, '*Macbeth*', *Guardian*, 31 October 1974.
14 Coveney, '*Macbeth*', 19.
15 John Barber, 'Williamson Dominates *Macbeth*', *Daily Telegraph*, 31 October 1974.
16 Michael Coveney, '*Macbeth. Twelfth Night*', *Plays and Players*, Vol. 22, no. 8 (May 1975), 31–2 (31).
17 Frank Marcus, 'All in the Mind', *Sunday Telegraph*, 3 November 1974.
18 Harold Hobson, *Sunday Times*, 3 November 1974.
19 Beauman, *The Royal Shakespeare Company*, 327.
20 Programme, *Romeo and Juliet*, 1976, n.p.
21 Trevor Nunn, 'Back to Stage One', *Sunday Times*, 28 March 1976.
22 John Barber, 'Designs on the Audience', *Daily Telegraph*, 19 April 1976.
23 Jim Hiley, 'A Company with Direction', *Plays and Players*, Vol. 25, no. 1 (October 1977), 14–21 (19).
24 Ibid., 20 (Pennington had played Angelo in the 1974 production of *Measure for Measure*).
25 B.A. Young, '*Romeo and Juliet*', *Financial Times*, 2 April 1976.
26 Michael Billington, *Guardian*, 2 April 1976.
27 Felix Barker, *Evening Standard*, 2 April 1976.
28 Frank Marcus, 'The return of O', *Sunday Telegraph*, 4 April 1976.
29 Robert Cushman, 'Simple Stratford', 'Romeo and Juliet', *Observer*, 4 April 1976; John Elsom, *Listener*, 8 April 1976.
30 John Barber, 'This Romeo is a likeable odd-ball', *Daily Telegraph*, 3 April 1976.
31 Michael Coveney, '*Romeo and Juliet/Much Ado*', *Plays and Players*, Vol. 23, no. 9 (June 1976), 19–20 (20).
32 Richard David, *Shakespeare in the Theatre* (Cambridge: Cambridge University Press, 1978), 116.
33 Irving Wardle, 'Life and Death Polarities Extended', *The Times*, 5 April 1976.

34 Kenneth Hurren, 'All Lit Up', *Spectator*, 10 April 1976.
35 David Nathan, 'No Love-light in Romeo's Eyes', *Jewish Chronicle*, 9 April 1976.
36 Sheridan Morley, 'Four Hours' Traffic', *Punch*, 14 April 1976.
37 David, *Shakespeare in the Theatre*, 118.
38 Ibid., 117.
39 Michael Coveney, '*Romeo and Juliet*', *Financial Times*, 7 July 1977.
40 Michael Billington, '*Romeo and Juliet*', *Guardian*, 7 July 1977.
41 Irving Wardle, *The Times*, 5 June 1976. The twelve figures on the screens were explained in the programme as signs 'of middle European origin' outlining the play's plot. As Patricia Tatspaugh observes (*Shakespeare at Stratford. The Winter's Tale*, 19), without this information they would not have been intelligible to the audience.
42 Robert Cushman, review of *The Winter's Tale*, *Observer*, 13 June 1976.
43 Michael Billington, '*The Winter's Tale*', *Guardian*, 5 June 1976.
44 John Barber, '*Winter's Tale* Must Be a Great Success', *Daily Telegraph*, 5 June 1976.
45 J.W. Lambert, review of *The Comedy of Errors*, *Sunday Times*, 3 October 1976.
46 John Higgins, 'Trevor Nunn in Search of Fresh Pastures', *The Times*, 29 September 1976. Most of the interview focuses on Nunn's intention to establish full-company residencies outside London: 'I'm a believer in regularity and familiarity because this is the only way to build up a public.' He suggests that the move to the Barbican as a London venue will take place somewhere in 'the middle of 1979'.
47 Anthony Everitt, '*The Comedy of Errors*', *Birmingham Post*, 30 September 1976.
48 Robert Cushman, 'Theatre', *Observer*, 3 October 1976.
49 Irving Wardle, '*The Comedy of Errors*', *The Times*, 1 October 1976.
50 Robert Cushman, review of *The Comedy of Errors*, *Observer*, 20 November 1977.
51 Michael Billington, '*Comedy of Errors*', *Guardian*, 16 November 1977.

52 Jonathan Croall, *Performing King Lear. Gielgud to Russell Beale* (London: Bloomsbury Arden Shakespeare, 2015), 52.
53 John Higgins, 'The Road to Lear', *The Times*, 29 November 1976.
54 Milton Shulman, 'Lear out of Step', *Evening Standard*, 30 November 1976.
55 Michael Billington, '*King Lear*', *Guardian*, 1 December 1976; Irving Wardle, *The Times*, 1 December 1976.
56 Billington, '*King Lear*'.
57 Michael Coveney, '*King Lear*', *Plays and Players*, Vol. 24, no. 2 (February 1977), 18–19.
58 Wardle, *The Times*, 1 December 1976.
59 Herbert Kretzmer, 'Going from Madness to Majesty', *Daily Express*, 1 December 1976.
60 Croall, *Performing King Lear*, 55.
61 Roger Warren, 'Shakespeare at Stratford and the National Theatre, 1979', *Shakespeare Survey*, Vol. 33 (Cambridge: Cambridge University Press, 1980), 169–80; 169.
62 Michael Billington, '*Merry Wives*', *Guardian*, 4 April 1977
63 B.A Young, review of *Merry Wives*, *Financial Times*, 5 April 1977.
64 Michael Billington, '*As You Like It*', *Guardian*, 10 September 1977; Robert Cushman, review of *As You Like It*, *Observer*, 11 September 1977.
65 Robert Smallwood, *Shakespeare at Stratford: As You Like It* (London: Arden Shakespeare, 2003), 14.
66 Roger Warren, 'Comedies and Histories at Two Stratfords, 1977', *Shakespeare Survey*, Vol. 3 (1978), 141–53; 146.
67 Ibid., 147.
68 Timings from RSC/SM/1/1977/AYL1 (promptbook) and AYL2 (stage manager's book).
69 John Peter, 'The Spy Who Came in from the Cold', *Sunday Times*, 11 September 1977 (includes review of *As You Like It*).
70 Irving Wardle, '*As You Like It*', *The Times*, 10 September 1977.
71 Noel Witts, '*As You Like It*', *Plays and Players*, Vol. 25, No. 2 (November 1977), 22–3; 23.

72 Changes made for the Aldwych are shown in the second of the promptbooks. The text of the 'Prologue' is filed with the production records (RSC/SM2/1977/3–7): it is not clear whether this page was removed from the promptbook during or after the Stratford run.

73 B.A. Young, review of '*As You Like It*', *Sunday Times*, 18 September 1978.

74 Peter Hepple, '*As You Like It*', *Stage*, 21 September 1978.

75 Peter Jenkins, 'What you will', *Spectator*, 23 September 1978.

76 Leon Rubin, *The Nicholas Nickleby Story. The Making of the Historic Royal Shakespeare Company Production* (London: Heinemann, 1981), 13–14.

77 Ibid., 178–9.

78 Clive Priestley, *Financial Scrutiny of the Royal Shakespeare Company. Report to the Earl of Gowrie, Minister for the Arts* (London: HMSO, 1984), 107.

79 Rubin, *The Nicholas Nickleby Story*, 114.

80 Quoted by Irving Wardle, 'Before Chekhov', 19 November 1981.

81 Gareth Lloyd Evans, *Stratford-upon-Avon Herald*, 27 November 1981.

82 Scripts in the RSC archive: RSC/SM/1/1981/ALL1 (promptbook) and RSC/SM/1/1981/ALL1 (stage manager's script), both used at Newcastle-on-Tyne and the Barbican as well as in Stratford.

83 John Elsom, 'Change of Heart', *Listener*, 26 November 1981.

84 *The Complete Plays of Bernard Shaw* (London: Odhams, 1931), 399.

85 Michael Coveney, '*All's Well That Ends Well*', *Financial Times*, 18 November 1981.

86 Wardle, 'Before Chekhov', *The Times*, 7 July 1982.

87 Nicholas Shrimpton, 'Shakespeare Performances in Stratford-upon-Avon and London, 1981–2', *Shakespeare Survey*, Vol. 36 (Cambridge: Cambridge University Press, 1983), 149–56 (149).

88 Jack Tinker, 'A Scene Change, and All's Well', *Daily Mail*, 18 November 1981.

89 Michael Billington, '*All's Well*', *Guardian*, 18 November 1981.

90 Stanley Wells, *TLS*, 26 November.
91 Michael Billington, 'Nunn's Fine Tale', *Guardian*, 7 July 1982.
92 Shrimpton, 'Shakespeare Performances in Stratford-upon-Avon and London, 1981–2', 149.
93 Ibid., 150.
94 J.L. Styan, *Shakespeare in Performance: All's Well That Ends Well* (Manchester: Manchester University Press, 1984), 84.
95 James Fenton, 'All's Well with the Age of Chivalry', *Sunday Times*, 22 November 1981.
96 Shaw, *Complete Plays*, 399.
97 Stanley Wells, 'When the Music Stops', *TLS*, 27 November 1981; Shaw, 'Preface' to *Man and Superman*, in Edwin Wilson, ed., *Shaw on Shakespeare* (Harmondsworth: Penguin Books, 1969), 257.
98 Robert Cushman, 'Nunn's *All's Well*', *Observer*, 22 November 1981.
99 Styan, *Shakespeare in Performance*, 113.
100 Carol Rutter and Faith Evans, eds, *Clamorous Voices. Shakespeare's Women Today* (London: The Women's Press, 1988), 88.
101 James Fenton, *Sunday Times*, 13 June 1982.
102 Irving Wardle, 'A Hal as Never Seen Before', *The Times*, 10 June 1982.
103 Stephen Wall, 'Theatre of the Metropolis', *TLS*, 25 June 1982.
104 Michael Billington, 'There's a Hole in Hal's Buckler', *Guardian*, 11 June 1982.
105 Shrimpton, 'Shakespeare Performances in Stratford-upon-Avon and London, 1981–2', 153.
106 Francis King, 'Filling Up the Barbican', *Sunday Telegraph*, 13 June 1982.
107 Michael Billington, *Guardian*, 29 September 1978; Billington, *State of the Nation. British Theatre Since 1945* (London: Faber and Faber, 2007), 292–3.

Chapter 3

1. Tim Pigott-Smith, *Do You Know Who I Am? A Memoir* (London: Bloomsbury, 2017), 78–9.
2. Information on Buzz Goodbody from Chambers, *Other Spaces*, 26–7.
3. Chambers, *Inside the Royal Shakespeare Company*, 67, 68.
4. Peter Thomson, 'Towards a Poor Theatre: The Royal Shakespeare Company at Stratford in 1975', *Shakespeare Survey*, Vol. 29 (Cambridge: Cambridge University Press, 1976), 151–6 (153).
5. Eyre, *Talking Theatre*, 63–4.
6. Pringle, *The Theatres of Stratford-upon-Avon*, 71–2.
7. Interview in Curry, *Shakespeare on Stage*, 152.
8. Michael Billington, '*Macbeth*', *Guardian*, 15 December 1977.
9. Sue Dommett, '*Macbeth* at The Other Place, 1976: A production study', unpublished MA dissertation, University of Birmingham, 1977. The promptbook (RSC/SM/1/1977/MAC1) was used throughout the run in Stratford and London, and is catalogued with the year of the Warehouse performances.
10. Bernice W. Kliman, *Shakespeare in Performance, 'Macbeth'* (Manchester: Manchester University Press, 1992); Lois Potter, *Shakespeare in Performance. 'Othello'* (Manchester: Manchester University Press, 2002); Virginia Mason Vaughan, *Othello: A Contextual History* (Cambridge: Cambridge University Press, 1994).
11. Ned Chaillet, 'The stage is a circle', *The Times*; Michael Billington, 'Macbeth', *Guardian*: both 11 September 1976.
12. Kliman, *Shakespeare in Performance*, 102.
13. Robert Cushman, 'Triumphant Tragedy', *Observer*, 12 September 1976.
14. Eyre, *Talking Theatre*, 64
15. J.W. Lambert, *Sunday Times*, 12 September 1976.
16. David, *Shakespeare in the Theatre*, 87–8.
17. Dommett, '*Macbeth* at The Other Place, 1976', 7.
18. Gareth Lloyd Evans, 'The RSC's *King Lear* and *Macbeth*', *Shakespeare Quarterly*, Vol. 28, no. 2 (Spring 1977), 190–5 (194).

19 Benedict Nightingale, 'Black Russian', *New Statesman*, 17 September 1076.
20 McKellen in Curry, 152.
21 Irving Wardle, '*Macbeth*', *The Times*, 15 September 1977.
22 Dommett, '*Macbeth* at The Other Place, 1976', 100.
23 Ibid., 118.
24 Ibid., 35, 43.
25 Kliman, *Shakespeare in Performance*, 116.
26 Evans, 'The RSC's King Lear and Macbeth', 194.
27 Dommett, '*Macbeth* at The Other Place, 1976', 219 (omitting the indications in which letters are keyed to a ground plan specifying the exits and entrances used).
28 Dommett, '*Macbeth* at The Other Place, 1976', 82.
29 Ibid., 207.
30 Dennis Kennedy, *Looking at Shakespeare. A Visual History of Twentieth-Century Performance*, 2nd edition (Cambridge: Cambridge University Press, 2001), 255.
31 Details from promptbooks RSC/SM/1/1989/OTH1 and OTH2 (photocopy).
32 Kenneth Hurren, 'Glenda's Hedda', *Spectator*, 26 July 1975.
33 Christopher Small, 'Skill, Spirit and Taste in Chekhov's Most Moving Play', *Glasgow Herald*, 30 April 1978.
34 Trevor Nunn, 'Notes from a Director: *Three Sisters*', in Vera Gottlieb and Paul Allain, eds, *The Cambridge Companion to Chekhov* (Cambridge: Cambridge University Press, 2000), 101–10 (103).
35 Ibid., 105.
36 Ibid., 106.
37 Michael Ratcliffe, 'Theatre', *Observer*, 27 August 1989.
38 Jack Tinker, 'Catching the Soul of the Eternal Outsider', *Daily Mail*, 26 August 1989.
39 Norman Sanders, programme essay, TOP 1991. In the introduction to his New Cambridge Shakespeare edition Sanders discusses the manner in which 'every effort is made to circumscribe the effects and implications of the

characters' actions', while 'the geographical narrowing of focus is reinforced by the absence of the allusive scope normally present in Shakespearean tragedy' (18–19).

40 Stanley Wells, 'Shakespeare Production in England in 1989', *Shakespeare Survey* 43 (1991), 183–202 (191); Robert Smallwood, 'Shakespeare at Stratford-upon-Avon, 1989 (Part I)', *Shakespeare Quarterly*, Vol. 41, no. 1 (Spring 1990), 101–14 (111).

41 John Peter, *Sunday Times*, 27 August 1989.

42 Vaughan, *Othello: A Contextual History*, 219.

43 Quoted in an interview with Gwyn Morgan, 'Three Women in *Othello*', *Plays and Players*, October 1989, 16–18.

44 Michael Coveney, 'A monumental Othello', *Financial Times*, 26 August 1989.

45 Wells, 'Shakespeare Production in England in 1989', 194.

46 Adam Mars-Jones, 'Web of magic', *Independent*, 26 August (1989).

47 J.C.Trewin, '*Othello*', *Birmingham Post*, 25 August 1989.

48 Michael Billngton review of *Othello*, *Guardian*, 26 August 1989.

49 Wells, 'Shakespeare Production in England in 1989', 194.

50 Harry Eyres, *The Times*, 26 August.

51 Anne Barton, 'Other Places, Other Customs', *TLS*, 8 September 1989.

52 Morgan, 'Three Women in *Othello*', 17.

53 Potter, *Shakespeare in Performance*, 190.

54 Smallwood, 'Shakespeare at Stratford-upon-Avon, 1989 (Part I)', 114.

55 Wells, 'Shakespeare Production in England in 1989', 192.

56 'Diabolic Intellect and the Noble Hero: or, *The Sentimentalist's Othello*' (*Scrutiny*, 1937), reprinted in *The Common Pursuit* (London: Chatto and Windus, 1952). Chapter 2, 'Love and Identity', in Bayley's *The Characters of Love* (London: Chatto and Windus, 1960), defends the play and its hero against Leavis, whose approach is likened to that of Iago.

57 Vaughan, *Othello: A Contextual History*, 219.

58 Smallwood, 'Shakespeare at Stratford-upon-Avon, 1989 (Part I)', 113.

59 Vaughan, *Othello: A Contextual History*, 224.
60 Hunt in Morgan, 'Three Women in *Othello*', 17.
61 Michael Coveney, 'Blue Angel Delight', *Observer*, 1 September 1991.
62 Pringle, *The Theatres of Stratford-upon-Avon*, 73.
63 Paul Taylor, review of *Timon of Athens*, *Independent*, 8 March 1991.
64 Ian Dodd, review of *Timon of Athens*, *Tribune*, 15 March 1991; Peter Holland, *TLS*, 15 March 1991.
65 Carl Miller, review of *Timon of Athens*, *City Limits*, 14 March 1991.
66 Irving Wardle, review of *Timon of Athens*, *Independent on Sunday*, 10 March 1991.
67 Taylor, review of *Timon of Athens*.
68 John Peter, review of *Timon of Athens*, *Sunday Times*, 10 March 1991.
69 Textual information from the promptbook, RSC/SM/1/1991/MEA1.
70 Robert Smallwood, 'Shakespeare at Stratford-upon-Avon, 1991', *Shakespeare Quarterly*, Vol. 43, no. 4 (Autumn 1992), 341–56; 353.
71 Peter Holland, 'Shakespeare Performances in England 1990–1', *Shakespeare Survey* 20 (1992), 115–44; 135–6.
72 Michael Billington, review of *Measure for Measure*, *Guardian*, 20 September 1991.
73 Paul Taylor, review of *Measure for Measure*, *Independent*, 20 September 1991.
74 Charles Spencer, review of *Measure for Measure*, *Daily Telegraph*, 20 September 1991.
75 Martin Hoyle, review of *Measure for Measure*, *Independent on Sunday*, 22 September 1991.
76 Smallwood, 'Shakespeare at Stratford-upon-Avon, 1991', 356, emphasis in original.
77 John Gross, review of *Measure for Measure*, *Sunday Telegraph*, 22 September 1991.
78 Billington, review of *Measure for Measure*.

79 Holland, 'Shakespeare Performances in England 1990–1', 134.
80 Billington, review of *Measure for Measure*.
81 Hoyle, review of *Measure for Measure*.
82 Gross, review of *Measure for Measure*.
83 Smallwood, 'Shakespeare at Stratford-upon-Avon, 1991', 354.
84 Michael Romain, *A Profile of Jonathan Miller* (Cambridge: Cambridge University Press, 1992), 48–9.
85 Ibid., 168.

Chapter 4

1 Nicholas Hytner, *Balancing Acts. Behind the Scenes at the National Theatre* (London: Jonathan Cape, 2017), 21.
2 Details of the innovations proposed and implemented in 'Transformation' are given in Rosenthal, *The National Theatre Story*, 659–66.
3 Robert Smallwood, 'Shakespeare Performances in England, 1999', *Shakespeare Survey*, Vol. 53 (2000), 244–73 (271).
4 Charles Spencer, review of *Love's Labour's Lost*, *Daily Telegraph*, 22 February 2003.
5 Robert Butler, *Independent on Sunday*, 21 March 1999.
6 Nicholas de Jongh, *Evening Standard*, 16 March 1999.
7 David Nathan, *Jewish Chronicle*, 2 April 2003; Nicholas de Jongh, *Evening Standard*, 24 February 2003.
8 John Gross, *Sunday Telegraph*, 2 April 2003; Alistair Macaulay, *Financial Times*, 25 February 2003.
9 Michael Dobson, 'Shakespeare Performances in England, 2003', *Shakespeare Survey*, Vol. 57 (Cambridge, 2004), 258–89 (264).
10 Smallwood, 'Shakespeare Performances in England, 1999', 269. In *Shakespeare in Production. The Merchant of Venice* (Cambridge: Cambridge University Press, 2002) Charles Edelman identifies this as 'the traditional Hebrew prayer, Eshet Chayil, "A Woman of Virtue"'. In an appendix (265–6), Edelman notes the verse sung by Jessica at the end of the play: 'She will do him good and not evil all the days of her life.'

11 John Gross, review of *The Merchant of Venice*, *Sunday Telegraph*, 20 June 1999.
12 Charles Spencer, review of *The Merchant of Venice*, *Daily Telegraph*, 21 June 1999.
13 Smallwood, 'Shakespeare Performances in England, 1999', 269.
14 Hal Jensen, review of *The Merchant of Venice*, *TLS*, 2 July 1999.
15 Michael L. Greenwald, *Direction by Indirections. John Barton of the Royal Shakespeare Company* (Newark: University of Delaware Press, 1985), 73–4.
16 Allan Brien, review of *Troilus and Cressida* (RSC), *Spectator*, 29 July 1960.
17 Smallwood, 'Shakespeare Performances in England, 1999', 257.
18 Alastair Macaulay, review of *Troilus and Cressida*, *Financial Times*, 17 March 1999.
19 Benedict Nightingale, review of *Troilus and Cressida*, *The Times*, 17 March 1999.
20 Michael Billington, review of *Troilus and Cressida*, *Guardian*, 17 March 1999.
21 John Gross, review of *Troilus and Cressida*, *Sunday Telegraph*, 21 March 1999.
22 Smallwood, 'Shakespeare Performances in England, 1999', 258.
23 Michael Coveney, review of *Troilus and Cressida*, *Daily Mail*, 19 March 1999.
24 Smallwood, 'Shakespeare Performances in England, 1999', 257. This is the conclusion from the 1609 Quarto. The Folio text ends with 5.11 and Troilus' 'Hope of revenge' lines. On Nunn's revisions, see Alan C. Dessen, *Rescripting Shakespeare.The Text, the Director and Modern Productions* (Cambridge: Cambridge University Press, 2002), 72–3.
25 Bridget Escolme, *Talking to the Audience. Shakespeare, Performance, Self* (London: Routledge, 2005), 36–7.
26 Susannah Clapp, review of *Troilus and Cressida*, *Observer*, 21 March 1999.
27 Robert Gore-Langton, review of *Troilus and Cressida*, *Daily Express*, 20 March 1999.

28 Reviews of *Troilus and Cressida*: Paul Taylor, *Independent*; Charles Spencer, *Daily Telegraph*, both 17 March 1999.

29 Robert Butler, review of *Troilus and Cressida*, *Independent on Sunday*, 21 March 1999.

30 Sheridan Morley, review of *Troilus and Cressida*, *Spectator* 27 March 1999.

31 Georgina Brown, review of *Troilus and Cressida*, *Mail on Sunday*, 21 March 1999.

32 John Peter, review of *Troilus and Cressida*, *Sunday Times*, 21 March 1999.

33 Benedict Nightingale, review of *Love's Labour's Lost*, *The Times*, 22 February 2003.

34 John Peter, review of *Love's Labour's Lost*, *Sunday Times*, 2 March 2003.

35 Reviews of *Love's Labour's Lost*: Charles Spencer, *Daily Telegraph*, 22 February 2003; Jane Edwardes, *Time Out*, 26 February 2003; Susannah Clapp, *Observer*, 2 March 2003.

36 Michael Coveney, review of *Love's Labour's Lost*, *Daily Mail*, 22 February 2003.

37 Peter, review of *Love's Labour's Lost*.

38 Nicholas de Jongh, review of *Love's Labour's Lost*, *Evening Standard*, 24 March 2003.

39 John Thaxter, review of *Love's Labour's Lost*, *Stage*, 27 February 2003.

40 Kate Bassett, review of *Love's Labour's Lost*, *Independent on Sunday*, 2 March 2003.

41 John Gross, review of *Love's Labour's Lost*, *Sunday Telegraph*, 2 March 2003.

42 Sheridan Morley, review of *Love's Labour's Lost*, *New Statesman*, 10 March 2003.

43 Imogen Stubbs, 'Gertrude', in Michael Dobson, ed., *Performing Shakespeare's Tragedies Today. The Actor's Perspective* (Cambridge: Cambridge University Press, 2006), 29–39 (33).

44 Ibid., 34.

45 Ibid., 38.

46 Lloyd Evans, review of *Hamlet*, *Spectator*, 8 May 2004.

47 Kate Bassett, review of *Hamlet*, *Independent on Sunday*, 2 May 2004.
48 John Nathan, review of *Hamlet*, *Jewish Chronicle*, 30 April 2004.
49 Alastair Macaulay, review of *Hamlet*, *Financial Times*, 29 April 2004.
50 Nathan, review of *Hamlet*.
51 Michael Dobson, 'Shakespeare Performances in England, 2004', *Shakespeare Survey*, Vol. 56 (Cambridge: Cambridge University Press, 2005), 268–97 (294).
52 Michael Billington, review of *Hamlet*, *Guardian*, 28 April 2004.
53 Mark Shenton, review of *Hamlet*, *Sunday Express*, 2 May 2004.
54 Sarah Sands, review of *Hamlet*, *Daily Telegraph*, 30 April 2004.
55 *What's On*, review of *Hamlet*, 5 May 2004 (uncredited).
56 Details from Patricia Tatspaugh, 'Shakespeare on Stage in England. March to December 2005', *Shakespeare Quarterly*, Vol. 57, no. 3 (Autumn 2006), 318–43 (323), and Michael Dobson, 'Shakespeare Performances in England, 2005', *Shakespeare Survey*, Vol. 57 (Cambridge: Cambridge University Press, 2006), 298–337 (322).
57 Reviews of *Richard II*: Carole Woddis, *Herald*, 6 October 2005; Susannah Clapp, *Observer*, 9 October 2005.
58 Tatspaugh, 'Shakespeare on Stage in England', 325.
59 Dobson, 'Shakespeare Performances in England, 2005', 322.
60 Benedict Nightingale, review of *Richard II*, *The Times*, 5 October 2005.
61 Quentin Letts, review of *Richard II*, *Daily Mail*, 5 October 2005.
62 Jane Edwardes, review of *Richard II*, *Time Out London*, 12 October 2005.
63 Michael Billington, review of *Richard II*, *Guardian*, 5 October 2005.
64 Kate Bassett, review of *Richard II*, *Independent on Sunday*, 9 October 2005.
65 Dobson, 'Shakespeare Performances in England, 2005', 323.

66 Julian Curry, ed., *Shakespeare on Stage, Volume 2* (London: Nick Hern Books, 2017), 131.

67 Michael Dobson, 'Shakespeare Performances in England, 2007', *Shakespeare Survey*, Vol. 58 (Cambridge: Cambridge University Press, 2008), 318–50 (334).

68 Curry, *Shakespeare on Stage, Volume 2*, 139.

69 Dobson, 'Shakespeare Performances in England, 2007', 336.

70 Charles Spencer, review of *King Lear*, *Daily Telegraph*, 1 June 2007.

71 John Peter, review of *King Lear*, *Sunday Times*, 10 June 2007.

72 Michael Billington, review of *King Lear*, *Guardian*, 1 June 2007.

73 Benedict Nightingale, review of *King Lear*, *The Times*, 1 June; Curry, *Shakespeare on Stage, Volume 2*, 144.

74 Susannah Clapp, review of *King Lear*, *Observer*, 3 June 2007.

75 Curry, *Shakespeare on Stage, Volume 2*, 156.

76 Dobson, 'Shakespeare Performances in England, 2007', 336.

Conclusion

1 Reviews of King Lear: all published 1 June except *Independent on Sunday*, 3 June.

2 Dobson, 'Shakespeare Performances in England, 2007', 338.

3 Simon Trussler, 'A Man for All Seasons', *Flourish*, Vol. 2, no. 1 (Autumn 1968), n.p.

4 Hall, *Diaries*, 314; Blakemore, *Stage Blood. Five Tempestuous Years in the Early Life of the National Theatre* (London: Faber and Faber, 2013), 154; Holland, *English Shakespeares. Shakespeare on the English Stage in the 1990s* (Cambridge: Cambridge University Press, 1997), 7; Martin White, 'Trevor Nunn', in John Russell Brown, ed., *The Routledge Companion to Directors' Shakespeare* (London and New York: Routledge, 2008), 304.

5 Interview with Anthony Clare, 'Centre Stage', *Listener*, 2 August 1990.

BIBLIOGRAPHY

RSC promptbooks at Shakespeare Centre, Stratford-upon-Avon

All's Well that Ends Well, 1981–2: RSC/SM/1/1981/ALL1 (promptbook) and RSC/SM/1/1981/ALL1 (stage manager's script).
Antony and Cleopatra, 1972–3: RSC/SM/1/1972/ANT1-2 (promptbook) and 3 (stage-manager's book).
As You Like It, 1977–8: RSC/SM/1/1977/AYL1 (promptbook) and AYL2 (stage manager's book) and RSC/SM2/1977/3-7 (production records).
Macbeth, 1976–7: (RSC/SM/1/1977/MAC1 (promptbook, used in Stratford and London).
Measure for Measure, 1991: RSC/SM/1/1991/MEA1.
Othello, 1989: RSC/SM/1/1989/OTH1 and OTH2 (photocopy).
Romeo and Juliet, 1976: RSC/SM/1/1976/ROM1-2 (promptbook) and 3 (stage manager's book).
The Winter's Tale, 1969–70: RSC/SM/2/1970/Wint (promptbook, used in Stratford and London).

Books

Addenbrooke, David, *The Royal Shakespeare Company: The Peter Hall Years* (London: William Kimber, 1974).
Adler, Steven, *Rough Magic. Making Theatre at the Royal Shakespeare Company* (Carbondale and Edwardsville: Southern Illinois University Press, 2001).
Beauman, Sally, *The Royal Shakespeare Company: A History of Ten Decades* (Oxford: Oxford University Press, 1982).
Berry, Ralph, *On Directing Shakespeare. Interviews with Contemporary Directors* (London: Croom Helm, 1977).

Billington, Michael, *One Night Stands. A Critic's View of Modern British Theatre*, revised edition (London: Nick Hern Books, 2007).
Billington, Michael, *State of the Nation. British Theatre Since 1945* (London: Faber and Faber, 2007).
Blakemore, Michael, *Stage Blood. Five Tempestuous Years in the Early Life of the National Theatre* (London: Faber and Faber, 2013).
Bogadnov, Michael and Michael Pennington, *The English Shakespeare Company: The Story of 'The Wars of the Roses', 1986–1989* (London: Nick Hern Books, 1990).
Brown, John Russell, *Free Shakespeare* (London: Heinemann, 1974).
Burian, Jarka, *The Scenography of Josef Svoboda* (Middletown, CN: Wesleyan University Press, 1971).
Callow, Simon, *The National. The Theatre and Its Work, 1963–1997, with a Preface by Trevor Nunn* (London: Nick Hern Books/Royal National Theatre, 1997).
Chambers, Colin, *Other Spaces. New Theatre and the RSC* (London: Eyre Methuen/Theatre Quarterly Publications, 1980).
Chambers, Colin, *Inside the Royal Shakespeare Company. Creativity and the Institution* (London: Routledge, 2004).
Cochrane, Claire, *Twentieth-Century British Theatre. Industry, Art and Empire* (Cambridge: Cambridge University Press, 2011).
Cousin, Geraldine, *Shakespeare in Performance: King John* (Manchester: Manchester University Press, 1994).
Croall, Jonathan, *Performing King Lear. Gielgud to Russell Beale* (London: Bloomsbury/Arden Shakespeare, 2015).
Curry, Julian, ed., *Shakespeare on Stage Thirteen Leading Actors on Thirteen Key Roles* (London: Nick Hern Books, 2010).
Curry, Julian, ed., *Shakespeare on Stage*, Vol. 2 (London: Nick Hern Books, 2017).
David, Richard, *Shakespeare in the Theatre* (Cambridge: Cambridge University Press, 1978).
Dessen, Alan C., *Shakespeare in Performance: Titus Andronicus* (Manchester: Manchester University Press, 1989).
Dessen, Alan C., *Rescripting Shakespeare: The Text, the Director and Modern Productions* (Cambridge: Cambridge University Press, 2002).
Edelman, Charles, ed., *Shakespeare in Production: The Merchant of Venice* (Cambridge: Cambridge University Press, 2002).
Ellis, David, *Memoirs of a Leavisite. The Decline and Fall of Cambridge English* (Liverpool: Liverpool University Press, 2013).

Escolme, Bridget, *Talking to the Audience. Shakespeare, Performance, Self* (London: Routledge, 2005).
Eyre, Richard, *National Service. Diary of a Decade* (London: Bloomsbury, 2003).
Eyre, Richard, ed., *Talking Theatre: Interviews with Theatre People* (London: Nick Hern Books, 2011).
Fay, Stephen, *Power Play. The Life and Times of Peter Hall* (London: Hodder and Stoughton, 1995).
Gaskill, William, *A Sense of Direction* (London: Faber and Faber, 1988).
Gottlieb, Vera and Paul Allain, eds, *The Cambridge Companion to Chekhov* (Cambridge: Cambridge University Press, 2000).
Greenwald, Michael L., *Direction by Indirections. John Barton of the Royal Shakespeare Company* (Newark: University of Delaware Press, 1985).
Hall, Peter, *Peter Hall's Diaries. The Story of a Dramatic Battle*, ed. John Goodwin (London: Hamish Hamilton, 1983).
Hall, Peter, *Making an Exhibition of Myself* (London: Sinclair-Stevenson, 1993).
Hampton-Reeves, Stuart and Carol Chillington Rutter, *Shakespeare in Performance: The Henry VI Plays* (Manchester: Manchester University Press, 2006).
Hartley, Andrew James, *Shakespeare in Performance: Julius Caesar* (Manchester: Manchester University Press, 2014).
Hartley, Andrew James, ed., *Shakespeare on the University Stage* (Cambridge: Cambridge University Press, 2015).
Hayman, Ronald, *Leavis* (London: Heinemann, 1976).
Hodgdon, Barbara, *The End Crowns All. Closure and Contradiction in Shakespeare's History* (Princeton, NJ: Princeton University Press, 1991).
Holland, Peter, *English Shakespeares. Shakespeare on the English Stage in the 1990s* (Cambridge: Cambridge University Press, 1997).
Hytner, Nicholas, *Balancing Acts. Behind the Scenes at the National Theatre* (London: Jonathan Cape, 2017), Itzin, Catherine, *Stages in the Revolution. Political Theatre in Britain Since 1968* (London: Methuen, 1980).
Kennedy, Dennis, *Looking at Shakespeare. A Visual History of Twentieth-Century Performance*, 2nd edition (Cambridge: Cambridge University Press, 2001).
Kliman, Bernice W., *Shakespeare in Performance: Macbeth* (Manchester: Manchester University Press, 1995).

Lambert, J.W., *Drama in Britain, 1963–1973* (London: Longman Group for the British Council, 1973).

Leavis, F.R., *The Common Pursuit* (London: Chatto and Windus, 1952).

Marowitz, Charles, *Burnt Bridges. A Souvenir of the Swinging Sixties and Beyond* (London: Hodder and Stoughton, 1991).

Marowitz, Charles, ed., with Tom Milne and Owen Hale, *The Encore Reader. A Chronicle of the New Drama* (London: Methuen, 1965).

Marr, Andrew, *A History of Modern Britain* (London: Pan Books, 2008).

Middleton, Thomas and Cyril Tourneur, *The Revenger's Tragedy*, ed. R. A Foakes (Manchester: Manchester University Press, 1996).

Morley, Sheridan, *Our Theatres in the Eighties* (London: Hodder and Stoughton, 1990).

Ormsby, Robert, *Shakespeare in Performance: Coriolanus* (Manchester: Manchester University Press, 2014).

Pigott-Smith, Tim, *Do You Know Who I Am? A Memoir* (London: Bloomsbury, 2017).

Porter, Roy, *Madness. A Brief History* (Oxford: Oxford University Press, 2002).

Potter, Lois, *Shakespeare in Performance: Othello* (Manchester: Manchester University Press, 2002).

Priestley, Clive, *Financial Scrutiny of the Royal Shakespeare Company. Report to the Earl of Gowrie, Minister for the Arts* (London: HMSO, 1984).

Pringle, Marian J., *The Theatres of Stratford-upon-Avon, 1875–1992* (Stratford-upon-Avon: Stratford-upon-Avon Society, 1994).

Rees, Roland, *Fringe First. Pioneers of Fringe Theatre on Record* (London: Oberon Books, 1992).

Romain, Michael, *A Profile of Jonathan Miller* (Cambridge: Cambridge University Press, 1992).

Rosenthal, Daniel, *The National Theatre Story* (London: Oberon Books, 2013).

Rubin, Leon, *The Nicholas Nickleby Story. The Making of the Historic Royal Shakespeare Company Production* (London: Heinemann, 1981).

Rutter, Carol, *Enter the Body: Women and Representation on Shakespeare's Stage* (London: Routledge, 2001).

Rutter, Carol Chillington and Faith Evans, *Clamorous Voices. Shakespeare's Women Today* (London: The Women's Press, 1988).

Saunders, Graham, ed., *British Theatre Companies 1980–1994* (London: Bloomsbury Methuen Drama, 2015).

Selbourne, David, *The Making of 'A Midsummer Night's Dream'. An Eye-witness Account of Peter Brook's Production from First Rehearsal to First Night*, with an introductory essay by Simon Trussler (London: Methuen, 1982).

Shaw, Bernard, *The Complete Plays of Bernard Shaw* (London: Odhams, 1931).

Shewring, Margaret, *Shakespeare in Performance: Richard II* (Manchester: Manchester University Press, 1996).

Smallwood, Robert, *Shakespeare at Stratford: As You like It* (London: Arden Shakespeare/Thomson Learning, 2003).

Steinberg, Micheline, *Flashback: A Pictorial History 1879–1979: One Hundred Years of Stratford-upon-Avon and the Royal Shakespeare Company* (Stratford-upon-Avon: RSC Publications, 1985).

Styan, J.L., *Shakespeare in Performance: All's Well that Ends Well* (Manchester: Manchester University Press, 1984).

Tatspaugh, Patricia, *Shakespeare at Stratford: The Winter's Tale* (London: Arden Shakespeare/Thomson Learning, 2002).

Vaughan, Virginia Mason, *Othello: A Contextual History* (Cambridge: Cambridge University Press, 1994).

Walter, Harriet, *Other People's Shoes. Thoughts on Acting*, 2nd edn (London: Nick Hern Books, 2003).

Warren, Roger, *Staging Shakespeare's Late Plays* (Oxford: Oxford University Press, 1990).

Webber, Andrew Lloyd, *Unmasked. A Memoir* (London: Harper Collins, 2018).

Wells, Stanley, *Royal Shakespeare: Four Major Productions at Stratford-upon-Avon* (Manchester: Manchester University Press, 1977).

Wells, Stanley, ed., *Summerfolk. Essays Celebrating Shakespeare and the Stratford Theatres* (Ebrington; Long Barn Books, 1997).

Articles

Amory, Mark, 'Emperor Trev', *Sunday Times Colour Magazine*, 19 September 1978, 32–6.

Anon, 'Trevor Nunn and the RSC', *RSC News* (1986, Supplement (n.p., n.d. [1986]).

Ansorge, Peter, 'Director in Interview: Trevor Nunn Talks to Peter Ansorge', *Plays and Players*, Vol. 17, No. 12 (September 1970), 16–17.

Ansorge, Peter, 'A Pride of Hamlets', *Plays and Players*, Vol. 18, No. 5 (February 1971), 16–19 (18).

Bakewell, Joan, 'Profile by Joan Bakewell: Trevor Nunn', *Illustrated London News*, 1 September 1977, 44–5.

Bury, John, 'Against Falsehood', *Flourish* (Winter 1965), 6.

Cordner, Michael, 'George Rylands and University Shakespeare', in Andrew James Hartley, ed., *Shakespeare on the University Stage* (Cambridge: Cambridge University Press, 2015), 43–59.

Cushman, Robert, 'Profile: Trevor Nunn. The Years at Stratford', *Observer*, 15 May 1977.

Dobson, Michael, 'Shakespeare Performances in England, 2003', *Shakespeare Survey*, Vol. 55 (Cambridge: Cambridge University Press, 2004), 258–89.

Dobson, Michael, 'Shakespeare Performances in England, 2004', *Shakespeare Survey*, Vol. 56 (Cambridge: Cambridge University Press, 2005), 268–97.

Dobson, Michael, 'Shakespeare Performances in England, 2005', *Shakespeare Survey*, Vol. 57 (Cambridge: Cambridge University Press, 2006), 298–37.

Dobson, Michael, 'Shakespeare Performances in England, 2007', *Shakespeare Survey*, Vol. 58 (Cambridge: Cambridge University Press, 2008), 318–50.

Dommett, Sue, '*Macbeth* at the Other Place, 1976: A Production Study', unpublished MA dissertation, University of Birmingham, 1977.

Evans, Gareth Lloyd, 'Interpretation or Experience? Shakespeare at Stratford', *Shakespeare Survey*, Vol. 23 (1970), 131–5.

Evans, Gareth Lloyd, 'The RSC's *King Lear* and *Macbeth*', *Shakespeare Quarterly*, Vol. 28, No. 2 (Spring, 1977), 190–5.

Evans, Gareth Lloyd, 'Shakespeare in Stratford and London, 1981', *Shakespeare Quarterly*, Vol. 33, No. 2 (Summer 1982), 184–8.

Hiley, Jim, 'A Company with Direction', *Plays and Players*, Vol. 25, No. 1 (October 1977), 14–21.

Hobson, Harold, 'Where's the Greatness?' and Trevor Nunn, 'Plays Come Before Stars', *Flourish*, Vol. 2, No. 2 (Spring 1969), n.p.

Holland, Peter, 'Shakespeare Performances in England, 1990–1', *Shakespeare Survey*, Vol. 45 (Cambridge: Cambridge University Press, 1993), 115–43.

McKellen, Ian, 'Ian McKellen on Shakespeare', *Shakespeare Quarterly*, Vol. 33, No. 2 (Summer 1982), 135–41.

Morgan, Gwyn, 'Three Women in *Othello*', *Plays and Players* (October 1989), 16–18.

Nunn, Bill, 'Variable Geometry at Stratford', *Tabs*, Vol. 30, No. 2 (June 1972), 72–6.

Nunn, Trevor, 'A Time for Help', *The RSC Newspaper*, No. 1 (Winter Season 1974/5), 2.

Nunn, Trevor, 'Looking Back, Looking Forward', in Stanley Wells, ed., *Summerfolk. Essays Celebrating Shakespeare and the Stratford Theatres* (Ebrington: Long Barn Books, 1999), 129–46.

Rutter, Carol Chillington, 'Shakespeare Performances in England (and Wales)', *Shakespeare Survey*, Vol. 65 (2012), 445–83.

Sargant, James, 'Barbican: A One-Room Relationship', *RSC Yearbook* (1978), n.p.

Shrimpton, Nicholas, 'Shakespeare Performances in Stratford-upon-Avon and London, 1981–2', *Shakespeare Survey*, Vol. 36 (Cambridge: Cambridge University Press, 1983), 149–55.

Smallwood, Robert, 'Shakespeare at Stratford-upon-Avon, 1989 (part 1)', *Shakespeare Quarterly*, Vol. 41, No. 1 (Spring 1990), 101–14.

Smallwood, Robert, 'Shakespeare Performances in England, 1999', *Shakespeare Survey*, Vol. 53 (Cambridge: Cambridge University Press, 2000), 244–73.

Speaight, Robert, 'Shakespeare in Britain', *Shakespeare Quarterly*, Vol. 19, No. 4 (Autumn 1968), 367–75.

Speaight, Robert, 'Shakespeare in Britain', *Shakespeare Quarterly*, Vol. 20, No. 4 (Autumn, 1969), 435–41.

Speaight, Robert, 'Shakespeare in Britain – The Stratford Season', *Shakespeare Quarterly*, Vol. 23, No. 4 (Autumn 1972), 383–7.

Stott, Catherine, 'Buzz Goodbody talks to Catherine Stott', *Guardian*, 27 October 1971.

Stredder, James, 'John Barton's Production of *Richard II* at Stratford-upon-Avon', *Shakespeare Jahrbuch* (West) 1976, 23–42.

Stubbs, Imogen, 'Gertrude', in Michael Dobson, ed., *Performing Shakespeare's Tragedies Today. The Actor's Perspective* (Cambridge: Cambridge University Press, 2006).

Tatspaugh, Patricia, 'Shakespeare Onstage in England: March to December 2005', *Shakespeare Quarterly*, Vol. 57, No. 3 (Autumn, 2006), 318–43.

Thomson, Peter, 'A Necessary Theatre: The Royal Shakespeare Season 1970 Reviewed', *Shakespeare Survey*, Vol. 24 (Cambridge: Cambridge University Press, 1971), 117–26.

Thomson, Peter, 'No Rome of Safety: The Royal Shakespeare Theatre Season, 1972 Reviewed', *Shakespeare Survey*, Vol. 26 (Cambridge: Cambridge University Press, 1973), 139–50.

Thomson, Peter, 'The Smallest Season: The Royal Shakespeare Company at Stratford, in 1974', *Shakespeare Survey*, Vol. 28 (Cambridge: Cambridge University Press, 1975), 137–48.

Thomson, Peter, 'Towards a Poor Shakespeare: The Royal Shakespeare Company at Stratford in 1975', *Shakespeare Survey*, Vol. 29 (Cambridge: Cambridge University Press, 1976), 151–6.

Tierney, Margaret, 'Direction and Design. Trevor Nunn and Christopher Morley Talk to Margaret Tierney', *Plays and Players*, Vol. 19, No. 12 (September 1972), 23–7.

Trussler, Simon, '*The Greatest Whore of them All*: Peter Hall at Stratford, 1960–1968', *The Drama Review: TDR*, Vol. 13, No. 2 (Winter 1968), 169–74.

Trussler, Simon, 'A Man for All Seasons', *Flourish*, Vol. 2, No. 1 (Autumn 1968), n.p.

Warren, Roger, 'Theory and Practice: Stratford 1976', *Shakespeare Survey*, Vol. 30 (Cambridge: Cambridge University Press, 1977), 169–79.

Warren, Roger, 'Comedies and Histories at Two Stratfords, 1977', *Shakespeare Survey*, Vol. 31 (Cambridge: Cambridge University Press, 1978), 141–54.

Warren, Roger, 'Shakespeare at Stratford and the National Theatre, 1979', *Shakespeare Survey*, Vol. 33 (Cambridge: Cambridge University Press, 1980), 169–80.

Wells, Stanley, '*The Revenger's Tragedy* Revived', in G. R. Hibberd, ed., *The Elizabethan Theatre VI* (Toronto: MacMillan, 1978), 105–33.

Wells, Stanley, 'Shakespeare Production in England in 1989', *Shakespeare Survey*, Vol. 43 (Cambridge: Cambridge University Press, 1990), 183–204.

White, Martin, 'Trevor Nunn', in John Russell Brown, ed., *The Routledge Companion to Directors' Shakespeare* (London and New York: Routledge, 2008).

Online source

Rycroft, Charles, 'Laing, Ronald David (1927–1989)', rev. *Oxford Dictionary of National Biography*, Oxford University Press, 2004; online edn., May 2009 [http://www.oxforddnb.com/view/article/40071, accessed 28 March 2017].

Videos

The Comedy of Errors (1978: 'conceived for TV' by Trevor Nunn, directed by Philip Casson).

King Lear (2008: production designer Eric Walmsley, directed by Trevor Nunn and Chris Hunt).

Macbeth (1978: designed for TV by Mike Hall, directed for TV by Philip Casson, producer Trevor Nunn).

The Merchant of Venice (2001: original stage production directed by Trevor Nunn, production and costume designer Hildegarde Bechtler, art director Eric Walmsley).

Othello (1990: design for TV adapted from Bob Crowley's stage design by David Myerscough-Jones, directed by Trevor Nunn).

INDEX

Ackland, Joss 124
Actors Company, The 148
Addenbrooke, David 23
Afore Night Come (Rudkin) 128
Alchemist, The (Jonson) 4, 127, 130
Allam, Roger 181
All's Well that Ends Well 31, 35, 113–23, 124–5, 168, 198
Annis, Francesca 99, 104
Ansorge, Peter 8, 51, 55, 67–8
Antony and Cleopatra 62–3, 68–73, 79, 83, 87, 128
Anything Goes (Porter) 27, 174
Appia, Adolphe 59
Arms and the Man (Shaw) 115
Arts Council of Great Britain 11, 13–14, 16, 63
Ashcroft, Peggy 54, 113, 116–17
Aspects of Love (Lloyd Webber) 25
As You Like It 31, 35, 108–11, 125
Ayrton, Randall 39

Baker, Sean 151
Bakewell, Joan 22
Balcony, The (Genet) 58
Ball, John 77
Bamber, David 175
Bannock, Sheila 38
Barber, C.L. 45

Barber, John 52, 57, 71, 81, 82, 92, 98, 102
Barker, Felix 97
Barton, Anne 89, 153, 154, 159
Barton, John 4, 17, 21, 28, 29, 35, 43, 88–90, 101–2, 105, 127, 144, 147, 172, 178, 185
Bassett, Kate 183, 186, 191, 197
Bayley, John 159
Beale, Simon Russell 178
Beauman, Sally 6, 13, 60, 93
Beckett, Samuel 39, 162
Berliner Ensemble 65, 77–8
Berry, Cicely 23, 29
Bethell, S.L. 45
Billington, Michael 54, 68, 71–2, 75, 89, 92, 97, 101–2, 105–6, 108, 116–17, 118, 124, 130, 132, 142, 153, 165, 166–7, 187, 190–1, 194
Bjornson, Maria 163, 169
Blakeley, Colin 74–5, 82
Blakemore, Michael 198
Blue Angel, The (Gems) 25, 127, 161, 163–4
Bogdanov, Michael 15–16
Bonham Carter, Helena 171
Boyd, Michael 178
Brecht, Bertolt 1–2, 54, 64, 65, 77–8, 112
Brien, Allan 80

Brook, Peter 6, 7–8, 13, 38–9, 73, 97, 103
Brown, Georgina 181–2
Brown, John Russell 83, 90
Bruce, Brenda 52, 53, 58
Bryden, Ronald 3, 40, 42, 51, 54–6
Butler, Robert 181

Caesar and Cleopatra (Shaw) 70
Caird, John 111, 123, 125, 198
Campbell, Cheryl 118–19
Casson, Philip 131
Cats (Lloyd Webber) 25, 125
Caucasian Chalk Circle, The (Brecht) 1–2
Chaillet, Ned 132, 146
Chambers, Colin 4, 8, 13, 26–7, 85, 128–9
Chekhov, Anton 4, 113, 115, 127, 128, 149, 150
Cherry Orchard, The (Chekhov) 115
Chess (Lloyd Webber) 25–6
Chorus Line, A (Hamlisch) 111
Churchill, Caryl 162
Clapp, Susannah 181, 189, 195
Cochrane, Claire 11
Comedy of Errors, The 31, 35, 60, 101, 102–5, 108, 125, 130–1
Compass Theatre Company 14
Cordner, Michael 22–3
Coriolan (Brecht) 65, 77–8
Coriolanus 60, 61–2, 63–5, 66, 77–8, 80–2, 128
Cornwell, Charlotte 110
Coveney, Michael 90, 91–3, 98, 100–1, 106, 115, 161, 179–80, 182
Cox, Frank 64

Croall, Jonathan 105
Crotty, Derbhle 176–8
Crowley, Bob 148
Curry, Julian 41
Cushman, Robert 2, 91, 97, 98, 102–3, 108, 122, 133–4, 144, 147
Cymbeline 44, 51

Dance of Death, The (Strindberg) 150
Daniels, Ron 178
David, Alan 111
David, Richard 98–9, 134
da Vinci, Leonardo 46–7
de Jongh, Nicholas 180–1, 183, 197
Dench, Judi 50–1, 52, 103–4, 136–40, 146
Dickson, Andrew 26
Dignam, Mark 66
Dobson, Michael 187, 191–3, 195, 197
Dodd, Ian 162
Doll's House, A (Ibsen) 121
Dommett, Sue 131, 139, 144, 145
Dostoevsky, Fyodor 127
Dury, Susan 132
Dyer, Chris 93

Edgar, David 9, 111–12
Edwardes, Jane 182, 190
Elsom, John 97–8, 121
English Shakespeare Company 15–16
Evans, Edith 116
Evans, Gareth Lloyd 42, 43, 52, 113, 135, 143
Everitt, Anthony 103
Eyre, Richard 18, 27, 129, 171
Eyres, Harry 154

Farrah, Abd' Elkader 93
Farrell, Nicholas 171
Fellini, Federico 73
Fenton, James 120, 121, 123
Fiennes, Joseph 174
Fitzgerald, Scott 162
Flannery, Peter 162
Fleetwood, Kate 183
Foco Novo (theatre company) 12
Forster, E.M. 18
Foster, Barry 162
Franklin-Robbins, John 123
Franks, Philip 118
French, Philip 39
Freud, Anna 163
Freud, Sigmund 46, 163, 165, 168
Frye, Northrop 45

Garai, Romola 193
Gaskill, William 10–11
Geeson, Judy 82
Genet, Jean 58
Gibbon, Edward 76
Gill, Peter 90
Glasgow Citizens Theatre 14–15, 90
Glover, Julian 189
Glyndebourne Festival Opera 27
Goodbody, Buzz 88, 127–9, 147
Goodman, Henry 174, 175–6
Gore-Langton, Robert 181
Grace, Nikolas 104
Grandage, Michael 151
Grass, Günter 77–8
Greenwich Theatre 168
Greer, Germaine 70–1
Griffiths, Trevor 128
Gross, John 167, 174, 176, 179, 183
Gunter, John 114

Guys and Dolls (Loesser) 27
Gwilym, Mike 117–20

Hack, Keith 90
Haig, David 165
Hair (MacDermot) 49
Hall, Peter 1–3, 6, 10, 16–17, 19, 22, 24, 27, 28, 33, 44, 55, 83, 172, 178, 198
Hall, Stuart 49–50
Hamlet 2, 3, 28, 32, 35, 55–9, 128, 147, 184–8
Hands, Terry 10, 17, 24, 29, 43, 47, 93, 107, 124, 127
Hanson, Alex 175
Harrison, George 46
Harte, Judith 132
Harvey (theatre, Brooklyn) 192
Havergal, Giles 14–15
Hayman, Ronald 21
Haymarket Theatre (London) 28
Heath, Edward 77
Hedda Gabler (Ibsen) 88, 148
Heilpern, John 8
Henry IV, Parts 1 and 2 18, 35, 123–4
Henry V 93, 124, 190
Henry VI, Parts 1–3, 4, 124. *See also Wars of the Roses*
Henry VIII (Shakespeare and Fletcher) 35, 44, 51, 53–4
Hepple, Peter 110
Higgins, John 105
Hiley, Jim 23, 95
Hobson, Harold 36–7, 38, 40, 41, 43–4, 58, 63, 73–4, 75, 93
Hodgdon, Barbara 54
Hogg, Ian 63–4
Holland, Peter 78, 162, 165, 167, 198

INDEX

Hope-Wallace, Philip 48, 54
Howard, Alan 41, 56–7, 178, 186
Howell, Rob 178
Hoyle, Martin 166, 167
Hunt, Marsha 151, 160
Hurren, Kenneth 98
Hytner, Nicholas 172, 190

Ibsen, Henrik 88, 121, 148
Ingham, Barrie 52
Itzin, Catherine 11–12

Jackson, Glenda 88, 148
Jacobs, Sally 35
James, Oscar 81–2
Jenkins, Peter 111
Johnson, Richard 68, 70, 72
Jones, David 43, 77
Jones, Griffith 133
Julius Caesar 62–3, 65–8, 79, 82, 83

Kafka, Franz 168
Kean, Marie 132
Kennedy, Dennis 147
Kenny, Sean 33
Kermode, Frank 45
King, Francis 124
King Johan (Bale) 89
King John 88, 89, 128
King Lear 25, 28, 32, 35, 37–40, 58, 82, 102, 103, 105–7, 128, 147, 184, 191–5, 197
Kingsley, Ben 107, 171
Kliman, Bernice W. 131, 132, 143
Kott, Jan 187, 195
Kretzmer, Herbert 38, 48, 106

Kumalo, Alton 46
Kyle, Barry 35, 95, 101, 105, 106–7

Laing, R.D. 40, 46, 50, 56, 58
Lambert, J.W. 52, 72, 134, 143–4, 147
Laurenson, James 110
Leavis, F.R. 1, 21–3, 36, 45, 159
Leigh-Hunt, Barbara 102
Leigh, Vivien 73
Letts, Quentin 190
Levin, Bernard 112
Lewsen, Charles 69
Linklater, Kristen 79
Lloyd, Bernard 41
Lolita (Nabokov) 166
Love's Labour's Lost 28, 32, 173–5, 182–3
Lynne, Gillian 25, 103, 108

Macaulay, Alastair 179, 187
Macbeth 4, 31, 32, 87–8, 90–3, 109, 125, 130, 131–47, 169, 198
Mackintosh, Cameron 9, 125
Madoc, Philip 164
Man and Superman (Shaw) 115, 120–2
Marcus, Frank 41, 63, 84, 92, 97
Marlowe Society (Cambridge) 1, 22
Marowitz, Charles 12
Mars-Jones, Adam 153, 158
Mason, Brewster 54
McCoy, Sylvester 194
McDiarmid, Ian 145
McEnery, Peter 110
McKellen, Ian 98–100, 130, 135–46, 148, 150, 151, 156, 160, 191–5

Me and my Girl (Gay) 182
Measure for Measure 25, 32, 90, 125, 127, 161–9
Mendes, Sam 178
Merchant of Venice, The 32, 169, 173–8, 184
Merry Wives of Windsor, The 17–18, 44, 107–8, 127–8
Midsummer Night's Dream, A 7–8, 35, 97, 184
Miles, Ben 189
Miller, Carl 162
Miller, Jonathan 168
Mirren, Helen 56–7, 58, 92–3
Misérables, Les 9, 25, 125
Moore, Jean 128
Morley, Christopher 2, 34, 36, 40, 41, 44, 51, 55, 61, 65, 82–3
Morley, Sheridan 99, 181, 183–4
Mortimer, John 67, 107
Much Ado about Nothing 17, 34–5, 36, 40–1, 84, 101
Murphy, Gerard 124
My Fair Lady (Lerner and Loewe) 27

Nabokov, Vladimir 166
Napier, John 36, 93, 107, 111, 123, 129, 148–9
Nathan, David 98, 174, 187
National Theatre 5, 6, 10–11, 18–19, 25, 28, 40, 65, 168, 169, 171–84
Nelligan, Kate 110
Nicholas Nickleby (Edgar, after Dickens) 9, 111–12, 123–4
Nightingale, Benedict 45–6, 52, 54, 70–1, 73–4, 75, 80–1, 135, 179, 190–1, 194

Norman, Ned 197
Notes from the Underground (after Dostoevsky) 127
Novello, Ivor 116
Nunn, Trevor
  early career 1–4, 21–3, 26
  influence 5–6
  interviews and other statements 7, 18–19, 21, 24, 25, 26, 30, 61, 78–9, 94, 129 (*see also* programme notes)
  musicals 9, 25–7, 125
  National Theatre, policies as artistic director 172–3, 183–4
  productions of musicals (with composer's name)
    Anything Goes (Porter) 27, 174
    Cats (Lloyd Webber) 25, 125
    Chess (Lloyd Webber) 25–6
    Guys and Dolls (Loesser) 27
    Misérables, Les (Schönberg and Boublil) 9, 25, 125
    My Fair Lady (Lerner and Loewe) 27
    Oklahoma! (Rodgers and Hammerstein) 27
    Porgy and Bess (Gershwin) 27, 160
    South Pacific (Rodgers and Hammerstein) 27
    Starlight Express (Lloyd Webber) 25, 29, 125

Sunset Boulevard (Lloyd
  Webber) 25
productions of non-
  Shakespearean plays
  Alchemist, The (Jonson)
    4, 127, 130
  Blue Angel, The (Gems)
    25, 127, 161, 163–4
  *Caucasian Chalk Circle,
    The* (Brecht) 1–2
  Hedda Gabler (Ibsen)
    88, 148
  *Life and Adventures of
    Nicholas Nickleby,
    The* (Edgar) 9,
    111–12, 123–4
  Relapse, The (Vanbrugh)
    2
  Revenger's Tragedy, The
    (Middleton, attrib.
    Tourneur) 2–4, 24,
    36–8, 73, 75, 178
  Seagull, The (Chekhov)
    25, 28, 115
  Three Sisters (Chekhov) 4,
    113, 127, 148–9, 157
productions of plays by
  Shakespeare (with year of
  first performance)
  Antony and Cleopatra
    (1972) 62–3, 68–73,
    79, 83, 87, 128
  As You Like It (1977)
    31, 35, 108–11, 125
  Comedy of Errors, The
    (1976) 31, 101, 102–5,
    108, 125, 130–1
  Coriolanus (1972) 60,
    61–6, 77–9, 80–2,
    128
  Hamlet (1970) 28, 32, 35,
    55–9; (2004) 184–8
  Henry IV, Parts 1 and 2
    (1981) 18, 35, 123–4
  Henry VIII (Shakespeare
    and Fletcher) (1969)
    35, 44, 51, 53–4
  Julius Caesar (1972)
    62–3, 65–8, 79, 82, 83
  King Lear (1968) 28, 32,
    35, 37–9, 58; (1976),
    102, 105–7; (2007)
    25, 184, 191–5, 197
  Love's Labour's Lost
    (2003) 28, 32, 173–5,
    182–4
  Macbeth (1974) 31, 32,
    97–8, 90–3; (1976)
    4, 109, 125, 130,
    131–47, 169, 198,
  Measure for Measure
    (1991) 25, 32, 125,
    161–9
  *Merchant of Venice,
    The* (1999) 32, 169,
    173–8, 184
  *Merry Wives of Windsor,
    The* 44, 107–8
  *Midsummer Night's
    Dream, A* (2016) 184
  *Much Ado about
    Nothing* (1968) 17,
    34–5, 36, 40–1, 84,
    101
  Pericles (2016) 28, 184
  Romeo and Juliet (1976)
    31, 35, 94–101
  *Taming of the Shrew,
    The* (1967) 2, 19, 21,
    23, 36–7, 41

Tempest, The (2011) 184
Troilus and Cressida 32, 173–4, 178–82, 184–5
Twelfth Night (film, 1996) 171–2
Wars of the Roses, The (from 1963 RSC script, adapted by Hall and Barton) 184
Winter's Tale, The (1969) 31, 35, 44–53, 84–5, 90, 157, 187, 198; (1976) 101–2
programme notes 45, 76–8, 95–6
rehearsal techniques 18, 19–20, 29–30, 78–80, 83, 95–6, 112, 149, 160, 198

Occupations (Griffiths) 128
Oh What a Lovely War (Littlewood/Theatre Workshop) 116
Oklahoma! (Rodgers and Hammerstein) 27
Old Vic Theatre 28, 65
Oliver, Stephen 108, 111
Olivier, Laurence 11, 27, 73
Omambala, Chu 177
Oram, Christopher 191–2
Ormsby, Robert 78
Othello 4, 32, 113, 125, 128, 130–1, 147–61, 169, 175

Palace Theatre (London) 125
Pasco, Richard 52, 89

Peck, Bob 142
Pennington, Michael 15–16, 95, 98–9, 101
Pericles 28, 44, 47, 184
Peter, John 110, 150, 162–3, 182, 184
Piggott-Smith, Tim 128
Pirandello, Luigi 57
Place, The (London theatre) 128
Plebeians Rehearse the Uprising, The (Grass) 77–8
Porgy and Bess (Gershwin) 27, 160
Porter, Eric 39–40
Porter, Roy 50
Potter, Lois 131, 157
Priestley, Clive 10
Prospect Theatre Company 14
Proust, Marcel 115

Ratcliffe, Michael 150
Redgrave, Corin 68
Rees, Roger 104, 142
Rees, Roland 12
Relapse, The (Vanbrugh) 2
Renaissance Theatre Company 14
Revenger's Tragedy, The (Middleton Tourneur) 2–4, 24, 36–8, 73, 75, 178
Richard II 28, 32, 88–9, 144, 147, 184–5, 188–91
Richard III 4
Richardson, Ian 2, 89
Rich, Frank 25
Roberts, Peter 42–3, 57
Robeson, Paul 159

Romeo and Juliet 15, 31, 35, 94–101, 112
Rosenthal, Daniel 28
Royal Court Theatre 90
Royal Hunt of the Sun, The (Shaffer) 65
Royal Shakespeare Company
 administration and finance 7–10, 13, 24–5, 30–1
 'company style' 3, 5, 17, 23–4, 41, 84–5
 design and architecture 31, 59–61, 87, 93–5, 101, 107, 161
 ensemble principle 6–7, 9, 10–11
 'Theatregoround' 88, 128
 'Theatre of Cruelty' season (1963–4) 14, 133
 theatres (owned or leased)
  Aldwych (London) 3, 6, 13, 35, 48, 53, 61, 77, 80, 87, 104, 127, 130
  Barbican Theatre (in Barbican Centre, London) 4, 5, 24, 35, 61, 118
  Courtyard (temporary theatre, Stratford) 28, 191–2
  Other Place ('new', from 1991) 25, 32, 127, 161
  Other Place ('old,' 1973–89) 4, 13, 14, 24, 31, 88, 108, 113, 125, 127–61, 169
  Pit (in Barbican Centre) 4
  Royal Shakespeare Theatre 13, 33–4, 93–5
  Swan 5, 31, 73, 162, 191
  Warehouse (London) 4, 13, 14, 88, 130, 137, 147
Rubin, Leon 111, 112
Rudkin, David 128
Rutter, Carol Chillington 77
Rylands, George ('Dadie') 22–3

Saint-Denis, Michel 128
Sanders, Norman 150
Sands, Sarah 188
Sargant, James 61
Satyricon (Fellini) 73
Saunders, Graham 13
Say, Rosemary 37
Scofield, Paul 39
Seagull, The (Chekhov) 25, 28, 115
Senecan tragedy 75
Serious Money (Churchill) 162
Seymour, Di 101
Shaw, George Bernard 70, 113, 115, 118, 120–1, 167
Shorter, Eric 111
Shrimpton, Nicholas 115, 117–8, 124
Shulman, Milton 42, 105
Sinden, Donald 53, 54, 105–6, 194
Singer (Flannery) 162
Skinner, Claire 165–6
Smallwood, Robert 89, 150, 160, 164, 166–7, 175–6, 177, 178–80
Smith, Derek 49
Soloski, Alexis 28–9
South Pacific (Rodgers and Hammerstein) 27
Spacey, Kevin 185, 190–1
Spall, Tim 107

Speaight, Robert 39, 48, 50, 70
Spencer, Charles 174, 176, 182, 194, 197
Spriggs, Elizabeth 53
Starlight Express (Lloyd Webber) 25, 29, 125
Steinberg, Michelle 25
Sternberg, Josef von 161
Stewart, Patrick 65, 67, 72, 81–2, 124
Stone, Oliver 162
Strachey, Lytton 45
Strindberg, August 118, 150
Stubbs, Imogen 152, 155, 171, 185–6
Styan, John 122
Suchet, David 162
Sunset Boulevard (Lloyd Webber) 25
Suzman, Janet 37, 41–2, 68, 70–2, 75, 82
Svoboda, Josef 59
Swift, Clive 153

Taming of the Shrew, The 2, 15, 19, 21, 23, 36–7, 41–2
Tatspaugh, Patricia 48, 189–90
Taylor, Paul 162
Tempest, The 27, 44, 51, 128, 184
Thaxter, John 183
Theatre for a New Audience (New York) 28
Thomson, Peter 55, 65, 72, 73, 74, 78, 83–4, 129
Three Sisters (Chekhov) 4, 113, 127, 148–9, 157
Tierney, Margaret 61, 70
Timon of Athens (Shakespeare and Middleton) 162–3, 185
Tinker, Jack 116, 150

Titus Andronicus 60, 62, 73–7, 79–80, 83
Traversi, D.A. 45
Trewin, J.C. 38–9, 43, 51, 80
Troilus and Cressida 17, 32, 49, 101, 173–4, 178–82, 184–5
Troublesome Reign of King John, The (anon.) 89
Trussler, Simon 23, 198
Twelfth Night 44, 90, 148, 171–2
Two Noble Kinsmen, The (Shakespeare and Fletcher) 5
Tyzack, Margaret 82

Uncle Vanya (Chekhov) 128

Vaughan, Virginia Mason 131, 151, 159–60
verse speaking 22–3, 30

Waiting for Godot (Beckett) 162
Waller, David 58
Wall, Stephen 123–4
Wall Street (film) 162
Walter, Harriet 18, 113, 115, 121–3
Wanamaker, Zoë 155–6, 158
Wardle, Irving 17, 36, 41, 42, 61–2, 63, 65, 66, 74, 82–3, 98, 105–6, 115, 120, 123–4, 137, 162
Warner, David 3, 186
Warner, Deborah 73
Warren, Roger 53, 107, 109
Wars of the Roses, The (adapted by Hall and Barton) 4, 9, 28, 65, 90, 184
Webber, Andrew Lloyd 25–6, 29

Wells, Stanley 4, 116–17, 150, 154
Whishaw, Ben 185–7
White, Martin 198
White, Willard 152, 159–60
Whiting, Margaret 82
Whittaker, Samantha 185
Williams, Clifford 60, 103
Williams, Michael 37, 104, 106, 194
Williamson, Nicol 80–1, 91–3
Will Shakespeare (Mortimer) 107
Winstanley, Gerrard 77

Winter's Tale, The 31, 35, 44–53, 84–5, 90, 101–2, 157, 187, 198
Witts, Noel 110
Wood, John 67–8, 74, 82
Woodvine, John 107–8, 130
Woolfenden, Guy 2–3, 46, 49, 75, 83, 84, 91, 103–4

Young, B.A. 108, 110
Young Vic (theatre) 4, 162–3

Zeffirelli, Franco 40

www.ingramcontent.com/pod-product-compliance
Lightning Source LLC
Chambersburg PA
CBHW050324020526
44117CB00031B/1756